"Dig Those Freeways"

L.A. Bizarro!

The Insider's Guide to
the Obscure, the Absurd,
and the Perverse in Los Angeles

Anthony R. Lovett   **Matt Maranian**

Designed by Margo A. Mooney

A Buzz Book

St. Martin's Press
New York

L.A. BIZARRO!: The Insider's Guide to the Obscure, the Absurd, and the Perverse in Los Angeles

All photographs copyright © 1997 by Anthony R. Lovett and Matt Maranian except the following: *Night of the Stars* (p. 73) Courtesy of Adult Video News; photos by Mark Kernes; *Amok* (p. 46) Interior photos by Fredrik Nilsen; *Shadow Lane* (p. 91) Courtesy of Shadow Lane; *Jayne Mansfield* (p. 144) Courtesy of Archive Photos; *The Chicken Boy Catalogue for a Perfect World*™ (p. 184) Courtesy of Future Video; photos by Andy Caufield.

Web Site: http://www.buzzmag.com

Book design by Margo A. Mooney.

Library of Congress Cataloging-in-Publication Data

Maranian, Matt.
  L.A. Bizarro! : the insiders guide to the obscure, the absurd, and the perverse in Los Angeles / Matt Maranian, Tony Lovett.
    p. cm.
  ISBN 0-312-15562-x
  1. Los Angeles (Calif.)—Guidebooks. I. Lovett, Tony. II. Title.
F869.L83M36 1997
917.94'940453—dc21
                                                              97-919
                                                                CIP

First Buzz Book Edition: June 1997
10 9 8 7 6 5

Acknowledgments

Matt: We need to do our dedication. Where do you think we should start?

Tony: How about, "This book is dedicated to all the jerks who picked on us in school and are now assistant managers at Wal-Marts—or worse, lawyers."

Matt: Maybe we should start with something a little more practical. Like a dedication to our lovely wives.

Tony: Good idea. I'd like to dedicate this book to my lovely wife, Marianne, without whom I'd still be a lonely, booze-swilling, pill-popping, gun-toting, agoraphobic loser.

Matt: And I dedicate this book to my lovely wife, Loretta—my sweet sugar plum—who has been an absolute living doll throughout her eight-month tenure as a book widow. A dedication also goes to my exemplary parents—who actually laughed at the most vulgar portions of this book—and my adorable sister, Jill. But I also have about a million people to thank for helping me: ultra-thanks to Carol Katz, for being a constant source of encouragement and much-valued sounding board, and to Don Favareau (you can see Don's ass in the entry for "Naked City") for allowing me to drag him along on dozens of ridiculous field trips for the research of this book (I also thank Don for his brilliant observations and for letting me claim some of his best quotes as my own). Mega-thanks goes to Mark Frauenfelder and Carla Sinclair for their invaluable friendship and unconditional generosity. There are lots of other people who will get a personal thank you because we obviously don't have enough room here.

Tony: You mean this isn't just filler? In that case, I also want to thank my marvelous mother and my late, great father, both of whom always encouraged me to do whatever I wanted with my life—short of blowing up a nuclear power plant, shooting the President, or becoming a male exotic dancer. And I'd also like to thank Paul Young at *Buzz* for getting our proposal into the right hands. Most importantly, I kowtow at the feet of our graphic designer, Margo Mooney, who read our minds and improved upon whatever paltry ideas were careening around our tiny, dessicated brains.

Matt: All hail Margo Mooney!! You're a goddess, Margo.

Tony: And then there are all the people who helped me in ways they probably don't even realize: Russ Hampshire, who cut me a lot of slack and displayed undue generosity; Alan Smith, "The Mad Scanner;" and Irwin Allen, for making the film version of *Voyage to the Bottom of the Sea*, which I watched incessantly throughout the writing of this book. Finally, I'd like to thank you, Matt, for being the best writing partner a guy could ask for, next to Rod McKuen, of course.

Matt: Likewise. It's been a pleasure.

Tony: Well, I guess that just about covers it.

Matt: Except for one thing—where's our fucking check?

Tony: You mean we're getting paid for this?

table of contents

Introduction

You know, Los Angeles isn't much different than the smoke-and-mirrors movie industry for which it's famous. L.A. is a town fraught with facades and phoniness, where tanning salons take the place of going to the beach, where cosmetic surgery is as routine as having your teeth cleaned, and where the sun attempts to shine almost every day through a dazzling multi-layered miasma of toxic air. So it isn't surprising that the City of Angels is a place where the superficial is valued far more than the sublime. Here, growing old isn't a sin; showing your age, however, is. In this way, Los Angeles is like an aging, high-priced callgirl trying to keep her dwindling clientele happy. Subsequent coats of makeup and the occasional facelift may provide temporary relief, but all the Beverly Centers, Universal Citywalks and Disneylands can't save the old girl. Plain and simple, she's become a boring lay.

That's what prompted us to seek out and sample the lesser known assets of our fair city, many of which are, ironically, in plain sight and easily accessible. The best of L.A.'s offbeat underbelly is what this book is really about, but when we use the term "underbelly," we use it fondly. We look at it as a selection of those peculiar cultural treasures that are so often overlooked, if not ignored altogether. By way of example, when Americans eat sushi they tend to shy away from tuna belly ("Toro") for fear of the name—yet it's the most tender, tasty, and highly valued cut of tuna. Likewise, some of our entries may appear unsavory at first glance—and indeed, some are—but there are also some real gems hidden beneath the veil of apparent freakishness.

If it appears that we're a little mixed-up about our feelings towards L.A., we aren't alone. In fact, most of the world shares a love-hate thing with Los Angeles. It seems that just about everyone would like to come here to be a star, but no one wants to be swallowed whole by the earth, or be shot to death by gang members, or worse, pulled over for a traffic violation by the LAPD. Most Angelenos share that same love/hate relationship with one exception: We're on the inside looking out. Those on the outside looking in tend to think of Los Angeles as some kind of pre-apocalyptic amusement park for the damned, a smog-shrouded Gomorrah where the water is as unpalatable as the regurgitated ideas splattered on our TV and movie screens. And they're right! Tragically, here in L.A. there is no life for art to even imitate. Instead, art just imitates itself, a snake eating its tail, a dog eating its own vomit. And that's what gives our town its inimitable charm.

So never mind the fact that the earth around here moves more often than not. Forget the overwhelming potential to be consumed in a conflagration. Don't think about the fact that you stand a good chance of being yanked at gunpoint from your luxury car as you sit at an intersection listening to your new Kenny G CD, only to be shot right there in the middle of the street like some kind of washed-up, helpless Power Ranger. Why? Because that's life in Los Angeles! Enjoy it!

And to help you do just that—and to take your mind off all of the above—we've put together what we think is a somewhat unusual little guide to the place we affectionately call Hell on Earth. It's just the tip of the iceberg, a mere smattering of all the strangeness this metropolis has to offer, but it should be enough to keep you amused in the bathroom for quite some time, depending on your regularity.

By now you may have gathered that L.A. BIZARRO isn't for everyone. But if you have a sense of humor, a lust for adventure, some pocket change, and optional nerves of steel, prepare yourself for the discovery and exploration of a weird new world that's waiting just outside your front door. And if you aren't in the mood to budge from your plush Strato-lounger, you can vicariously experience the glory and glamor via our decidedly biased exposes and adventures in that wonderful aforementioned underbelly.

And if, for some inexplicable reason, you decide this book isn't for you, may we kindly suggest you place it back on the shelf, back slowly away, and return to your sad, pathetic, sheltered excuse for a life?

Thank you.

—Anthony R. Lovett and Matt Maranian

October, 1996

chapter one

Enjoy Life,
Eat Out
More Often!

"Where do you wanna eat?"

Whether you're an out-of-towner or you've made Los Angeles your home for more years than you care to admit, it's the one question that has a tendency to instantaneously turn otherwise sprightly brains into hashed browns.

You can always go the easy route and dig the latest edition of the L.A. Times Restaurant Review out of your recycling bin, or thumb through that yellowed Zagat Guide you keep in your glove compartment–but who died and made them the last word on dining out? What if you want more than a fastidiously presented microscopic portion of nouvelle cuisine, or the chance of spotting an overpaid movie actor pushing crab cakes into his or her face just a table away from yours? Can the celebrity-spotting of The Ivy compete with the 98 bubbling fluorescent fish tanks of Bahooka? Will the swans dotting the quiet streams outside the dining room of The Bel-Air Hotel mark your memory as indelibly as the overkill of stuffed monkeys hanging from the ceiling at Damon's Steak House? Could the upscale westside crowd and cuisine eclectica of Röckenwagner hold a candle to the winos and waterfalls of Clifton's Cafeteria?

We don't think so.

Unfortunately, the phone book doesn't list the city's eating establishments under headings like "Restaurants with Talking Parrots," "Diners That Haven't Remodeled Since 1945," or "Steak Houses with Garish South Seas Themes"–and since the ratio of restaurants to people in Los Angeles is about three to one, this additional obstacle can make the already maddening decision-making process considerably tougher.
But that's why you've got us.

So here you go: a low-class and high-trash listing covering some of Los Angeles' most outlandish, outrageous, and egregious eateries. Restaurants that the Times or the Zagat Guide may have carelessly overlooked...or completely misunderstood.

Holding our noses at *Cole's*

For Your Malodorous Dining Pleasure

Cole's has always reminded me of a filthy stinking Parisian public urinal trough, the kind you can't flush. If you like the acrid aroma of a real honest-to-goodness dive, you'll absolutely adore *Cole's*.

They claim to be the oldest operating restaurant in Los Angeles, and judging from the smell I'd say that they're probably correct. *Cole's* opened in 1908 and was declared a historical landmark in 1974, so there's something here for winos and local history buffs alike. The turn-of-the-century interior (dark wood, brass, red booths) may have at one point in time been charming. There's sawdust on the floor (for camouflage?) and "antiqued" signs that say things like "We Do Not Extend Credit to Stockbrokers" and "Avoid Sinful Enterprises" hang over the bar.

You might want to pop a couple of aspirin before you enter because you may be in for the headache of your life. The air is almost opaque with cigarette smoke even when no one's smoking. Once you've gotten used to the stale cigarette effluvium you'll detect

a putrid sub-odor; hard to place, but something akin to the scent of the repeatedly pissed-in pants of an elderly man who's recently consumed a large plate of steamed asparagus. It's a good idea to take the booth next to the open door; you'll need the ventilation—and a quick and easy exit.

Cole's atmosphere is unique on many levels. The ambience is like "The Iceman Cometh" meets "Cheers" on morphine. Most of the clientele look like they'd chew their mother's face off for breakfast. Strangely, a good number of them carry duffle bags or ominous looking cheap black briefcases. Since *Cole's* is basically a roach motel for humans, it's a wonderful place to eavesdrop. As I walked in, a young woman seated at the bar was chatting with the very inebriated man slouched next to her. "Stop slobbering and GET YOUR FINGER OUT OF YOUR NOSE!" she said, followed by a wheezing cackle. He ignored her and continued picking his nose, all the while successfully copping feels off of her with his other hand.

Great conversations like these are fairly scarce though, because most of the patrons appear so shitfaced (the bar being the most popular section of *Cole's*) that all they're able to do is affix their drunken gaze to the television set—the deafening volume of which will have largely contributed to the migraine that you'll undoubtedly acquire. *Cole's* is pure charm.

There's a cafeteria style steam table, and *Cole's* offers a fairly ambitious menu that I'd advise anyone to approach with great caution. We love *Cole's* and don't want to knock it, but don't believe the food to be their forté. This however is an unqualified judgement having not actually eaten anything there ourselves. There's something about the *Cole's* environment that makes consuming solid food quite difficult—it might take everything you've got just to choke down half a beer.

Cole's is not a place for ladies, fops, or those who take life too seriously, since it's conceivable that you may see a patron puke on himself or piss his pants or both.

Bon appetit!

–MM

Cole's
118 East 6th Street
Downtown Los Angeles
(213) 662-4090

Rare are the 40s and 50s burger joints that didn't fall prey to the hands of greedy real estate developers. Rarer still are ones that didn't get ruined with an "upgrade" in the 70s or 80s. Fortunately, **The Apple Pan** survived, and although it now stands dwarfed in the shadow of the frighteningly proportioned and aesthetically distasteful West Side Pavilion shopping mall, it still caters to a loyal following, often lined up through the quaint screened door and ready to pounce on the next available red vinyl stool. *The Apple Pan* evokes flashbacks of that "I Love Lucy" episode where Lucy, Ricky, Fred and Ethel decide to go into business together and buy a small lunchcounter diner. Unchanged since it first opened in 1947, *The Apple Pan* remains the best place to pretend you're a Ricardo or a Mertz. Or if you prefer, Mrs. Trumbull.

The beauty of *The Apple Pan* lies in its simplicity. They've found their winning formula and they haven't messed with it in fifty years. Burgers, fries and pie and not much more. The grill stands towards the back of the small room, bordered by a formica countertop along three sides. No tables. The original wood-bladed ceiling fans still oscillate above, and the back wall is papered in an understated plaid. The waiters, too, look like they've been there since 1947, with their little paper hats and white aprons. Patrons thrill to details like the paper cones set into red plastic cup holders used for soda and water, or the fact that *The Apple Pan* is one of the few places in town that still serves real cream with their coffee.

Any time spent waiting in line is soon overcompensated for by the greased lightning service. As soon as you grab a seat, a no-nonsense waiter slams a menu and a blank ticket down on the counter in front of you and glares blankly in anticipation of your order. Crumbling under the pressure to make a snap decision, a quick look at the menu (a quick look is all you need anyway) prompts an exchange between waiter and customer—*The Apple Pan* rite of passage—which usually goes something like this:

> **"WHAWOUDYLIKE?"**
> **"Um...I think I'll have a Hickory Burg..."**
> **"CHEESE?"**
> **"No thank..."**
> **"FRIES?"**
> **"Yes plea..."**
> **"COKE?"**
> **"Ye..."**

BAM!—the paper cup filled with ice hits the formica. **BAM!**—an ice cold can of Coke. **BAM!**—an order of perfect fries.

> **"KETCHUP?"**
> **"Yes, plea..."**

BAM!—a small brown paper plate filled with ketchup. Seconds later, a perfect burger wrapped in wax paper—not a monster, not a fancy bastard Southwestern hybrid, but what once must have been what all real burgers tasted like—is tossed in your direction. *The Apple Pan* doesn't waste time with superfluous dishware.

"Quality Forever" is *The Apple Pan*'s slogan, and since their food may seem a little heavy by today's standards, forever won't take long if you eat here every day. And no matter what your doctor has told you, and no matter how terminally you've stuffed your gut, you can't leave without a slab of pie. The banana cream is like flying a cholesterol cloud straight to heaven (or Valhalla if you're of Nordic descent).

The Apple Pan
10801 Pico Blvd.
Westwood
(310) 475-3585

Dining at *Phillipe, The Original*

Callow plagiarism and undue credit-mongering are but two more of the charming traits we Angelenos are so proud of, and claiming to be the "Home of the French Dip" is certainly no exception. Indeed, a trip to downtown L.A. can be a vexing experience in and of itself when one is faced with the duality of both Cole's and **Phillipe, The Original** claiming credit for inventing the French Dip sandwich. Slice some beef, cut a french roll in half and dip the non-crust faces in *au jus*, put it all together and there you have the concoction that has sparked countless debates as to its origin.

And You Thought Marcel Marceau Was The Original French Dip!

In the end, who gives a hoot? All such claims become moot when faced with the question of originality versus quality. In this debate, *Phillipe, The Original*, is clearly the winner when it comes to actually putting food in your mouth, chewing, swallowing, and keeping it down.

In fact, *Phillipe* serves some of the best sandwiches in Los Angeles, consistently, day in and day out, as they have been for the past 60 years. And not just beef sandwiches. The pork and ham are also excellent, and the lamb sandwich is one-of-a-kind, carved from the leg as you look on with drooling anticipation. The custom-made mustard is a sub-atomic formula that will lift the top of your cranium and send your sinuses reeling. Salads range from cole slaw, to macaroni, to potato and beyond...the extensive menu of sides mounted on the wall will take you half a year to read—if you have perfect eyesight. The stew and chili are hearty staples, and the purple pickled eggs are nothing less than a semi-hallucinatory treat. They leave your tongue a wonderful shade of ultra-violet. Even the Coke with ice is the best in town, something that we have never been able to figure out, other than the fact that it must be the ice and the neat little glass, or both. The Coke is from the can.

Walking into *Phillipe* is akin to stepping back in time a few decades. The sawdust covered floor is lined with long community tables and stools. Counters along the back walls allow those in a hurry (or with an aversion to sitting) to stand, eat, and run. The service counter is a five-foot-high glass and steel affair that stretches the length of the main room, and is staffed by a phalanx of unintentionally retro-uniformed ladies who take your order, make your sandwich, and ring you up with all the charming efficiency of Barbara Billingsley. Due to the location of the place, wedged between Chinatown's east side and just north of Terminal Station and Olvera St., you can expect to meet a wonder-fully mixed—and often confused—selection of characters standing in line at the place.

That is, if you can tell what's a line and what isn't. The large beams that flank the counter sometimes serve to block direct access to an open register, and often you'll find people completely ignoring an open berth...until you walk up to it and order. Then you'll hear some grumbling behind your back, but so what? First come, first serve—it's the law of the land at *Phillipe, The Original*. If the patrons happen to be sharp on the day you visit, we suggest you scan the place from the raised stair entranceway, and you will find a shorter line every time. Now the only problem will be getting to it, since the place tends to be crowded at the usual—and sometimes unusual—feeding hours. *Phillipe's* feeds over a half-million people a year, and sometimes it would seem that they've all shown up at once. Still, with over eight lines to chose from, you can play the odds just like at Santa Anita and go for the big win. Parties of three or more may wish to attempt a "Trifecta" approach and "spread out" over several lines. Whoever gets to the front first is then joined by the others, much to the dangerous chagrin of the rank and file. Mooooo!

There are some huge high-backed booths in the back room, with room enough for the entire Manson family and Shorty O'Shea's head—so bring the whole family!

DID YOU KNOW?

Each year, Phillipe, The Original uses:

ONE MILLION SPECIALLY BAKED FRENCH ROLLS

200,000 POUNDS OF CHOICE BEEF

100,000 POUNDS OF LEAN EASTERN PORK

36,000 POUNDS OF SPRING LAMB

37,000 POUNDS OF BAKED HAM

Phillipe, The Original
1001 North Alameda St.
Los Angeles
(213) 628-3781

Giovanni's Salerno Beach Restaurant

As a rule of thumb it's always advisable to stay completely clear of Playa Del Rey. But it's worth venturing out into the land of sun and fun luvin' beer- swilling swingles to experience **Giovanni's Salerno Beach Restaurant**. You can't miss it, it's the place covered in Christmas lights—with Santa, snowmen, and toy soldier figures on the roof 365 days a year.

Apparently no one ever told Giovanni that less is more. Not to our knowledge has any restaurant in Los Angeles achieved the kind of visual chaos found here, *Giovanni's* decor is the kind that could only happen by accident. But how, one can't help but wonder, did every visible inch of the walls and ceiling get covered with layer upon layer of Christmas lights, Pez dispensers, bunches of plastic grapes, varnished loaves of bread, pinatas, dolls, streamers, a scarecrow, motorized miniature witches, stuffed animals, zillions of Christmas tree ornaments, jack-o-lanterns, giant plastic candy canes, miles of garland, birthday decorations, Hanukkah decorations, flags, hundreds of Chianti bottles, banners for every occasion, pine cones, a veritable tornado of thrift store bric-a-brac and the kind of yard sale refuse that should have been thrown out to begin with? The nine bird cages and five fish tanks almost get lost. And no, it's not one of those flashbacks you've been anxiously awaiting, the walls in *Giovanni's* really do breathe!

Curiosity, confusion, and wonder nearly killing us, we asked Giovanni just how his restaurant evolved into the charming little firetrap it is today. The explanation was a simple one. Giovanni, a robust man who resembles an Italian Tennessee Williams, said that about twenty-seven years ago he pulled out all the stops and decorated the place up for Christmas. Once Christmas passed, he decided taking all the decorations down was just more than he could deal with, so up they stayed. Forever. But the overwhelming Christmas theme hasn't kept him— or his charming partner Adelina— from adding generously to the mess year after year, creating one of the most breathtaking interiors we've ever experienced firsthand. And you thought the Sistine Chapel was awe-inspiring.

We'll eat anyplace that serves dishes with names like "Linguini with Clams a la Sophia Loren." Although among our friends the general consensus in regard to the food has always been along the lines of "the worst meal of my life," we must honestly say that while the food doesn't rival that of Rex II Ristorante, our personal meals at *Giovanni's* have always been satisfactory, and besides, the portions are enormous.

Giovanni's Salerno Beach Restaurant
193 Culver Blvd.
Playa Del Rey
(310) 821-0018

Clifton's Cafeteria

Don't be fooled by the modest facade. Just as the story goes that Africa and South America were once a part of the same continent before the earth shifted millions of years ago, we believe that by the same principle **Clifton's** was once a part of the Snow White ride at Disneyland.

Immediately after entering you'll detect a familiar smell (A rest home? A thrift store?) and file into a line for *Clifton's* extensive array of less than mouthwatering cafeteria cuisine. For those of you with a delicate constitution we suggest limiting your meal to coffee. For those of you with a cast-iron stomach, we suggest you turn your meal into a game: See which one of you can eat the largest and most varied feast (extra points for meat and fish dishes), pick the item that looks like it's been aging on the steam table longest and have three servings!

The *Clifton's* decor looks like the kind of hallucination a glue sniffer might have if he used pine-scented air freshener instead of model airplane cement. The main wall inside *Clifton's* stretches two stories high and is painted floor to ceiling to look like a forest clearing complete with cedar tree trunk relief and an illuminated full moon. Perched high on a stone ledge you'll spot a deer (it's not real) surrounded by artificial foliage, astroturf and fake rocks. In the opposite corner is a miniature chapel, also made of "stone" and topped with a neon cross.

There's seating on five levels with enough tables and chairs to accommodate a party of, we would assume, several thousand, but the best spots—and most coveted—are on the terrace next to the waterfall. The third floor bears no resemblance to the rest of the cafeteria, but it's worth a trip up the stairs just to take a look-see; sort of a colonial ballroom with red flocked bordello wallpaper delicately splattered with flecks of gravy and chicken broth by overzealous patrons.

If you're thinking of ending your life, you'll be hard-pressed to find a more beautifully macabre setting than *Clifton's*. The lighting induces the same sensation as waiting in a bus terminal at 3:00 A.M., so don't be alarmed if you begin to feel a bit punchy. You'll soon lose all sense of day or night because *Clifton's* has thoughtfully painted forest scenes over all the windows to shelter you from the nasty reality of downtown Los Angeles—besides, the reality of *Clifton's* main dining room can be nasty enough. The window treatments do however create an interesting, albeit third-rate, forest inside/forest outside illusion.

E.J. Clinton was a Salvation Army captain who established Clinton's "Cafeteria and Puritan Dining Rooms" in San Francisco at the turn of the century. He came to Los Angeles (changing one consonant in his last name for no reason that we can discern) and founded *Clifton's Cafeteria* in 1931. As you exit, be sure to pick up a copy of "*Clifton's* Food For Thot," a monthly pamphlet of inspirational "thots," poems and "useful truths." *Clifton's* is a delightfully dingy wonderland where only true urban adventurers have a good time.

Clifton's Cafeteria
648 South Broadway
Downtown Los Angeles
(213) 627-1673

Clifton's Pacific Seas

The facade alone featured a waterfall cascading three stories above the sidewalk—accented with rock grottos, palm fronds, and neon flowers. This was easily the most spectacular commercial structure in all of downtown—perhaps the entire city. Inside, the facade kept its promise: another surreal masterwork in the *Clifton's Cafeteria* bloodline. Owner E.J. Clinton and his architects proved that you don't have to sacrifice glamour just because you're scarfing down a mass-produced, forty-five cent heat-lamp-and-steam-tray meal. The exotic glitz of **Clifton's Pacific Seas Cafeteria** rivaled any Hollywood nightclub, all the while catering to senior citizens, families on a budget, and down-and-out winos. Opened in 1931, and demolished just four short decades later.

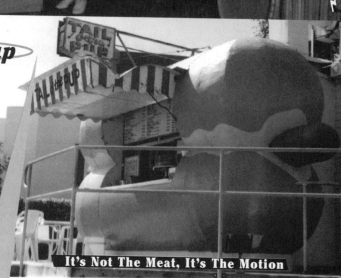

Clifton's Pacific Seas Cafeteria
Formerly at 618 South Olive, Downtown Los Angeles

Tail O' the Pup

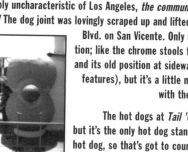

Tail 'O the Pup is, tragically, one of the last remaining gems of mimetic architecture in Southern California. Oddly enough, this 1938 *chef-d'oeuvre* designed by Milton J. Black originally stood at 311 North La Cienega Blvd., exactly one block east of where it stands today. How does a hot dog stand get bumped an entire city block? In the late 80s most of the corner was razed to make way for the monstrous eyesore, the Hotel Sofitel. In a shocking display of architectural integrity discernibly uncharacteristic of Los Angeles, *the community actually rallied to preserve a famed landmark!* The dog joint was lovingly scraped up and lifted to its current site, just above Beverly Blvd. on San Vicente. Only minute details were lost in the translation; like the chrome stools that used to sit in front of the counter, and its old position at sidewalk's edge (one of Orson Wells' favorite features), but it's a little more convenient to eat there now, what with the shaded tables and little parking lot.

It's Not The Meat, It's The Motion

The hot dogs at *Tail 'O the Pup* aren't really all that great, but it's the only hot dog stand in town that's shaped like a giant hot dog, so that's got to count for something.

Tail O' the Pup
329 North San Vicente
West Hollywood
(310) 652-4517

Dining on Sloppy Tube Steak at *Pink's*

You won't find quaint mimetic architecture at **Pink's** because the best hot dog stand in L.A. doesn't even begin to resemble a gargantuan mock-up of a frankfurter and its ubiquitous beige bun. That's the raison d'etre for **Pink's** nearby competition, *Tail O' the Pup*. No, **Pink's** is just a plain white building that sits by itself on La Brea, just north of Melrose, where it services an almost constant flow of hungry customers from 9:30 in the morning until 2 A.M. (3 A.M. on Fridays and Saturdays).

What's A Weenie Without A Bun?

Pink's is truly an L.A. hot dog stand. Aside from its nocturnal hours, the place boasts its own parking attendant; and as if to thumb its nose at its tony neighbor Beverly Hills, *Pink's* offers free parking. When was the last time you heard those two words used in the same breath? *Pink's* was originally a simple hot dog wagon which Paul Pink parked at the corner of Melrose and La Brea in 1939 when the depression was still in full swing. Here you could find a meal in bun, slathered in onions and chili, for a mere dime. Better still, *Pink's* beats the pants off *Del Taco* (with their one-minute service policy) by serving up a hot dog with all the fixings in about thirty seconds!

It's been said that Orson Welles once ate 15 chili dogs in one sitting, and used to frequent *Pink's* in the dead of night—though the same has been said for his visits to such culinary landmarks as *Tommy's*, *Tail O' the Pup*, and just about every other food vendor located within the obese legend's arm's length from a street curb. Ever the romantic, Bruce Willis proposed to Demi Moore over chili dogs at *Pink's*, and before he became the most famous midget in Hollywood, Michael J. Fox used the place as his office. How charming.

As you might have already gleaned from the latter paragraph, *Pink's* is a prime spot for potential star sightings. Imagine the thrill of watching the mega-talented Roseanne stuffing her gaping maw with a dripping bacon cheeseburger, or the chub-inducing sight of Kim Basinger wrapping her lips around a turkey frank other than Alec Baldwin's? Super-cool crooner Barry White gets off on the mild Polish sauerkraut dog, also a fave of Richard Dreyfuss. Even Diana Ross, known for her hermetic ways, has been seen in line at *Pink's* (with her driver next to her, of course) waiting for her food as her Rolls Royce idles in the lot.

Chili dogs are *Pink's* strong suit, maybe because they've been manufacturing the sloppy concoctions for almost sixty years. Perhaps that explains the heavenly perfection of what is usually an otherwise grotesque assault on the taste buds and gastrointestinal tract. One bite of *Pink's* fare, however, and you will find yourself filled with visions of the Great Welles in the back of his limo, scarfing a baker's dozen of chili dogs and washing down the whole mess with a case of Kosher soda.

Now you, too, can pretend to be the ill-fated director of *Citizen Kane*.

Wear a bib.

Pink's
709 North La Brea
(Melrose & La Brea)
Los Angeles
(213) 931-4223
(recording only)

Dinner and a show at *El Cid*

El Cid is another one of those places nearly everyone's heard about, but only a committed few actually take the time to check out. It's a damn shame too, because *El Cid* remains one of the best bets for your entertainment buck.

It sits just off the edge of an extremely unglamorous section of Sunset Boulevard towards Silverlake. The nondescript facade doesn't look especially inviting, but as soon as you step beneath the front awning and begin the walk down the oblique brick stairways, past the blooming flowers and trickling fountains of *El Cid*'s sunken, multi-leveled courtyard and patio—*Ole! You're suddenly transported to Espania!* Or at least a reasonably cartoonish facsimile, as the restaurant claims to be "...an authentic replica of a 16th-Century Spanish Tavern."

Is That A Pair Of Castanets In Your Pocket Or Are You Just Happy To See Me?

The building that now houses the histrionic elegance of this restaurant and bar was, as the story goes, originally the site of Hollywood's first movie studio and served as the location for D.W. Griffith's epic *Birth of a Nation*. Although there exists some debate over the site of Hollywood's "first" movie studio, it is a fact that *El Cid* had a second incarnation as a cabaret in the 1950s, and since 1961 exists as it is today, *a dinner-and-flamenco thrill ride!*

Who doesn't become wildly inspirited by the jackhammer rat-ta-tat of castanets, the stomping of heels, and the synchopated hand claps by a troupe of feisty flamenco dancers—especially when scored by a live flamenco guitarist and wailing Spanish vocalist! The dinner probably won't knock you off your seat, but there are some very tasty appetizers like the marinated mushrooms and the stuffed mussels, and you really can't go too wrong with the paella and most all the entrees, which are surprisingly better than one would expect from an authentic replica of a 16th-Century Spanish Tavern. But once the red curtains are drawn and the dancers take their positions on the small stage, it's *all* about the show—you may as well be eating dogshit and you wouldn't know it, *or care!* Making Spanish eyes at the dancers is half the fun, and I nearly wet my seat when Angelita—one of the more dramatic flamenco dancers to take the *El Cid* stage —locked her heavily mascara-laden eyes with mine during her castanet solo. It made me feel like an authentic Spanish Prince in an authentic replica of a 16th-Century Spanish Tavern.

You're in good company here. In addition to the eclectic and very grown-up crowd, *El Cid* has played host to an eclectic list of luminaries—as the menu will inform you—from Leonard Nimoy to Marlon Brando. Bette, Lana, and even Raquel nibbled quesadillas here too. You'll probably work into this motley equation somewhere between David Bowie and "Fonzie." Get there early, about an hour before the show starts, so you can get real smashed. You also need some time to have dinner and peruse the 8 x 10 glossies of *El Cid*'s roster of performers posted in the lobby, peek into the curio cabinets filled with flamencoabilia, hang at the bar, and wander the balcony. Early arrival will also ensure a ringside table—but don't sit too close; the whipping of flamenco skirts and projectile perspiration could make for an unsavory experience if you're in the wrong line of trajectory.

The timing of the show is impeccable—it lasts almost a full hour and concludes just when all that clicking and tapping starts to work your last raw nerve.

—MM

El Cid
4212 West Sunset Blvd.
Hollywood
(213) 668-0318

The Brown Derby
They Tore Up the Parking Lot and Put Up a Blasphemy

L.A. is a town where stars come crashing down as quickly and as often as they are sent into orbit. If fame is fleeting, then respect is virtually non-existent in La-La Land, and there is no better architectural metaphor for L.A.'s gross negligence of its own than **The Original Brown Derby**.

There were two *Brown Derbys*, actually. One was an eaterie on 1628 Vine Street in Hollywood that opened on Valentine's Day in 1929, and was soon thereafter dubbed "Restaurant of the Stars" due to its star-studded roster of clients. It closed in 1985 and burned down three years later. Despite its name, this *Brown Derby* resembled most other restaurants and was not built in the fashion of a gigantic article of clothing one wears on their head.

The Brown Derby most people conjure up in their minds, however, is the coffee shop that was constructed in the shape of nothing other than a big brown derby back in 1926 by the husband of actress Gloria "I'm ready for my close-up Mr. DeMille" Swanson. This mimetic marvel—called *The Original Brown Derby*—sat at 3377 Wilshire Boulevard, just across the street from the famed Coconut Grove and infamous Ambassador Hotel. In 1984, when I moved into the Gaylord apartment building that was separated from the *Brown Derby* by a parking lot, the historical eyesore was already closed and beginning to decay. Of course, that never stopped my friends and me from climbing on the giant hat and trying to break into it, and when we finally succeeded on gaining access one hallucinogenically inspired evening, we found nothing inside but darkness, dusty cobwebs, and lots of objects to stumble over. Looking back, I wonder what we were expecting to find after all—the carcass of the maitre d' perhaps? The only gratifying experience I had that evening was standing atop the derby and taking a refreshing leak as the world whizzed past me on Wilshire.

Still, it was always heartening to see that wee bit o' Hollywood history every time I stepped out of my apartment building, and I optimistically assumed that the kind soul who put up the parking lot spared the *Derby* out of sheer respect for the past. Then, a few years later, the parking lot succumbed to the spreading architectural cancer known as the "mini-mall." *The Brown Derby* was to be spared—kind of—by placing it atop the mini-mall *as if it were an actual* hat. Oh, the indignities this town forces upon its finest symbols!

When I returned to photograph the place for this book in 1996, one can imagine my mixed emotions when I discovered that *The Original Brown Derby* was alive again (albeit under another name) in the form of a karaoke bar/cafe—but it was no longer brown. Instead, it now looked like the victim of a manic spray-paint graffiti artist commissioned by Reynolds Aluminum, having been completely resurfaced in a ghastly bright metallic silver hue. Appropriately, the ex-*Derby* has been renamed "Xcess," which certainly describes the mind-set of the new Korean owners who transmogrified the stately old edifice into a hyperbolic facsimile of a U.F.O. The interior now resembles a cross between a harem's den and a disco, which might have gone over well with Gloria Swanson's demented character from *Sunset Blvd.*, but made me slightly nauseous. When I called the establishment to ask a few questions about their operations, the person with whom I spoke was completely unfamiliar with the term "Brown Derby," much less the English language.

Too bad they didn't just tear the thing down and give its remains a proper burial. Where's Jack Kervorkian when you really need him?

Gaze upon the glaring blasphemy at its original location, only slightly higher (on the second floor) and much tackier than originally intended. Enter at your own karmic risk.

—ARL

Xcess Cafe
(in what was once *The Original Brown Derby*)
3377 Wilshire Blvd.
Los Angeles
(213) 480-1223

Enjoying the Fresh-Killed Birds at *Superior Poultry*

Alot of vegetarians take great pleasure in telling meat-eaters that if they could only see where their meat comes from, they wouldn't eat it anymore. Well, that may or may not be true. In a similar vein, there are plenty of folks out there who, after regurgitating their first round of Tequila shots swore they'd never touch the stuff again. Then there are those who, despite the hideousness of the hangover, were unswayed by the experience and returned to the bottle like babes to their mothers' bosoms. We call these people "alcoholics."

Likewise, some people are put off when they find out what are really in hot dogs, or when they read graphic accounts of what goes on in slaughterhouses (i.e., slaughtering), or even when they perchance to walk through a Chinese kitchen. On the other hand, those of us who have given in to the carnivorous demon—or worked in a restaurant—know that nothing in the culinary world is perfect, especially when it comes to the systematic killing

Is That A Chicken Head In Your Pocket Or Are You Just Happy To See Me?

of animals for our eating pleasure. But unless your taste buds have taken a permanent vacation, you already know that freshness is perhaps the most important factor in the food chain—and when it comes to chicken, you can't get it any fresher than at **Superior Poultry** in Chinatown. That is, unless you happen to kill it yourself.

Located on bustling Broadway, *Superior* is definitely not a place to bring the kids, especially if they are fond of baby chicks. The front of the simple store is stacked with metal cages which are in turn packed with chirping chickies. Correct that—*doomed* chirping chickies. For a mere ten paces from these cages you will find a long counter awaiting you, and behind it, a team of industrious uniformed chicken murderers practicing their trade. And they do it well.

Fortunately, they don't stop at simple, senseless chicken murder: they also pluck, wash, clean, and prepare their victims as you see fit. No vats of "fecal soup" as seen on *60 Minutes*, no assembly line peopled by workers with loose hairnets, no styrofoam trays, and best of all, no days spent in a refrigerated truck and meat cases waiting for that magical expiration date to come around.

One trip to any Chinatown market—with their countless roasted ducks hanging by their necks and plastic tubs full of odd, smelly sea creatures—will teach you that when it comes to food, the Chinese are neither squeamish nor gentile. They have no problem with the carnivore/death connection, and will even gleefully flaunt it in your face. Like at *Superior Poultry*, for example. And that's good, because the last thing we Americans need is to believe that the meat we buy in our pristine supermarkets has somehow found its way there in anything less than a bloody and violent manner. In the good ol' days on the farm, the favorite pig was raised as a member of the family and then summarily dispatched to provide the Easter ham. Now you can get in touch with that early American spirit—in a Chinese sort of way—at *Superior Poultry*.

This is one retail store that actually lives up to its name, though it is definitely not for the faint-of-heart. But then again, if freshness comes first on your shopping list, or if you simply enjoy watching chickens meet their maker, a trip to *Superior* is in order.

Just try not to worry about all the bad karma.

> **Superior Poultry**
> 750 Broadway
> Los Angeles
> (213) 628-7645

Maria's Ramada

Maria's Ramada
1604 Kingsley Drive,
Hollywood
(213) 669-9654

Maria's has always seemed misplaced to us. It belongs along a dusty roadside near a sleepy border town. Instead, this being glamorous Hollywood, it's located just a hop, skip and a tombstone past the graves of Cecil B. DeMille, "Alfalfa" Switzer and Bugsy Siegal at The Hollywood Memorial Cemetery on Santa Monica Blvd.

Don't let the stench of the garbage Dumpster near the front door scare you off, *Maria's* really is one of the best Mexican restaurants in town. It's also proof that Christmas lights, plastic vegetables, and crudely woven god's eyes go a long way in dressin' up a place if you know what you're doing. We're unsure whether the decorator—perhaps Maria herself— got exactly what they were aiming for or simply made the most of a minimal design budget, but in either case it's dazzling. Each booth is slapped together out of old boards and corrugated tin not too unlike an outhouse, and is reminiscent of a cute little *barrio* absent of sewer rats.

Because of the *manana* mindset, we always wonder if the server hasn't taken a siesta or dropped dead in the kitchen. But no matter, the chips, salsa (the hottest around!) and pickled vegetables will keep you pacified quite nicely and the food is always worth the wait. There's a Seeburg Disc-o-theque in the corner with an excellent selection of Latino tunes. Making random choices is a good way to kill time while waiting for your order, and it's impossible to pick a bad song.

On a good night, if your lucky, you might spot cult film sensation Kitten Natividad tucked away in a corner booth, uproariously guzzling tequila. Kitten, a native of Juarez Chihuahua, Mexico, claims *Maria's* food is the best in Los Angeles. But then, she could have been drunk when she said that.

Phil's Diner

Their matchbook cover claims "extra ordinarily (sic) fine food in a unique atmosphere." Though we're unsure what "extra *ordinarly*" food is, you can sure as hell bet on the atmosphere being unique!

Phil's is actually a derailed dining car that has sat near the corner of Chandler and Lankershim in North Hollywood for the past two million years. Don't expect to find the manufactured and studied cuteness of a place like Carney's on Sunset though; *Phil's* is a slightly harder-core experience. Once you step past the sliding wood door you may notice that the original tiled floor slants considerably to the south. Each of the fourteen green vinyl stools have an inordinate wobble which require a strong sense of balance and equilibrium, and it's best not to touch anything if sticky surfaces and greasy dust offend you. There's not much flash here: some dusty souvenirs and mugs sit on a high shelf, and a 70s Peter Max-ish pinball machine stands in one corner. *Phil's* is the perfect place to stop for a break from Valley thrift shopping—in fact the Phil's experience is a lot like dining in a junk shop.

If you're in a quandary over what to order, proprietor and chef Mr. "Phil" Hong will yank the menu from your hands and point to the "Specialties" column—four of the best dishes served in any diner anywhere. For only a few bucks (everything here is dirt cheap) you can get supersavory Mongolian BBQ beef, fried potatoes, and a salad with what seems to be an oil and water dressing. It's always best to order one of *Phil's* specialties (try the steak sandwich!); however they do offer a comprehensive traditional diner menu as well.

Phil's has always been most popular among the blue collar crowd that work nearby (*Phil's* offers a "He-Man Breakfast"), but these days, you're likely to find just as many hipsters perched atop those precariously shaky stools. Get there early, Phil's keeps the working he-man hours of 9:00 A.M. to 3:00 P.M. Monday through Saturday.

Phil's Diner
11138 Chandler Blvd.
North Hollywood
(818) 763-1080

Dr. Hogly Wogly's Tyler Texas BBQ

Stuff Your Colon!

Dallas, Texas is known mostly for:

1) The TV show
2) The football team
3) JFK's last stand
4) Good barbecue

Of these, I am most interested in the last two, and as I get older and more confused about what may have really gone down that crisp November day at Dealey Plaza, I give up on conspiracies altogether and remember the wonderful barbecue that my father and I used to enjoy at a humble smokehouse called *Red Bryan's.* This was the most tender brisket imaginable, meat that needed no sauce, which is the case for any good Texas BBQ. It stood on its own merit, namely hours and hours of basting and slow-smoking that imparts a flavor only a true carnivore can even begin to appreciate. Vegans have given up their ways for real Texas BBQ.

When I first came to L.A., I stumbled across a few noteable soul food/BBQ joints by USC, but nothing could prepare me for the day when I found *Dr. Hogly Wogly* and all my dreams came true—in the Valley, no less. Tucked on Sepulveda Blvd. just south of Van Nuys, **Dr. Hogly Wogly's Tyler Texas BBQ** occupies an unassuming building in not the best of neighborhoods, but then again, you're there for the meat, not the scenery, and the place has curtains, so relax. The fact of the matter is that The Doctor's is about as close to the real thing as you're going to find in these parts, unless you consider the Lone Star state to be Freeway close.

Personally, I avoid eating at the restaurant itself not because of the cheesy wood-panelled decor (in fact, that's a plus), but because of the daunting crowds and ensuing waiting lists that accompany prime-time dining hours on Fridays and Saturdays. Fortunately, The Doctor offers take-out of both the a la carte and full dinner variety, complete with either mild or hot BBQ sauce on the side—in a glass bottle no less! This last amenity is simply astonishing in this age of plastic, and a slap in the face to all establishments that would serve their customers BBQ sauce—or any sauce for that matter—in anything less than a glass bottle. This fact alone would make *Dr. Hogly Wogly's Tyler Texas BBQ* a surefire bet for this book.

Fortunately for you, they also serve some damn good 'Q to go with the sauce—if you swing that way. Like at home, the meat at *Dr. Hogly Wogly's Tyler Texas BBQ* can go it alone—especially the brisket, baby back ribs, and pork loin—though both the hot and so-called "mild" are two of the best I've ever tasted, so much so that I sloshed it all over my meat by the end of the meal. Old habits and decorum, out the window in one suicidal leap.

If you choose to experience the anti-decor that is *Dr. Hogly Wogly's Tyler Texas BBQ,* then you'd also be best prepared for no-nonsense waitresses who work hard for a living hauling steaming trays of smoked meat all day and don't have the time to stand there while you go, "Um...uh...hold on a second...uh...do you have anything like a boneless, skinless grilled chicken breast—plain?" This is the best rib joint in town, plain and simple, so if you're on some candy-ass diet that means you can't eat like a normal Texan, do us all a favor and stay the hell away.

Having said that, perhaps I will now be able to get a table on the weekends.

—ARL

Dr. Hogly Wogly's Tyler Texas BBQ

8136 Sepulveda Blvd.

Van Nuys

(818) 782-2480

HOLSTEIN

GUERNSEY

HEREFORD

ABERDEEN-ANGUS

SHORTHORN

Digging The Monkeys *Damon's*

I think **Damon's** means "Denny's" in Samoan. Though the cuisine of this South Sea-inspired steak house doesn't compete with that of *Trader Vic's*, the prices sure as hell do; you'll pay here for an entire meal what you'd pay for one measly tropical drink at *Trader Vic's*. Most importantly, *Damon's* decor has a higher kitsch quotient, so leave your fine-tuned palate at home.

Juicy Steaks, Baked Potatoes, and Stuffed Monkeys

We live in a time when tropical decor is scarce among restaurants, which makes *Damon's* such a treasured retreat. Although *Damon's* has been in business since 1937, its original location— an extremely charming, old Hollywood affair— was senselessly bulldozed to make way for the Glendale Galleria. Which I wouldn't object to, had the Glendale Galleria taken on a Hawaiian theme.

Damon's has done nicely at their current location on Brand Avenue since 1983; but somehow, their new spot seems just stale enough to pass itself off as fifty-nine years old and no one would think to question. With a large tropical fish tank as its centerpiece, the *Damon's* decor is reminiscent of the well-trod tourist food-traps that pimple Waikiki: an abundance of bamboo and thatched roofing, vintage murals of island scenes lining the walls, and tabletops of slick, get-'em-in-get-'em-out formica. Some of the wiggiest "nautical" light fixtures ever to illuminate a dining room hang low over the tabletops, offsetting the Brobdingnagian macrame spectaculars draping dangerously close to your dinner plate. Suspended from the tall, A-frame ceiling looms a kayak swarming with stuffed monkeys.

You can still enjoy all that is *Damon's* even if you haven't got the stomach for surf and turf. Cozy up to the bar and drink your dinner, whiling away happy hour to *Damon's* continuous efflux of luau tunes. If you drink enough, the nasty reality of The Glendale Galleria is slightly easier to take.

—MM

Damon's Steak House

317 North Brand Blvd.
Glendale
(818) 507-1510
(818) 956-9056

OUT-AND-ABOUT

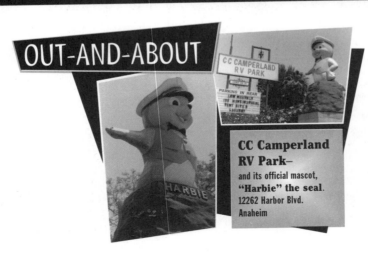

CC Camperland RV Park–
and its official mascot,
"Harbie" the seal.
12262 Harbor Blvd.
Anaheim

Dining inferno at *Bahooka Ribs and Grog*

f you thought those great 1960's Polynesian restaurants were all but extinct, journey back with me into the world of **Bahooka**, a hyper-surrealistic Polynesian wonderland right in our own backyard. If you can imagine a veritable labyrinth of aquariums, tiki gods, plastic light-up parrots, U.S. Marine memorabilia and a vegetarian bulemic fish appropriately named "Bahooka Joe," then you have only just begun to envision the garish glory that is *Bahooka*.

Bahooka is all the things that your psychoactive Tahitian dreams (or nightmares as the case may be) are made of. For me personally, *Bahooka* is further validation that real life is in fact far better than fiction. At the very least, it's worth the drive.

All This And *Go Go* Too!

Clearly the shining star of *Bahooka* is a waitress named Go Go. That's really her name, swear to God. Not only is Go Go a complete doll and a laugh riot, she can garnish a Polynesian cocktail like nobody's business. And when Go Go's in the mood to garnish, stand back. She'll load a landfill's worth of maraschino cherries, pineapple and orange slices and miniature paper umbrellas onto every drink she serves. But most importantly, Go Go sets it all on fire. Go Go has actually served my water and coffee on fire, bless her heart. She brought a flaming near-beer to my dinner companion. But her pyromaniacal cocktail garnishing hardly ends with cocktails. She's the only waitress I know of that can make a side order of fries look like a Singapore sling. Go Go has even set my Jell-O ablaze. She really outdid herself one evening when I informed her that I was in need of silverware. She quickly returned with a tray, on which was presented a knife and fork...*entirely engulfed in flames!* Go Go brings fun fun fun, Polynesian style, wherever she goes. I strongly encourage you to request Go Go as your waitress. Call ahead to see if she's working that night and be sure to tip her at least 30%. Go Go is a Goddess.

Fortunately, *Bahooka* doesn't attract a "fun" crowd and the clientele seem to run mostly toward senior citizens, large families, and teenagers on first dates. But don't let that scare you away, the dimly lit booths and alcoves are private enough to have sex in—although not recommended—and I've never gotten in trouble for whooping it up and having a real good time. And with 98 (count 'em, 98) fluorescent fish tanks bubbling away, it's the closest you can come to having dinner on the "Submarine Voyage" at Disneyland.

Start off with one of their "Polynesian Appetizers" like *Cheese Sticks Fried in Beer Batter* or *Onion Rings*. However, I highly recommend the Fish Puffs: small balls of something fishy deep fried and served with a variety of "Polynesian" sauces. As far as I'm concerned there's only one choice for your entree: Bahooka's Special Exotic Ribs. Not that these ribs are especially delicious, but they are "special" and "exotic," so that counts for something. Politically correct herbivores won't find Polynesian braised tofu on the menu, but you will find a baked yam or potato, corn on the cob, salad, vegetable soup or a vegetarian burger—just like in Tahiti! If you have trouble making a choice from the selection of eighteen entrees, ask Go Go for a recommendation. Have Go Go select your cocktail too. In fact, ask Go Go for marital advice, ask her why the sky is blue, ask her the meaning of life, ask her how the human brain works. She'll have an answer for you.

If you've been very well-behaved, make a polite request that Go Go show you the famous vegetarian bulemic fish, "Bahooka Joe." He's seventeen years old, is so large that he barely has room to turn around in his tank, and he chomps down carrot sticks like an angry rabid dog. Unfortunately, there's a limit to the number of carrot-eating fish presentations Go Go can give in one evening, since Joe tends to regurgitate his veggies once he's had more than his fill. So if Go Go is unable to meet your request, please understand, and come back another time.

Once you've experienced the magic of *Bahooka*, you'll want to return again and again and again....

—MM

**Bahooka Ribs
and Grog**
4501 North Rosemead Blvd.
Rosemead
(818) 285-1241

Dining and Dashing at *The Original Pantry*

The Original Pantry is noteworthy for a number of reasons:

1) It has survived for almost a century in one of L.A.'s less savory areas.

2) There is no lock or key for the front door, and has never been without a customer.

3) They print a pamphlet (sometimes available at the cashier) that enumerates the immense number of cabbage heads, dead cows, and other sundries consumed by this place in a single year (very impressive).

4) There is a myth that all the white-shirted and bow-tied waiters are ex-cons.

5) Current L.A. Mayor Dick Riordan owns the place.

6) Lastly, they don't seem to want any free publicity, wouldn't return my numerous phone calls, and refused to let me take any pictures of the restaurant's interior for this book when I paid a personal visit.

don't get it. All I wanted to do was write up *The Original Pantry* as one of L.A.'s best and brightest restaurants—but trying to get info out of the folks who run the place is harder than breaking into CIA headquarters in Langley and tapping into the mainframe. Without going into the dismal details, let me just say that I found it next to impossible to get a copy of the booklet above (#3) unless I made the 40-minute trek from my home to downtown, and when I did, they were pleased to inform me they were fresh out! Add to this the insult that they refused to let me take any photos of the frozen-in-time interior, and well, it was almost enough to make me want to drop the entry from the book altogether.

Considering the fact that L.A.'s current Mayor owns *The Pantry*, I thought that perhaps a call to his office would solve the communication problem. So I called. When I mentioned to one of the Mayor's aides that I was including the restaurant in the book as one of L.A.'s shining stars, she glibly replied "Have you ever eaten there?" Well, smarty-pants, the fact of the matter is that I have—many, many times. While attending USC in the early 80's, I took most of my meals at this joint...so I have what you might call a sentimental attachment to *The Pantry*. Though the frequency of my attendance has waned over the

Is That A Shiv In Your Apron Or Are You Just Happy To See Me?

years, my affection has only grown in light of the satanic spawn of chi-chi, nouvelle, micro-portioned eateries inspired by "Wolfgang" Puck and his cancerous clones in West Los Angeles. *The Pantry* is a *real* restaurant, the kind they simply don't make anymore, and that alone should warrant a visit. And all kidding aside from the Mayor's office, the food is simple but good.

The Original Pantry (the term "original" is obviously very big when it comes to naming downtown restaurants) sits on the corner of Figueroa and Ninth, just a few blocks north of the L.A. Convention Center. Open 24 hours a day, with no lock or key for the front door, *The Pantry* is proud to claim the slogan "Never without a customer." Quick to serve almost any meal at just about any time, it's a famished eater's paradise. A huge silver bowl filled with iced celery stalks, carrot sticks and radishes is already waiting on your table, and as soon as your buns hit the hard seat (usually still warm from the last customer), a plate of unusually good cole slaw is slid in front of you with all the speedy intent of an Indy pit crew. You'll also get an entire loaf of fresh-baked sourdough bread for your voracious appetite.

Visit *The Pantry* not just for the huge, delicious steaks (all less than $10 each) served all day and night (may I suggest you try the tenderloin, butterfly-style?), but for the pot roast, short ribs, and Spartan yet somehow charming high-ceilinged ambience. And, of course, there's the eclectic mix of clientele. If you happen to dine alone, take advantage of the large community table near the front door (it seats about eleven) or the traditional counter. Your eating companions just may include a variety of well-dressed lawyers, mumbling bag ladies, some grunge rockers, a few sailors, some 'SC frat boys, and God knows who else. No matter what the mix, the conversation is never dull...that is, if anyone bothers to speak up.

Breakfast at *The Pantry* would have made Henry the 8th quite proud—and even fatter. The portions are ridiculously huge—especially the chili and cheese omelette, which comes with a gargantuan portion of hash browns that must weigh in at close to a pound. You won't find some fancy-ass Northern Italian grill at *The Pantry* because everything —including the herculean slabs of meat—are cooked on the standard flat heating element you find at any respectable coffee shop. This sometimes makes for a bit of a greasy experience, although if you sit at the counter, you'll take some comfort as you notice that the industrious chefs clean the fry-grill with what seems like ludicrous frequency.

The waiters—who, as urban legend has it, are all ex-cons—are at worst, simply excellent waiters. There was one gentleman who worked there during my entire tenure at USC who looked just like Stan Laurel. He had such kind eyes, a meek manner, and always remembered my usual order—no matter if it was breakfast, lunch or dinner. Beyond this, he was so quick with the cole slaw you'd swear he must have been hovering overhead. He laughed off the ex-con story when I once mentioned it to him, although not without a hint of nervousness. It dawned on me then that perhaps there was some truth to the story after all, but I didn't really want to know. Why ruin your appetite by possibly discovering that your mild-mannered waiter was in fact once an ax-wielding maniac who hacked up the wife and kids, wrapped them in brown butcher paper and twine, and stored them in the meat locker? When I made my worthless visit to *The Pantry* for the pamphlet, I was fortunate enough to meet a security guard named Armando. He was the only employee other than another familiar waiter who would give me information on the place, and confirmed that the ex-con/waiter connection is indeed nothing but a nasty rumor.

The Original Pantry
877 South Figueroa
Los Angeles
(213) 972-9279

Whenever the rare occasion transpires that a customer dines and dashes without paying his check, you can sit back and enjoy a good show. Like greased lightning, one of the waiters will tear out after the offender, and invariably drag the sniveling snot back to the restaurant so that the LAPD can come and haul him/her away for a proper beating in the privacy of the downtown jail. Such a scene may well lead one to be convinced that these waiters in their crisp white shirts, bow ties, and aprons may have perhaps once been, if anything, *prison guards*, and not the ex-prisoners of myth. Wouldn't that be ironic in a Hollywood movie kind of way? Maybe Bruce Willis can play the head waiter.

No matter what the backgrounds of the waiters may be, *The Original Pantry* is a hell of a place to stuff your face. Check it out when you feel like digging in without getting soaked, because the prices are very reasonable—which is all the more reason not to skip out on the check. And when you're done with your meal, be sure to pick up a souvenir shirt, hat, and postcard; especially the latter, since they won't let you take photos of the precious interior. And who can blame them? After all, you might use the pix to recreate a similar success story in *The Pantry*'s glorious image. Or worse, sell the damn things to the commies. And while you're at it, don't forget to ask for a free *Pantry* button bearing the Mayor's smiling face.

(P.S.—A special tip of the hat to Armando, "The Peacekeeper," for taking the time to talk to me and straighten out a few facts. Perhaps he should be kicked upstairs to the publicity department— if only they had one.)

Speaking of whom, hey Mayor, why don't you tell your managerial goons to lighten up a bit when it comes to providing publicity? After all, if anyone knows the value of a photo op, it must be a shrewd politician and businessman such as yourself.

Then again, maybe pork barrels, not pork chops, are your strong suit.

—ARL

Luxuriating at *The Beverly Hills Hotel Fountain Coffee Room*

ew structures in Los Angeles are more steeped in Tinseltown legend than **The Beverly Hills Hotel**. It's been a favorite movie star trysting spot for decades (Marilyn Monroe and Yves Montand steamed up bungalow #5), it's also served as a valued celebrity hideout (John Lennon and Yoko Ono locked themselves into bungalow #11 for a solid week), and it's played host to the eccentricities of those too rich to question (Howard Hughes asked that room service perch his nightly roast beef sandwich orders in the branches of a tree just outside his favorite bungalow, #4). *The Beverly Hills Hotel* has also been a favored arena for several A-list adulterers (Desi Arnaz loved many a "Lucy" here), and set the scene for some of Hollywood's most volatile marriages (Elizabeth Taylor and Richard Burton played out a real-life "Who's Afraid of Virginia Woolf" in bungalow #5—with a standing room service order of four bottles of vodka a day: two at breakfast, two at lunch). Celebrated drunks W.C. Fields, Dean Martin, and Humphrey Bogart all tied one on here in The Polo Lounge bar.

> **Coffee Shop Dining At Its Swankiest**

Late 1992, *The Beverly Hills Hotel* closed its doors for a full two and a half years in order to undergo a $100 million restoration and remodeling. The moment the cyclone fencing went up around its 12 acres, I feared the famed landmark would be subject to the worst facelift in Beverly Hills history. Though the remodeling was limited mostly to the accommodations (252 rooms were knocked around and enlarged, shrinking the total to 194), and the work was necessary for the hotel to hold its own among the more contemporary luxury accommodations in the area, much of the original classic charm—sadly—was lost.

Worst of all, the hotel was repainted in the WRONG color pink, and for anyone familiar with the pre-facelifted *Beverly Hills Hotel* the difference was glaringly obvious. Once a timeless flamingo pink, the treasured centerpiece of Sunset Boulevard had been depreciated with a shade close to that of a pencil eraser. There are numerous other minor changes that only we freaks for detail would ever notice; the absence of the quaint downstairs drug store is sorely felt, as is Harry Winston Jewelers which used to be located in the lobby. Though still exquisite in anyone's estimation, the revamped hotel is undeniably contradistinctive to the original.

Fortunately, in spite of the extensive remodeling, the best spot in the entire hotel managed to slip by unaltered. Tucked away into a tiny, awkward, asymmetrical nook just inside the curved stairway leading down from the lobby, sits the little-known **Fountain Coffee Room**. The classic 1949 design by architect Paul Williams has an unrivaled charm evocative of a pharmacy soda fountain, but cross-pollinated with a dash of mid-century modern swank as a sweeping free-form black marble countertop lined with 19 stools cuts through the center of the narrow room. Above, recessed lighting set into a streamlined stucco overhang runs the length of the counter at ceiling level. Some walls are plate glass, others are covered with a vintage pattern of deep green banana leaves—the old trademark wallpaper pattern once featured throughout the hotel. Behind the counter within arm's reach of your pink vinyl seat, a cook with a tall chef's hat serves up the food from a sparkling chrome grill, handing it off to chirpy waitresses in pink uniforms who maintain the impeccable service standards of the hotel's "nicer" eateries. This is coffee shop dining at its finest.

Fresh ingredients and fastidious preparation (to the extreme that grease is blotted from a bacon strip before it's placed onto your plate) may not do much to justify a $5.00 bowl of dry cereal or a $10.00 hamburger, but the experience is worth the inordinate profit margin and the food is the best of its kind. Whatever the time of day, start out with an

**The Fountain
Coffee Room
The Beverly
Hills Hotel**

9641 Sunset Blvd.
Beverly Hills
(310) 276-2251

Orange Freeze, the apex of their fountain selections. Priced at $5.50, the Orange Freeze averages out to about .25¢ per sip, but it's worth every penny—plus the $5.00 you'll have to pay for parking.

The Fountain Coffee Room doesn't draw the tony crowd of The Polo Lounge, but it's a pretty sure bet that you'll spot at least one person who was a guest on "The Merv Griffin Show" interspersed among ladies who lunch, and a handful of characters straight from the pages of a Brett Easton Ellis novel sporting that just-rolled-out-of-bed-after-a-long-night-of-cocaine/sex/cigarettes/vodka look.

—MM

Did You Know?

—The 1992-1995 remodeling wasn't the only time the Beverly Hills Hotel closed its doors. The depression forced the hotel to shut down in 1930, until The Bank of America reopened it in 1932.

—The Polo Lounge used to be called El Jardin until 1941, when it was renamed in honor of regulars Will Rogers, Darryl Zanuck and Tommy Hitchcock who frequented the hotel after their polo matches—and for Charlie Wrightsman, whose championship polo team kept its silver trophy bowl there.

—"Rancho de las Aguas"—a piece of land once owned by the Mexican government—was developed in 1906 by Burton Green and renamed "Beverly Hills" in 1907, after his home in Beverly Farms, Massachusetts.

OUT-AND-ABOUT

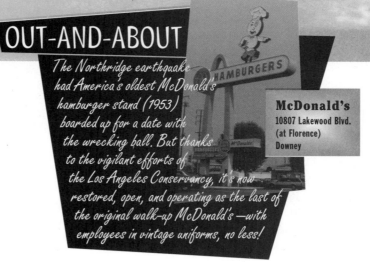

The Northridge earthquake had America's oldest McDonald's hamburger stand (1953) boarded up for a date with the wrecking ball. But thanks to the vigilant efforts of the Los Angeles Conservancy, it's now restored, open, and operating as the last of the original walk-up McDonald's—with employees in vintage uniforms, no less!

McDonald's
10807 Lakewood Blvd.
(at Florence)
Downey

Pastrami without Pretension at
Brent's Delicatessen

"Hungry People Eat At Brent's" (sic).

—Slogan for Brent's Delicatessen in Northridge

The Miracle Of Meatloaf

Just like New Yorkers enjoy prattling on about Wolff's and Carnegie Delicatessens as being the best in the world, Los Angeles Jews take pride in having their own firm opinions on which Southland Deli stands astride the top of the matzo heap. *Art's* in Studio City, *Nate and Al's* in Beverly Hills, *Canter's* in Fairfax—all popular and predictable picks— are more highly regarded than any of the "chain" delis (like *Jerry's* or *Bagel Nosh*), or worse, delis that are not in fact delis in the true sense of the word, but merely sandwich shops that pose as delis. In L.A., it seems that location has a lot to do with a deli's popularity, otherwise *Langer's* (across from the gang- and junkie-infested MacArthur Park), and **Brent's**, located in a less-than-glamorous Northridge shopping center, would also be on the lips of every Angeleno who knows the difference between corned beef and corn on the cob.

While we personally witnessed the tragic decline of *Langer's* dismal surroundings, we have only seen improvement in the expansion and service at *Brent's*. It would seem that the only thing wrong with *Brent's* is its location: not the fact that it's located two doors down from an *Office Depot*, but the fact that it's situated deep within that icky-poo wasteland they call the San Fernando Valley. Of course, not everyone looks on the Valley like it's a soiled diaper, especially if you happen to live in it, but city dwellers from the other side of the hill tend to turn up their noses at the thought of having to travel into the Valley, as if their pristine hell-hole has been sprinkled with magic pixie dust. And, in fact, it has—though in the Valley we're not ashamed to call it smog. So if the Valley does somehow manage to secede from Los Angeles and become its own city, then why not erect a big brick wall along the border, topped with barbed wire and broken glass, and torture the bastards on the other side by blowing the scent of *Brent's* corned beef over the damned thing. That'll teach 'em.

The *American Heritage Dictionary* says the word delicatessen is the plural of the German word for "delicacies." Isn't it pretty damn ironic that any restaurant that sells such heavy duty fare as blintzes, matzo ball soup and chubs—not to mention the ominous black pastrami—should find the origin of its name in such a gentile word as "delicate"? But then again, the Jews are no stranger to irony.

Speaking of irony, it also seems strange that a deli should serve up the best meat- loaf in town, considering the fact that meatloaf is a traditional mainstay of goyem dining. Oh meatloaf, bane of childhood, lowly leftover, pillar of budget cuisine, how you are misun- derstood! Oh meatloaf, odd conglomeration of ground cow and sundry fillers, long have you suffered at the hands of negligent chefs and uncreative housewives! Yet *Brent's* meat- loaf is a heavenly concoction that kicks ass on the same stuff served at posh poseur joints like Beverly Hill's *Kate Mantilini's*, which singlehandedly made *loaf de la meat* a chic menu

item. *Brent's* meatloaf won't cost you an arm and a leg, though, and is as substantial and savory as this dish comes. The homemade mashed potatoes on the side aren't bad, either.

Apparently, we are not alone in our reverence for *Brent's*. At noon the front lobby looks like a Tokyo subway car—except everyone is wearing lots of gold. You may have to wait for a table, but since their expansion after the '94 quake, you'll find it quite painless and well worth whatever time you spend cooling your heels. Best of all, *Brent's* is actually run by a real family, and a nice one at that. After the quake, when all the *7-Eleven*s were tripling their prices on batteries, *Brent's* was open that same morning, despite having incurred some nasty damages. But *Brent's* wasn't open for business—they were open to give away free loaves of bread and other surviving foodstuffs to those who were in need. With every food store closed in a ten-mile radius, and considering the extent of their own damages, this gesture on *Brent's* behalf would have brought a tear to Frank Capra's eye.

The employees at *Brent's* are an efficient lot, and as kind as they come—far kinder than the usual L.A. deli help, which seem to pride themselves on imitating nasty New Yorkers. Believe me, if we wanted a gum-smacking waitress with a curt attitude or a deli counter-man who says things like, "Yeah, what do you want? I don't have all day!", then we'd move back to The Rotten Apple. Some people may find a kind of charming bravado in such faux rudeness, but we simply find it, well, rude.

As if to further bolster my claims about this hinterland establishment, *Brent's* turned up as the #1 deli in the 1994 and 1995 *Zagat Guide*s, beating out all the other delis across the Santa Monica mountains where allegedly bonafide Angelenos live and breath and eat gefilte fish. So go ahead and secede, San Fernando, and do it with pride. After all, we have *Brent's* on our side.

Suck on that, L.A.

Brent's Delicatessen and Restaurant
19565 Parthenia St.
Northridge
(818) 886-5679

OUT-AND-ABOUT

One of the finest, best preserved, and ultra-wiggiest pieces of historic architecture in Los Angeles. This 1921 design by Henry Oliver was originally built on the lot of the now defunct Willat Movie Studios in Culver City. It was moved to its current location in the 1930s, where it functions as a private home. Boo!

The Witch House
516 Walden Drive
Beverly Hills

Dim Sum at *Ocean Seafood*

I'm not ashamed to say it. I *love MSG*. Maybe it's because when I was a child, my mother would pour some Accent in her hand while she was fixing dinner and let me lick it from her palm just to keep me at bay. So it only makes sense that I love Chinese food, especially the delicious dumplings and sundry items that come under the classification of Dim Sum. And when it comes to the latter, my favorite eaterie is a bustling place in Chinatown that is aptly named *Ocean Seafood*. Now, I don't know whether *Ocean* uses a lot of MSG in their Dim Sum or not, but I do know that they make the best damn dumplings in Chinatown and that's all I care about. Some will argue that the nearby *ABC Seafood*—a great name for those learning their alphabet—at 708 New High St. (not a drug dealers' hangout) is really the best, but let them argue. I still prefer *Ocean*.

Best Place To O.D. On MSG

In case you don't know about Dim Sum brunch, it's a weekend occurrence at many Chinese restaurants in Chinatowns across the U.S. It's like other brunches in that you get stuffed to the gills for a nominal price, but unlike other brunches, the food comes to you as soon as your cheeks hit the seat. This is accomplished through the miracle of many Chinese women pushing metal carts loaded with slotted steel or bamboo containers which in turn are loaded with tasty steamed stuffed dumplings of sundry shapes, sizes and flavors. You also have dessert carts, soup carts, broccoli/clam carts...you name it. Carts galore. And these babies constantly circulate throughout the room, so you are never far from a plate of Har Gow or Cha Shu Bao or Shu Mai. If you don't mind the drive, you can check out the plethora of opportunities in Monterey Park. Or just go to *Ocean*, where Dim Sum is served not only on the weekends, but every day of the week.

You enter *Ocean* downstairs, although in the past year or so, a dining room has been installed next to the first floor elevator. Avoid this area since you don't get to enjoy the vast, clamoring throng awaiting you upstairs. Once you've climbed the fountain-lined, mirror-encased stairs and find yourself at the top, give your name to the girl behind the counter. She'll hand you a piece of paper with a number (just like *Baskin-Robbins*), and then you'll stand and wait with the others while number after number—far from yours—are called. This is great if you're being drafted into the military, but not so amusing when your stomach is growling and you're faced with carts of aromatic food that jaunt by at a teasing rate on their way to some lucky sod who's already been seated. I combat this by pushing my way to the tiny bar which is not meant to serve patrons, smile, and buy about four beers for myself. Drinking and waiting go so well together, and *Ocean* also serves up a variety of tropical drinks in the *Trader Vic's* vein.

One tactic I use to get around the wait is to act like I'm famous. Of course, this requires you to dress like a Hollywood jerk and wear sunglasses indoors, but that's the price of avoiding the plebs. Here's how it works: 1) Look like a star. A real star. 2) Grab the arm of a passing waiter and tell him you are shooting on location down the street and you need to be back on the set in an hour or Mel Gibson, your notoriously nutty co-star, will hurt you. 3) Ask him to get you a cocktail while he finds your table. This usually clinches it, and you'll soon find yourself seated with a colorful drink in your hand—topped with a pretty umbrella, of course. This works for men or women, although women should choose a co-star like Barbara Streisand, Sharon Stone or someone equally as scary.

Sometimes the place is mobbed, sometimes semi-mobbed, but always one or the other. Go early if you can stomach pork bao at 11 A.M., or you may want to go around lunchtime and brave the wait. After all, once you're seated, you can loiter until they stop serving (around 3 P.M.)—so why not just relax, loosen your belt, yap a bit, and when you're hungry again, just grab another steaming serving of shu mai and presto, you're on your way.

Ocean specializes in seafood dumplings, but they also serve pork, beef, and chicken items as well as an entire menu of excellent Mandarin fare. Don't plan on eating again that day—unless you happen to take home some goodies from their downstairs take-out stand. The barbecued pork and salty fried shrimp are big-time winners. Two important pointers when patronizing the take-out stand: 1) Don't tell your cardiologist; and 2) Don't look into the kitchen, whatever you do—everything you've heard about Chinese kitchens is not only true, it's worse.

Another neat thing about *Ocean Seafood* is that you can have your choice of any number of live fish and crustaceans swimming around in the huge acrylic tanks just off the West dining room. All you have to do is point 'em out, pick your style of preparation, and bang—they're dead meat. Makes you feel kind of powerful. In the off-dumpling hours, *Ocean* also serves a great dinner menu and a wide variety of traditional, non-Dim Sum specialities.

So this weekend, skip the mediocre multitude of skeezy "champagne brunches" and give yourself completely to the Dim Sum experience. That is, unless you're one of those wimps who can't handle their Maoist beer or their Monosodium Glutamate...

—ARL

Ocean Seafood
750 North Hill St.
Chinatown
(213) 687-3088

Is That A Lamb Chop In Your Pocket Or Are You Just Happy To See Me?

Epicurean Delights After Midnight at the *Pacific Dining Car*

One of the few benefits of living in L.A. is the preponderance of establishments open 24 hours a day—other than crack houses, of course. The truth is, we Angelenos are a spoiled lot, fortunate enough to live in a town where you can go grocery shopping, stuff your face, or have your shirt pressed at 3 in the morning. Such nightcrawler conveniences are almost enough to make up for the San Andreas fault. *Almost.*

While *The Original Pantry* may be the most notorious never-closed eaterie in town, it is not alone in its distinction. Just northwest of *The Pantry* is the **Pacific Dining Car**, a top-notch restaurant that has been in business since 1921 and, though not inexpensive, is a late-night epicurean's wet dream come true. And like *The Pantry*, the *PDC* isn't located in the best of neighborhoods, yet still warrants a visit—especially if you have an insatiable craving for Maine lobster and filet mignon in the wee hours before dawn.

We like to think of ourselves as 25-hour-a-day guys in a 24-hour-a-day town, and rightly so. The entertainment business—not to be confused with the rigors of writing books such as this one—causes people to keep odd hours—which is where the *PDC* comes in handy. Sure, you can get a hearty blue-collar post-midnight meal at *The Pantry*—or even *Denny's* for that matter—but if you try to order a crab cocktail or a plate of ceviche or a beefsteak tomato & Maui onion salad all you'll get is a blank stare at best and at worst, thrown out on your ass. The *Pacific Dining Car* features all of these items, along with a great Caesar Salad, crab cakes, shrimp scampi and U.S.D.A. *Prime* Eastern Corn-Fed Beef that's aged on the premises, cut by their own butcher, and grilled over Mesquite charcoal. If *The Pantry* is the Wal-Mart of all-night diners, then the *PDC* is Nordstrom, plain and simple.

We could go into the colorful history behind the *PDC* and how it moved around a number of times before ending up at its current location, but all that drivel is secondary to the mere fact that it even exists. Fact is, most of you may never have the desire to eat a huge veal chop with a side of homemade red pepper sauce at 4 A.M., but if you ever do, you know it's there. And that alone is reason enough to sleep soundly and feel strangely secure in an otherwise precarious universe.

Dinner is served all day and night at the *PDC*, but if you're in the mood for some of the best eggs Benedict in town, you can get them—along with anything else on the incredible breakfast menu—between 11 P.M. and 11 A.M. on weekdays, and until 4 P.M. on the weekends. The lavish lunch menu is available from 11 A.M. 'til 4 P.M., and you can count on tasty specials every day of the week. Last time we stopped in, they were serving fresh asparagus, Mulligatawny soup, and soft shell crabs as but a few of their special offerings.

In October of 1990, the *Pacific Dining Car* opened another restaurant in Santa Monica with the same name, menu, and gracious service. The only glaring difference between the two is that the Santa Monica branch closes between 2 and 6 A.M. Both take reservations and offer valet parking, neither of which you will encounter at *The Pantry* or *Denny's*. Limeys will undoubtedly find the afternoon tea (served between 3 and 5 P.M.) an absolutely splendid affair, while non–tea-totalers will delight in the full bar. After all, what could go better with your California omelette than a perfectly mixed Bloody Mary? And while you're at it, make mine a double.

L.A. takes a lot of knocks for being a tacky, garish, classless culture of self-centered, drug-addled, Cliff-Note-educated mogul-heathens and tanned bag people—all of which is true—but for our money, the *Pacific Dining Car* beats the pants off any Manhattan diner you can name, any day of the week. And when the Big One finally does give L.A. the royal shakedown, this is one of the few places we hope is left standing. After all, any earthquake over 7 on the Richter scale can make you work up an appetite for a T-bone steak the size of your head, no matter what time it may be. And like the births of most babies, any respectable tremor of lethal proportions is bound to strike in the middle of the night, in which case, you probably won't need a reservation after all.

OUT-AND-ABOUT

And you thought "The Tonight Show" was Burbank's only cultural advantage! This much-maligned pocket of the San Fernando Valley is also a proud home to the oldest standing Bob's Big Boy in the country! Architect Wayne McAllister's Streamline-cum-Coffee Shop Modern design hasn't lost an iota of its original swank since its opening in 1949. Though the interior has been redecorated, the restaurant still—incredibly enough—features car-hop service Saturday and Sunday nights from 5:00 to 8:00 P.M., in the original cantilevered car-port towards the rear of the lot. Dig it!

Bob's Big Boy
4211 Riverside Drive
Burbank

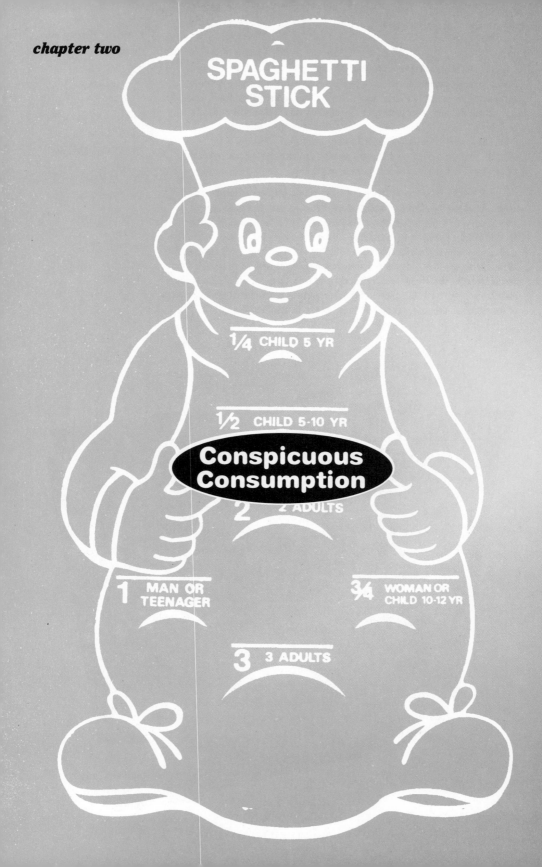

SPAGHETTI
STICK

1/4 CHILD 5 YR

1/2 CHILD 5-10 YR

Conspicuous Consumption

2 2 ADULTS

1 MAN OR
TEENAGER

3/4 WOMAN OR
CHILD 10-12 YR

3 3 ADULTS

Complete the following sentence:

When I've got some extra change in my pocket, I will generally...

A) ...put at least 10% into a savings, IRA, or investment account.

B) ...head straight for a liquor store.

C) ...comb the classified listings under the heading "erotic massage."

D) ...squander it foolishly on unnecessary items like rat skulls, religious statuary, head shop paraphernalia, vintage pornography, festive Polynesian cocktail mugs, toe-tag keychains, gigantic glow-in-the-dark rosaries, theatrical blood, full-color forensic manuals, photos of naked movie stars, and anything else truly bizarre.

If you answered "D," you'll be pleased to know that L.A. is a treasure trove of such trash; a veritable Valhalla of the valueless, where you can waste your hard-earned dollars on a seemingly endless assortment of way-cool junk (no, not heroin). And if you're unclear about where to start, may we suggest you begin with the following pages? You'll find that our outre shopping guide, packed with a sampling of everything odd from vintage lingerie to human skeletons, will be a welcome change of pace from your usual shopping regime—and will have you alternative consumers frothing at the mouth. Allow us to steer you to various vendors of the truly strange, and perhaps you'll discover a fabulous world of refuse that you never even knew—or cared—existed.

Indeed, the best things in life are not free— they're for sale among the obscure junk stores, curio shops, and gift emporiums of L.A. BIZARRO!

Diggin' the cool threads at *Hidden Treasures*

Never was a store more appropriately named. Just up the road from a filthy health food market and across the bend from the Topanga Canyon restaurant fixture, *Inn of the Seventh Ray*, stands a little mirage of tiki gods, nautical curiosities, trickling waterfalls and old clothes.

For the most part, **Hidden Treasures** is a vintage clothing store, but the wares—which also include quilts, vintage textiles, linens and sundry antiques—are almost secondary to this down-the-rabbit-hole, brain-ticklin' nautical encounter. Shuffling through the clothing racks here is a very different shopping experience; like someone slipped a little DMT into your Blue Hawaii. Blowfish poised in a frozen PUFF hang in high corners, miniature ships and mermaidabilia line narrow shelves, and taxidermied reptiles climb the walls and peek from behind rocks in the cascading waterfall dioramas just outside the open windows. Curios from the deep sea and primitive Polynesian carvings fill your field of vision and continue outdoors onto the patio where seashell-encrusted tropical love-grottos and a bamboo coffee bar line the vine-enclosed terrace (used only for special events—don't show up thinking you can hang out all day on the patio reading the paper, drinking coffee, and making a nuisance of yourself). Like a hidden corner of The Secret Garden, an enticing, narrow stairway spirals up the side of a steep hill through vines and trees, and levels off at a small sandy precipice landscaped with a shallow lily pond, a campfire and a full sized teepee. The only thing missing are Terence McKenna's machine elves.

Darrell Hazen is the humble creator-proprietor of this Topangan oasis. The source of his creative inspiration is due partly to being nautically influenced early in life, plus he also admits, "I like to trip people out." Originally planning to move his business to Hawaii, he decided instead to move Hawaii to Topanga. Hawaii never looked so good. His somewhat psychedelic interpretation of the islands couldn't have found a better home than in hippiefied Topanga Canyon, hence *Hidden Treasures* is twice removed from reality.

If the wealth of oceanic oddities aren't enough to challenge your focus, the clothing racks are so tightly packed into every corner of the piecemeal building that you're continually poked in the gut by rows of wire hangers. You may have to occasionally step over a snoozing dog, and the sheer number of dust mites must number in the zillion of trillions, but at these prices who's complaining? You can even find items with pricetags marked "FREE." They deal in everything from Victorian lace to David Cassidy-era cottage cheese polyknit, as well as scarves, hats, sunglasses and novelties. The *Hidden Treasures* staff is inordinately hospitable, and it's not unusual for one of them to graciously whip you up a complimentary cappuccino or serve you a pastry as you browse—a gesture heretofore exclusive to the couture salons of Rodeo Drive. You'd have to *beat* this kind of treatment from the vapid fashion victims working in some of the other vintage clothing shops around town!

No trip to *Hidden Treasures* should be considered complete without taking a peek at the toilet seat in the ladies' room.

A final word of caution: Topanga Canyon can appear to be a very beautiful—even charming—little community. Don't fall victim to the "Green Acres" syndrome; the city man thought moving to the country was an excellent idea until he met some of the locals.

Hidden Treasures
154 Topanga Blvd.
Topanga Canyon
(310) 455-2998

A vicarious vacation at *Adventure In Postcards*

Making the trek out to Sunland is an adventure in itself, but if you came home with a lurid color postcard of L.A.'s long defunct Zamdoanga South Sea Nite Club ("Home of the Tailless Monkeys"), or an autographed photo of Joyce DeWitt, wouldn't the trip be worth it?!

This hole-in-the-wall gold mine has a stock of postcards—turn of the century to the present—numbering well into the hundred thousands, all painstakingly sorted into categories with headings as obscure as "Insane Asylums," "Swastikas," "Outhouses," and "Amish, Mennonite & Shaker." You'll also find the obvious, with headings for each state, famous cities, foreign countries, animals, food, hotels, et al. And don't pass over the binder of cards titled "Ethnic and Macabre" or the collection of autographed celebrity photos and correspondence (Wayne Newton, Penny Singleton, Dom DeLouise, Isabelle Sanford, Bob Barker, Vincent Price...)

Wish You Were Here

Owner Lee Brown used to deal exclusively in depression-era glass, but seeing that she was "so close to the fault line," Lee figured she'd be better off with merchandise that didn't shatter into a million sharp pieces when it fell to the ground. She made the shift into the postcard biz twenty-five years ago, and has kept this Sunland shop for the past seven. Lee knows her stock well, and aside from being sweet as pie, she maintains the most extensive, varied, and reasonably priced collection in Southern California. Thousands of cards are priced at .25 cents, most range from $1 to $5.

Although Lee's collection is postcard-heavy, the store still has a few depression glass pieces, and carries most any kind of vintage paper matter: matchbooks, playing cards, tourist pamphlets, family snapshots, advertising displays, playbills and programs, promotional stills, luggage and travel stickers. Especially wondrous are the boxes marked "miscellaneous," where one can find sundry items like WWII ration stamps, old Disneyland tickets books (all absent of "E" tickets), or an "Alka-Seltzer Songbook" from 1937. Look deeper into the corners and you'll spot swizzle sticks, political buttons and God knows what else! Half the thrill is the digging, and *Adventure In Postcards* lives up to its name.

From kitty cats to cannibalism, Bozo the Clown to Hindu cremations, *Adventure in Postcards* covers it all. It's the absolute perfect place to while away a rainy afternoon, or if you have time, the rest of your life.

Adventure in Postcards
8423 Foothill Blvd.
Sunland
(818) 352-5663

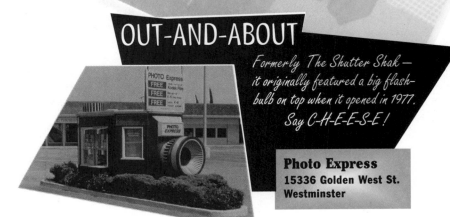

OUT-AND-ABOUT

Formerly The Shutter Shak — it originally featured a big flash-bulb on top when it opened in 1977. Say C-H-E-E-S-E!

Photo Express
15336 Golden West St.
Westminster

Roaming through the prop palm trees and thatched huts of **Oceanic Arts**, one half expects to spot Tina Louise sheathed in a silk sarong sipping pineapple juice from a coconut shell—because the place could easily pass for the "Gilligan's Island" soundstage. But

The Enchanted Tiki Room's Eastern Annex / *Oceanic Arts* isn't a soundstage. And it isn't a cocktail lounge, or a Polynesian steak house. It's also not a tiki pop-culture museum, a travel agency, nor a one-day crash course in the history of South Seas-themed restaurants of Southern California. It isn't a Tahitian peepshow, either.

However, *Oceanic Arts* could be easily misidentified as any of the above!

Oceanic Arts is a multi-faceted shopping experience; their 10,000-square-foot warehouse is an entire tropical universe unto itself. Part of the space is devoted to their huge collection of props for studio and party rental; eight-foot-high carved wooden tikis, treasure chests, life-size alligators, fiberglass waterfalls, automated gorillas, et al. The remainder of the warehouse is a maze of South Sea and nautical accoutrements—from tiki door pulls, plastic parrots, and blowfish lanterns, to tropical cocktail mugs, bamboo fencing, and tiki torches. Absolutely anything you'd ever need to replicate an establishment like *Don the Beachcomber's* or the *Enchanted Tiki Room* can be found within these walls. They've also got an excellent selection of exotic tunes on cassette, like "The Drums of Bora Bora" or "The Beat of Tahiti," and even the Jerry Vale of Hawaii, Don Ho. Allow yourself ample time to browse every inch of their isles, because there's always something really great tucked way in the back of a shelf covered with a thick layer of dust—and you could very well be the first person to have discovered it in twenty-five years.

In spite of the wares, the best part about a visit to *Oceanic Arts* is Bob Van Oosting and LeRoy Schmaltz. As charismatic as their names imply, Schmaltz and Van Oosting have been in the business of importing and manufacturing sundry South Sea decor well over three decades. You'll usually find LeRoy covered with sawdust in the *Oceanic Arts* workroom, grinding out one of his expert Polynesian carvings. As you enter, Bob is usually the one to bid you welcome as if he's just docked his houseboat so that you can hop aboard for a tropical cocktail. His white hair and pencil-thin moustache are always perfectly groomed—and like a matured beachboy on permanent summer vacation, he's forever sporting a festive Hawaiian print shirt. Both men are deeply enthusiastic about their work, and they've got more than a few stories to tell about their travels to the far corners of the South Pacific (ask LeRoy about the time he fell asleep in a Kangaroo nest). If you're planning a trip to Tahiti—or nearly any other island paradise—they'll probably have a few recommendations for you, and maybe even some visual aids.

Bob is a scholar in the comprehensive history of the Southern California Polynesian restaurant, and if you ask nicely, he'll unearth their awe-inspiring collection of original menus from those nearly forgotten establishments. You'll inevitably wind your way over to their glass display case crammed with a cache of original tiki cocktail mugs from these very same restaurants (not for sale), and Bob can make distinctions in markings, different molds, and tiki emblems with the passion and proficiency of Louis Leakey fondling a hominid cranium—it's the icing on the *Oceanic Arts* cake having this rare opportunity to cull a little of our tiki history. If you're feeling lucky, try to charm Bob into dragging out their old photo album filled with shots taken throughout their extensive travels; their collection of naked young natives rivals anything you've seen in *The National Geographic* or the latest N.A.M.B.L.A. newsletter. But only make a request to see this stuff if you've made a large purchase—after all, Bob and LeRoy's aim in life isn't to provide *you* with free entertainment, so don't make a damn nuisance of yourself.

Like a Polynesian Smithsonian, never in your lifetime will you feel like you've seen everything *Oceanic Arts* has to offer—so future trips are imperative. Their stock is always changing and many of their most unusual tiki collectibles are one-time only. If your budget can't accommodate an impetuous tropical getaway, a drive out to Whittier and an afternoon in the *Oceanic Arts* warehouse should pacify you until you've earned enough frequent flyer miles for a trip to The Big Island, and besides, you'll come home with just as many souvenirs.

Oceanic Arts
12414 Whittier Blvd.
Whittier
(310) 698-6960

The Smart & Final For Speed Freaks

Sugar buzzing at *Sun Valley Ice Cream*

n Los Angeles, some believe that you can tell a lot about an establishment by the cars parked out front. If so, the parking lot at **Sun Valley Ice Cream** is a good prognostic; it's crammed bumper to bumper with ice cream trucks plastered over with decals of 50-50 bars or large hand-painted red, white and blue popsicles. Oddly enough though, a visit to *Sun Valley Ice Cream* can serve as a lesson in reverse discrimination: if you're *not* an ice cream man the proprietors distrustfully eyeball your every move as though you're a machine-gun carrying member of the S.L.A.

There must be a Sun Valley ordinance that requires every commercial and residential structure to bear a striking resemblance to an auto wrecking yard. Though minus the pizazz, this is the Willy Wonka's of the San Fernando Valley, because it's not just ice cream we're talking about! Racks are stacked high with cases of bubble gum in every conceivable form and shape, from liquid gum in little jugs, squeeze tubes, and bubble tape, to bubble gum-shaped pizzas and cherry Blow Pops. To hell with vitamin supplements; when purchased in bulk, entire cartons of candy cigarettes, enormous boxes of crackling rocks, and novelty confections like "Yummy Mummies" or "Candy Filled Space Straws" are sure to give you that much-needed midday energy boost.

You can also pick through a varied selection of toys (all of which must be purchased in volume) like party poppers, sling shots, boomerangs or child-sized press-on nails—and all at prices that beat Pic 'n Save!

Has too much time passed since the ice cream man tinkled his tune down your street? Fuck the ice cream man! You're a busy person with a lot to do during the day—you can't sit around and wait to accommodate *his* erratic schedule. Go straight to the source: buy a whole case of missiles or drumsticks at *Sun Valley Ice Cream* and the next time your ice cream man cometh, wave a choco-taco at him with one hand, and give him the finger with the other!

Sun Valley Ice Cream
9740 Glenoaks Blvd.
Sun Valley
(818) 504-9230

Survival Books/The Larder

With a motto like "Something to Offend Everyone," you can expect to find plenty of controversial gift possibilities at **Survival Books/The Larder**. Got a grandma in the Viper militia? Is your nephew a diehard fan of that wacky fertilizer freak, Tim McVeigh? Does dad believe that the Black Panthers and Z.O.G. are mere moments away from launching a full-scale assault on all that is holy and American? Well, then, *Survival Books* is your one-stop shopping Mecca!

Is That A Bottle Of Pepper Spray In Your Pocket Or Are You Just Happy To See Me?

Whether you are in need of a can of pepper spray or a book on how to change your identity, *Survival Books* can help you out. I speak from experience: After a certain ex-fiancee of mine opted to practice for our honeymoon with a persistent and particularly over-sexed co-worker, I found solace (and instruction) in the art of revenge at *Survival Books*. I loaded up on books: Books on how to find anyone anywhere, books on retribution, books on surveillance--all of which I used to track down the bastard, confront him in the presence of *his* girlfriend, and make his life an instant living hell. Best of all, it felt good, and was much more effective than spurious and costly psychotherapy.

Now don't get me wrong: *Survival Books* isn't some clearinghouse for stalkers and homicidal spurned lovers—but it comes pretty damn close. There's also a wide variety of mercenary mags in case you're planning on a summer vacation in Bosnia or Rwanda. Compasses, survival foods, and even Tim McVeigh's favorite bathroom book, *The Turner Diaries*, are all waiting for you at *Survival Books*.

With the end of the world just around the corner, you might want to pay a visit to *Survival Books* just so you can bone up on your self-preservation tactics. You never know when evil aliens or the Christian Coalition might launch their final assault. Or perhaps you may simply be looking for some pepper spray to soak your philandering mate while they doze in a deep, peaceful slumber.

Say, why didn't I think of that before?

—ARL

**Survival Books/
The Larder**
111604 Magnolia Blvd.
North Hollywood
(818) 734-0804

OUT-AND-ABOUT

Pinch my weenie, I must be dreaming! Pushing Burbank's boundaries of surreal signage, the two-dimensional stage atop Papoo's Hot Dog Show features an angelic wiener—complete with halo and wings—hot-doggin' for the passing traffic on the otherwise sedate Riverside Drive.

**Papoo's Hot
Dog Show**
4300 Riverside Drive
Burbank

Perusing the photo albums at

Baby Jane
of Hollywood

Hey Look, I'm Naked!

Let's Play Naked Movie Star

Despite the overdose of movie memorabilia shops in Hollywood, film buffs can often have a tough time tracking down a specific photo of their favorite star. For example, where would you go to find an 8" x 10" glossy of your favorite 50s teen idol getting his dick sucked? Or a full body nude of the mega-schlonged Tony Randall? Are you a Monkees fan? Bet you don't have a shot of Davy Jones' asshole!

The aforementioned items are but a teensy-weensy sampling of the wares at **Baby Jane**. Their celebrity nudes are their hottest sellers—and since they cater to a primarily gay clientele, their photo books are stocked mostly with celebrity skin of the male variety. Every nude celebrity photo you've ever heard about (or seen ruined with "censored" bars in the tabloids) *Baby Jane* has for sale—and then some: from early shots of Yul Brynner, Victor Mature and Steve Reeves, to current shots of Brad Pitt, Arnold Schwarzenegger, and Sting. They've got some naked dames too, although the list is considerably less impressive.

Longtime infamous purveyors of bizarro-est celebriana in town, it was the '94 earthquake that put *Baby Jane* on the map. In the wake of the Northridge Temblor, fans could now purchase the shattered remains of housewares and floor tiles from their fave star's home; beautifully mounted, titled and numbered. Celebrity underwear has also done well in this West Hollywood shop, and owners Charles Moniz and Roy Windham keep their own private stash—from Schwarzenegger's jock strap ("padded for continuity") to Angelyne's pink lace thong—that they one day plan to showcase in the store.

Be sure to put your name on their mailing list for autograph signings; *Baby Jane* has played host to some sensational has-beens (Mamie Van Doren, Julie Newmar, Christopher Atkins) and the occasional cultish never-was (Joe Dallesandro). Their catalog of 8 x 10s is one of the most obscure in town. Favorite picks: a near 300-pound Marlon Brando in his underwear, rare 70s shots of Divine, and candid Lucy & Desi. From Hedy Lamarr to Chesty Morgan, take time to dig and you'll find it.

Baby Jane's is also beefcake headquarters, with dozens of b&w "physique" shots from the fifties (including a young Jack La Lane *sans* his red stretch bodysuit) and stacks of "fitness" magazines and photo booklets from the same period. They also carry full color, full boner shots of current porn stars. A word of caution: whatever you do, try to avert your eyes from the famed Burt Reynolds nudes hanging prominently behind the counter. *Yikes!!*

Baby Jane of Hollywood
7985 Santa Monica Blvd.
(in the French Market)
West Hollywood
(213) 848-7080

Fan Mail from Some Flounder at *The Dudley Do-Right Emporium*

Anyone who was watching Saturday morning TV in the late 60s and early 70s most likely has a particular affinity for Rocky, Bullwinkle, Super Chicken, and all the rest of these sophomoric yet sophisticated cartoon characters who transcended the banal likes of Scooby Doo and Sabrina the Teenaged Witch. From the late Jay Ward, the man who brought you the original *Crusader Rabbit*, grew the vast pantheon of animated maniacs who managed to deliver an anti-war statement couched in a comic context that could be just as easily digested by a six-year-old kid as an 18-year-old hippie stoner.

Despite the popularity of their minimalist yet colorful cartoons, Scott and Ward made most of their money from cereal companies, namely General Mills and Quaker Oats. Rocky and Bullwinkle were owned in part by General Mills (and still are), and Quaker Oats was the company that paid the duo to come up with Cap'n Crunch in 1963, and two years later, Quisp and Quake. Still, it was Bullwinkle, Dudley Do-Right, and their cohorts who put Jay Ward on the pop culture map.

"And Now Here's Something We Hope You'll Really Like"

Though the Cartoon Network is airing reruns of *The Bullwinkle Show* and *George of the Jungle*, you can get your hands on some solid Jay Ward action at his **Dudley Do-Right Emporium**, a retail/mail-order sales establishment with a quirky style (what else?) and equally eclectic merchandise. In business for well over two decades, the *Emporium* once offered everything from wristwatches bearing the likenesses of characters from Boris and Natasha to Buster Keaton and W.C. Fields, to Bullwinkle flight bags, Superchicken bath towels, and even build-it-yourself orange crate scooters. A later, more ambitious catalog expanded its merchandise into non-Bullwinkle territory with items like the Panasonic wrist radio, a post-coconut (imagine a real coconut in lieu of a simple postcard), and a gatefold of a provocatively posed Bullwinkle coupled with the slogan "Eat Your Heart Out Burt Reynolds." The *piece-de-la-resistance* of this catalogue was a fully functional FAA-approved Superchicken aircraft kit (Eat your heart out Neiman-Marcus!). Of course, you can't order any of this stuff anymore, but you can get an antique catalogue for a mere 50 cents—while the supply lasts, of course.

What you *can* order, however, are a number of wristwatches, production scripts, note pads, tee shirts, sweatshirts, ties, enameled pins, and really cool original scene cels from Ward's cartoons (oddly enough, Ward was neither an animator nor a writer, so go figure). Then there are the socks, the backward wall clocks, the metal lunch boxes, and perhaps the hottest item of all, the Boris and Natasha wristwatch which comes packaged in a neat little black bomb, fuse and all. And that's just mail order. A visit to the store will reveal all sorts of no-longer-available catalogue items, from "Moosylvania" stickers to the last of the bendable Boris and Natashas in existence. In short, *The Dudley Do-Right Emporium* is a treasure trove for purist pop trash hunters and perverted pack-rats alike.

Jay Ward had a rep as an eccentric of sorts, and he ruled his bizarre business with an iron fist of integrity until his death of kidney cancer in late 1989, after which his lovely widow and daughter took over. Since his death, the merchandising of Ward's characters has expanded, with new designs and items for sale, but no one can say how long the diminutive *Emporium* can endure on a street now fraught with high-rent, high-income entertainment venues like *The House of Blues* and the *Comedy Store*. A mere hundred yards west of the *Emporium*, you can still pay homage to the giant statue of Bullwinkle and Rocky that stands alone in the yard that was once another bastion of Ward's empire. Though to some it may seem like just another decaying prop, to those in the know it is much more, indeed. It's a shrine to all that is good and goofy, and, well, *innocent* about Hollywood—which these days is precious little.

God Bless Quisp. God bless George of the Jungle. God bless Jay Ward.

The Dudley Do-Right Emporium
8200 Sunset Boulevard
Hollywood
(213) 656-6500

Contemplating a world without polymers at *Plastica*

"In the nineties, Tupperware doesn't burp, *it whispers*."

—Pam Teflon

How can you not fall in love with a store that's so merchandise-specific that one could reasonably suspect the proprietors of being borderline compulsive: The only criterion for the wares at **Plastica** is that they be plastic. Any kind of plastic, but it's got to be plastic.

Is That A Hunk Of Polymethylmethacrylate In Your Pocket

This Silverlake store is owned and operated by Mike Calvert and Carla Denker—an adorable artist couple that

Or Are You Just Happy To See Me?

barely look old enough to have driver's licenses, much less put together a shop with as sophisticated an aesthetic and as flawless a presentation as *Plastica*. In business just since June of '96, the shop quickly made a name for itself with a varied mix of plasticabilia from the 1950s to the present: vintage dishware, handbags, jewelry, toys, vinyl clothing, inflatable Op Art pillows, molded modular furniture, even plastic-coated Mexican tablecloths and tote bags. Though the selection of items is broad, the sensibility remains consistent and—best of all—the prices are ridiculously low. After all, it's just plastic.

The store also features installations of Mike's inspired, large-scale weavings from plastic ribbon, and *Plastica* has served as a venue for the wildly popular Tupperware parties (complete with musical numbers) hosted by the Tupperware company's #1 grossing sales representative, Pam Teflon, who also happens to be a drag queen.

Plastica
3817 Sunset Blvd.
Silverlake
(213) 644-1212

When you think you're ready to ponder the virtues of polystyrene, polyethylene, and polyvinyl chloride, you might want to pay this atypical shop a visit.

Remember, plastic is forever.

Amok
The Little Bookstore from Hell

Shopping for some authentic autopsy photos to brighten up the kitchen? Looking for the best way to hang a man by his testicles? Or are you just hoping to bone up on your satanic rituals? Well, weird ones, you'll find all this and much, much more lurking for you among the aisles of the new, improved, and enlarged **Amok**—the all-purpose bookstore from Hell. Having grown from a tiny hole-in-the-wall to a much larger hole-in-the-wall, *Amok* serves up a breathtaking selection of the bizarre in book form as well as videos, mags, tee shirts, and assorted chachkies. *And* they do it with a smile.

Have you ever dreamed of walking into a bookstore without being assaulted by a six-foot-high stand-up for Tom Clancy's latest neo-fascist epic or Anne Rice's newest steaming pile of Vampire-tripe? At *Amok*, you will *not* find such wastes of paper, nor stum-

ble upon Harlequin Romances, cluttered "bargain tables" piled high with those huge, useless coffee-table photo books about World War II planes, porcelain dolls, and the like. What you will find, however, will be the entire works of Iceberg Slim, bios on everyone from Pier Paolo Pasolini to Paul Bowles, exposes on secret organizations like Freemasons and Scientology, illustrated pathology books, trashy reprints, highbrow philosophy tomes, voodoo manuals, and, perhaps most importantly, Catholic deprogramming instructions. And that's just the beginning. *Amok* also has an impressively vast cache of used and out-of-print books, from illustrated medical manuals to rare pulps from the 50s and 60s.

As bizarre as the store is the *Amok* catalogue itself. Although the *Amok Fourth Dispatch* is now out-of-print, this 350+ page book is packed with far more titles than the store could possibly ever shelve, and is as much fun to peruse as the establishment's shelves. The titles are divided by theme into various chapters, including "Mayhem," "Natas," (Satan spelled backwards), "Parallax," "Sensory Deprivation," "R & D," "Sleaze," and more. Detailed descriptions are given for almost every title, along with sundry excerpts from some of the works themselves, like this from Richard Krousher's *Physical Interrogation Techniques*:

"If you are going to gouge an eye, do it slowly, taking care not to damage the optic nerve. Then you can leave the eyeball hanging on his cheek still func-tioning. His brain will receive the vision information but will be unable to turn away or close eyelids as, for example, you mutilate his genitals."

Amok is putting together an even bigger and better catalogue, dubbed the *Amok Sourcebook*, for release in Spring 1997. In the interim, you may find temporary solace in the *Amok Journal: Sensurround Edition* (Stuart Swezey, *Amok*, 1995), a collection of passages from some of the store's more, uh, *colorful* selections. Check out the entry entitled "The Love Bug" to get an idea of just how far some people will go to get off. You may never look at a VW Bug the same way again.

Visit the store. Buy the new catalogue. Change your dull life.

Amok
1764 N. Vermont
Los Angeles
(213) 665-0956
Amok@Loop.com

Retail as God intended at

Cotter Church Supplies

Want to start your own church or maybe just lure some teenage runaways into your van? Everything you need to get the job done effectively is available at **Cotter Church Supplies**. Shopping at *Cotter* is literally a religious experience.

Who can honestly say they've never fantasized from time to time about being a Catholic priest? There's no better place to buy your dreams at retail. You'll be squealing "Hosanna!" as you shuffle deliriously through racks of albs, chasubles, copes, baptismal gowns and funeral palls. Complete your sanctified look with a genuine pastoral kit or hand-held thurible. Unfortunately, there are no dressing rooms.

For the tortured ex-Catholic, it's really much more fun and far more creative to shop for sex toys here than, say, *The Pleasure Chest*, and what's best is the I'm-going-to-burn-in-Hell-for-this tingle one may experience strolling the aisles while entertaining impure thoughts. Communion tables, three-foot altar candles, and prie dieu kneelers take on provocative new possibilities.

Next time you and your partner engage in some erotic role playing, give the "clergyman and the altar boy" game new realism with genuine raiment courtesy of the Theological Threads company! There's nothing quite like slipping your hand beneath the hem of an authentic altar boy cassock or choir robe, and *Cotter* has an ungodly selection. For the detail-oriented, *Cotter* also sells that unmistakably churchy-smelling incense, as well as processional crucifixes and pew torches.

Shop, Shop, Shopping At Heaven's Door

One certainly doesn't need to be a sex offender or a practicing Catholic to make use of *Cotter*'s merchandise. Their holy water bottles in the shape of The Virgin Mary of Guadalupe make great travel containers for shampoo, baptismal fonts are perfect for paper clips, and the wooden slide-top "sick call" crucifix kit functions beautifully as a cigarette box for the coffee table. Liven up the same tired hors d'oeuvres by serving pimento loaf on 2 ¾" host wafers, available in bulk. For the true prankster, try using the EMERGENCY CLERGY ON CALL laminated dashboard plaque to escape red-zone and street cleaning fines. A gallon jug of cheap sacramental wine always makes a good gift and you'll surely want to treat yourself to some of *Cotter*'s choice items like their glow-in-the-dark six-foot wall rosaries, or the equally luminescent glow-in-the-dark lightswitch plates that read in gold script, "Bless this house O Lord we pray/Make it safe by night and day"—but these items aren't always in stock, and don't stay on the shelves long when they are.

Be sure not to pass by the titles in their book department like *American Martyrs from 1592*, *Jokes Priests Can Tell*, or *The Dogma of Hell*—but you'll have to dig. These are stocked among hundreds of other titles, the kind we've all seen turning to stone in thrift stores.

One look at a few of *Cotter*'s price tags and you'll understand why churches are so insistent about passing those collection plates. Incidentally, they sell collection plates too. What you can't find available in store you're sure to find in their yellow pages-sized catalogue ($10)—which also makes for great bathroom reading.

Cotter Church Supplies
1701 West Ninth Street
Los Angeles
(213) 385-3366

Shopping for Animal Organs and Explosives at
Tri-Ess Sciences

Have you been shopping for a life-size, fully-posable, anatomically correct model of a newborn baby, complete with a "soft spot" on the head, diaper, ID bracelet and birth certificate? Been searching for some preserved sheep brains for your dissecting pleasure? Perhaps a gallon of theatrical blood is on your wish list; or maybe what your heart really desires is some "Super-Goop," a slimy substance available in almost any color of your choice and in three different consistencies? All these items, plus a vast selection of chemicals, special effects, skeleton models, and just about anything else from a science lab or a Hollywood action flick are yours for the asking at the amazing adult toy store known as **Tri-Ess Sciences Inc.**

Sheep Eyeballs, Pyro Gel, And So Much More!

Located in one of Burbank's more remote industrial areas, *Tri-Ess* has been supplying both students and SFX wizards for over 45 years, thanks to the seemingly boundless imagination and entrepreneurial energy of owner and operator, Mr. Ira Katz. Katz, an unimposing gentleman with short silver hair, glasses, and an officious yet friendly manner, has built *Tri-Ess* into a virtual monopoly without competition. No one else supplies more frogs and giant earthworms to schools around the country. No other company can claim to be as popular with special effects designers, providing everything from the standard smoke and fire elements to special, custom, hush-hush projects that may just end up winning an Academy Award®. Remember the exploding causeway-bridge at the end of *True Lies*? Katz helped to design the smoke and fire that made the miniature seem like the real thing. The white marshmallow goop and green slime from *Ghostbusters* were the same "super goop" that you can buy for your own enjoyment. In fact, just about every effect at *Tri-Ess* has shown up in one film or another, and as mentioned, Katz is quick to point out that there's also plenty of top-secret film projects being developed in the company's off-limits, high-security areas. Adding to this air of mystery, Katz may also tell you about other restricted areas which are strictly *verboten* "for reasons which can't be discussed." Almost makes you feel like you're at the Pentagon or something. *Tri-Ess* is also a well-trafficked one-stop for magicians, whether they simply need to purchase a new supply of flash paper or develop a whole new mega-illusion to dazzle the world—as David Copperfield often does. Perhaps Ira even played a part in Copperfield's mesmerization of Claudia Schiffer. And to think that you, a mere commoner, can also tap into this great resource of the unreal and the bizarre.

Besides offering two far-out catalogues—one for science supplies and the other for special effects—*Tri-Ess* also features a cool retail department that is open to the public Monday through Friday from 8:30 A.M. to 5:00 P.M., and on Saturdays from 8:00 A.M. to noon. Drop in during these hours to check out the shelves of bottled animal organs—like the dazzlingly blue sheep's eyeballs—or the vast array of science kits, warning stickers, and anatomical models of everything from dinosaurs to human ears. Whether you're in the market for a good microscope, or a drug dealer in need of a new triple-beam scale, or

simply looking to spruce up your walls with sundry arcane medical charts, this place is the answer to your prayers. And even if you're not a master of movie magic in need of realistic snow, or a practitioner of prestidigitation looking for a new gimmick, you can always amaze your friends and family with something simple like the "magician's wand," which will produce smoke on command. And just imagine the fun you'll have at airport security when you whip out the long-fused "simulated bomb," a menacing black spherical affair that will make you feel just like Boris Badanoff—especially when it lands you behind bars!

Whether you need a new radiation meter or simply wish to relive the glory days when you stood next to Candy Liebowitz in biology and tried not to puke when you cut open that putrid fetal pig, you can find them both (the meter and the pig, not Candy) at *Tri-Ess Sciences*.

And be sure to say hi to Ira...if he's not in the back blowing something up.

Did You Know...*that you can buy 5 pounds of aluminum powder for only $63.00 from Tri-Ess Sciences?*

Tri-Ess Sciences Inc.
1020 W. Chestnut St.
Burbank
(818) 848-7838

Getting into the groove at *Out of Our Heads*

You'll find an ever-increasing number of hip, funky, junky, retro-freaky shops dotting the otherwise seedy streets of the Vermont Ave./Sunset Blvd. area located just on the edge of Silverlake—which has been portentously dubbed as "The New Melrose" (a title shared with Lankershim Blvd. in North Hollywood, Abbot Kinney Blvd. in Venice, Montana Ave. in Santa Monica and parts of Ventura Blvd. in Sherman Oaks). Although it can't be denied that the area offers some of the most unusual merchandise to be had in Los Angeles, none of the businesses can hold a candle to the *ultra*store that is **Out of Our Heads.**

Is That An Adolph Hitler Pez Dispenser In Your Pocket
Or Are You Just Happy To See Me?

As their name may imply, *Out of Our Heads* is a mind-expanding shopping experience—like a Toys 'R Us on psilocybin mushrooms. The store is stuffed with an incomparable collection of vintage toys, adult novelties, board games, lunch boxes, promotional items, and every other kind of ephemera imaginable dating primarily from the 60s through the 70s. From H.R. Pufnstuf to Sonny & Cher, Boy George to Tony the Tiger, Burt Reynolds to E.T.—*Out Of Our Heads* runs the gamut. But what distinguishes them most from the handful of other shops that deal in similar stock is that *Out of Our Heads* infuses their retro-toyland fantasy with a 70s psychedelia aesthetic; the ceiling display of stoner art and vintage blacklight posters is awe-inspiring, and they also carry original contemporary paintings and art objects that tie in with the nudie-novelty-pothead theme of the store, like Adolph Hitler PEZ dispensers, original animation cells, and handmade puppets that'll rip Kermit the Frog a new asshole. The collection at *Out of Our Heads* often crosses the line between kitsch and high art, or a garage sale and a museum.

There's an enticing psychedelic tent pitched in the rear of the shop draped with twinkly lights and plastic beads—in here you'll find some super-wiggy "smoking accessories" to give credence to the store's name. For those equally out of their heads but under the age of eighteen, the shop offers a generous selection of candy and smoke bombs. "We sell a lot of stuff for kids to terrorize their teachers with," explains an employee, "but we're not anti-government, we're just pro-fun."

If the nude poster of Burt Reynolds, the Hee Haw memorabilia, and the David Cassidy jigsaw puzzles aren't enough to impress you, maybe owner Oscar Moreno and his congenial comrades manning the cash register will. The proprietors of *Out of Our Heads* actually have *personalities and communication skills*—something virtually unheard of among the hip haunts nearby. Elsewhere you're likely to be "welcomed" by an indolent shopkeeper who may seem genuinely annoyed by your presence—if they even bother to glance up (or wake up) when you enter. Think we jest? Pay a visit to Exene Cervenka's celebrated store *You've Got Bad Taste* (a.k.a. "We've Got Bad Attitudes") located right next door, where the employees seem to be under the dated, punk rock impression that it's cool to be rude (no, you just alienate customers), which is a shame because their stock is pretty great. Further north on Vermont Avenue, you'll find no shortage of poker-faced drones—all fashionably dressed, coiffed, pierced and tattooed of course—working the counters of the street's hipper-than-thou establishments, providing the anti-service that so many Los Angeles shoppers have come to expect and dread.

Hey, maybe this really *is* the "New Melrose" after all!

Out of Our Heads
3818 West Sunset Blvd.
Silverlake
(213) 665-TOYS

Grave robbing at *Necromance*

One of the best things about Los Angeles is that a shopper can find virtually anything here. Say, for example, that you need a dog brain, a pig embryo, an alligator skull, some snake vertebrae, a few monkey ribs, a handful of warthog tusks, a full set of human finger bones and a menacing plaster gargoyle to hang over the sofa. Who would you try first?

We suggest **Necromance**, by far one of the city's most unique boutiques. *Necromance* specializes in "natural history" and is a veritable Toys 'R Us for folks who like to play with dead things.

You find the darndest stuff displayed in their glass cases. Beaver, squirrel, cat, skunk and fox skulls, racoon penises, human ribs, beautifully preserved scorpions, spiders and exotic beetles and even human skulls and trilobites are pretty much all standard stock. Lotsa skull and coffin-shaped items, great tee shirts, candelabras and a select assortment of elegant accessories to compliment any haunted house, torture chamber or Church of Satan. *Necromance* also specializes in tasteful and exquisitely designed jewelry in silver made with bones and teeth, vermin skulls, seeds, stones and other natural materials.

Where The Living Shop For The Dead

Necromance is one of the very few places in town where one can purchase human remains legally. And a bundle of bones won't cost you an arm and a leg. A frog embryo or a bat submerged in a jar of formaldehyde are not only affordable (about $35), but also make great low-maintenance pets. And you can take home a genuine complete human skeleton for about the same price that you'd pay for a shar-pei puppy at *The Beverly Center*.

Necromance
7162 Melrose Ave.
Los Angeles
(213) 934-8684

Playing dress-up at *Junk for Joy*

This small Burbank shop reeks of mothballs and their "Silly and Ugly Clothing of Good and Bad Taste" is tightly crammed onto clothing racks, pushed into corners, and hung from every available inch of wall and ceiling space. For years **Junk for Joy** has been a well-kept secret of the entertainment industry; way off the beaten path of shopped-out Melrose Avenue but conveniently close to the movie studios, wardrobe people and stylists flock here taking advantage of their specialized and unused vintage stock.

Undergear fetishists take great delight in the 1950s bullet bras in their original boxes, seamed stockings, or thirty-five-year-old sanitary belts still tacked in place onto the original cardboard packaging. Hats, sunglasses, costume jewelry, belt buckles, linens, shoes, notions and ties help to round out their ever-evolving and varied inventory. Prices range from dirt cheap to near-cardiac arrest.

Combing the yellow pages and not having any luck? You can find it here. Whether it's brand-new pre-WWII flyswatters that you're in search of, or thirty identical 1970s majorette uniforms with matching white vinyl boots, *Junk for Joy* has got to be your best bet.

Junk for Joy
3314 Magnolia Blvd.
Burbank
(818) 569-4903

chapter three

Happy Hour!

Bars and Booze in L.A.

There are many places to get drunk in L.A., but there's nothing quite like an old-fashioned cocktail lounge to really strip down the relationship between you and bottle of Chivas. True, there's a big difference between The Polo Lounge and The Frolic Room, but not much. In the end, there's always the booze, being doled out one prescription at a time, and someone on the other end sucking it down.

Bukowski built his fame, gulp by gulp, writing about the barflies who inhabit these dim shrines to slow legal suicide. Spend some time with this subterranean breed and you'll understand why Charles had so many stories to write.

Sometimes, the very names alone of some of the cooler dives invite illicit and sinful thoughts: THE TENDER TRAP, THE ALIBI ROOM, THE DAILY PINT, THE LIQUID ZOO, and our favorite– once again–THE FROLIC ROOM.

This chapter is as much a tribute as it is a guide to such establish-ments, a dying breed in a world of prefab plastic watering holes like The Hard Rock Cafe and Planet Hollywood.

Cheers

Taking the Private Tour at the

Anheuser-Busch Brewery

Anheuser-Busch Brewery
15800 Roscoe Blvd.
Van Nuys
(818) 989-5300

The scent of brewing beer is much like that of a burning cigar—some people love it and some loathe it. Me, I've always enjoyed passing by the **Anheuser-Busch Brewery** and taking a big whiff of the sweet and sometimes pungent aroma that permeates the air for a good quarter-mile radius. There was a time when the Van Nuys brewery boasted a Busch Gardens attraction, with plenty of lush tropical flora, a parrot show, a tour of the brewery, and of course, free beer samples. Tragically, the gardens were eventually sacrificed in order to expand the factory's production capacity, and along with the parrots and the free beer went the scheduled tours as well.

Is That A Bud Light In Your Pocket

Or Are You Just Happy To See Me?

The good news—and a well-kept secret—is that *Anheuser-Busch* still offers tours of the brewery to the public, but by appointment only. There's no charge for the service, and although the birds and palm trees are history, you can still get a first-hand look at how they make all those wonderful beers from Bud Ice to Bud Dry. And if you behave yourself, you may even get a free glass of The King of Beers—or one of its many hybrids.

—A.R.L.

Diving into the Downtown Dive that is *Al's Bar*

I spent too many of my salad days at **Al's Bar**, and much of it was by choice. John Pork, my coworker at the 32 Market and cohort in the band Dead Pork, lived in the *American Hotel*, just upstairs from this crummy, seedy, amazingly popular dive. This made it easy to go down and get drunk even though we were underage, but next to impossible to sleep since the music and noise came up through the floor like a miasma of bad farts. That was okay, though, because we never slept since we were either downstairs watching bad art bands make noise onstage, or occasionally doing the same ourselves.

You Can Call Me Al, Then Call Me A Cab

A lot of things about *Al's* have changed over the years. For one, they patched up the pipe that used to look straight down onto the girls' toilet. I always expected to see Chuck Berry up there. Second, the clientele has changed. It used to be filled with ultra-hip, cynical downtown art-hopefuls. Now it's filled with *retro*-ultra-hip, cynical downtown art-hopefuls. Gone are the days when you could run into David Byrne in the squalid men's room as he emerged from the stall, sniffling and wiping his nose and talking fast—at least for him. And good riddance, I say.

But you can still get a cheap beer or play pool or listen to some cool tunes on the jukebox in an area of industrial downtown L.A. where in any other bar you would probably end up getting stabbed to death or sodomized in a back alley—or if you're lucky, both.

—ARL

Al's Bar
305 South Hewitt
Downtown
(213) 625-9703

Drinking at *The Frolic Room*

When Was The Last Time You Had A Really Good Frolic?

"frol·ic n. 1.) Gaiety; merriment. 2.) A gay, carefree time. 3.) A playful antic."—*American Heritage Dictionary*

When it comes to what I'd call a simple, old-fashioned, red Naugahyde bar, such bodegas can all seem very much alike very quickly—especially after a few stiff ones. But, given the "desert island scenario," and the option of picking but one cocktail lounge to service my fiefdom, I'd take **The Frolic Room** without hesitation—and not just because of the cheap drinks, eclectic jukebox, killer neon sign, or cool black facade. The moniker alone—*The Frolic Room*—would be enough for me.

Of course, the clientele doesn't hurt my decision, either. Unlike many other such bars, *The Frolic Room* attracts an offbeat, youngish Hollywood crowd, which is good news for you guys and gals trolling for semi-attractive, well-preened, and sometimes intelligent soul/bed mates. Not that the craggy, veteran drinkers of another respectable Naugahyde joint like, say, *The Chimney Sweep*, are lepers or anything, but sometimes you want to enjoy social intercourse with an amateur or junior league barfly and not another well-seasoned pro with his/her briefcase full of Blues. Don't expect the *Polo Lounge* when you walk in. Instead, leave your great expectations at the door. Walk in, belly up to the bar, sit down, order a drink, and let the frolicking begin.

—ARL

The Frolic Room
6245 Hollywood Blvd.
Los Angeles
(213) 462-5890

OUT-AND-ABOUT

Though the original signs were spared, the interior of this classic California coffee shop fell prey to an upgrade.

Jack's Salad Bowl
11533 Whittier Blvd.
Whittier

The H.M.S. Bounty

Sadly, the once-proud area of Los Angeles known as Mid-Wilshire has fallen on hard times of late. What once could be counted among L.A.'s classiest strips of hotels, apartments, restaurants and bars has slowly succumbed to the vagaries of time. Like a silent film beauty queen a half-century past her prime, the area now more resembles a babbling bag lady with osteoporosis. Still, there is solace to be found among the few remaining gems in this future slum, and one of them is the classic watering hole, the **H.M.S. Bounty**.

Yo Ho Ho And Barrel Of Grog!

In this age of unmitigated greed, who has ever heard of such a thing as a free juke-box—much less a player packed (as it has been for years) with 45's of Sinatra, Woody Herman, Tommy Dorsey, Sarah Vaughan, and sundry other dinosaurs now suddenly hip again with Gen-X'ers and their callow ilk? Well, that's exactly what you'll find at the *Bounty*, a Gothically dark, well-preserved relic from the days when a bar could also be a damn good restaurant. Here's a place where you can walk in the front door, sit down at the bar, and proceed to get completely pissed—knowing all the while that when Mr. Tummy begins to do the St. Vitus dance, there'll be something other than beer nuts, hard-boiled eggs and beef jerky for you to later regurgitate all over your shirt. Say, how does a plate of "L.A.'s Most Famous Pork Chops" sound? Or how about a steak, perhaps? In the mood for fresh fish (and we're not talking about Mrs. Gorton's)? Order another double and bolster that appetite without trepidation, for the *Bounty* serves real food (for the time being, at least) to sate the raging hunger within you.

Despite the rapid decay of its surrounding locale, the *Bounty* can still be counted among that rare breed of upscale watering holes without attitude, a dark place of drinking refuge in an otherwise blindingly gauche metropolis. Appointed in a dense walnut-and-leather decor and punctuated by the occasional authentic brass porthole and ship's lantern, the *Bounty* gives one the feeling of being safe and snug in the bowels of Captain Bly's most inner sanctum.

Of course, 36 years ago the *H.M.S. Bounty* wasn't even the *H.M.S. Bounty*. It was called *The Secret Harbor*. Then along came Mr. Gordon Fields, who stepped in and "Bounty-ized" the place, changing the name and adding the placard out front that promises "Food and Grog" as well as the aforementioned portholes and other items nautical. Another of Gordon's additions was the dark amber lighting, which, as he puts it, "makes ladies look younger and have less wrinkles." This effective bit of smoke-and-mirrors, combined with a few stiff doubles, would be enough to send any man home with a Rose Marie lookalike.

Over the decades, the *Bounty* has seen its share of megastars come in and get down. Jack Webb was a regular who held court with his cronies here on Monday nights in the early 70s. Whenever the New York Yankees were in town, Gordon could expect to see Yogi Berra, Mickey "What Liver?" Mantle, and their boozin' buddies slamming 'em down as only heavy hitters can. *The Coconut Grove* was just across the street at the *Ambassador Hotel*, and many of the performers from the *Grove* would board the *Bounty* for an open-ended liquid cruise. Van Johnson, Duke Ellington, and Sarah Vaughan (who could put away an entire bottle of Martel in an afternoon, according to Gordon) were among the many who often made the short walk from the *Grove* to the *Bounty*. Whether they made it back or not is another matter altogether.

The H.M.S. Bounty
3357 Wilshire Blvd.
Mid-Wilshire
(213) 385-7275

The *H.M.S. Bounty* sits cheek-by-jowl to the *Gaylord Apartments* (formerly the *Gaylord Hotel*), and when I was living in the latter, I would ride the elevator down to the lobby, turn right and walk straight through the *Gaylord*'s own "special" door into the *Bounty*. Talk about convenience! That padded brown leather portal was one of the more influential factors that governed my decision to make the *Gaylord* my home. How many stately rental dwellings can one find in this town that also boast their own private entrance into a 100 proof time-machine? Not many, I assure you.

Unfortunately, Jack Webb has gone to that great Dragnet in the sky, along with The Mick's liver, and the stars no longer shine at the *Bounty*. Gordon's still there, however, and God bless him. The man who started the *Bounty* is now being forced to play with the idea of downsizing the menu and slashing the food prices 60% to accommodate the influx of low-rent clientele—a grim foreshadowing of the end of civilization as we know it. Pay your homage to the *H.M.S. Bounty* before it becomes another tragic footnote in L.A.'s illustrious alcoholic history books.

—ARL

Going for a spin at *Windows on Hollywood*

n our estimation, any cocktail lounge that rotates warrants a visit. Add to this a panoramic bird's eye view of Los Angeles and its surrounding areas, a menu with entrees like "Universal Studios Salmon" and "Tinseltown Prime Rib," live entertainment that may even include a Sinatra impersonator—and you've got **Windows on Hollywood**, a veritable Sit-and-Spin for alcoholics!

What Goes Around Comes Around

Windows on Hollywood is the UFO-like appendage lodged into the side of the 23rd floor of the *Holiday Inn* on Highland Ave., just north of Hollywood Blvd. Since it's located in a part of town frequented only by tourists and crack addicts, it's not a spot most locals would consider when planning a night out (unless of course you're a crack addict), but it is a wonderful place to get completely bombed and should be taken into consideration next time you're looking for a change of scenery...literally! Cozy up to one of the window seats and get blitzed as your view of Los Angeles changes from south to north—and back again. At this altitude even Hollywood Blvd. looks beautiful...well, at night, after a few drinks. On a clear day you can see to Century City and beyond. On any other day, you can gain new perspective on just exactly how hideous the air quality really is in Los Angeles. Watch the sunset with a tequila sunrise and don't be afraid to get a little sloppy; *Windows on Hollywood* is unequivocally casual.

In addition to a dazzling view of the homeless teens panhandling on the streets below, *Windows on Hollywood* offers live music and dancing at 8:00 P.M. Tuesday through Saturday, and serves a full dinner menu. Cocktails and dinner service commence at 6:00 P.M., the kitchen closes at 11:00, but you can swill hooch till 2:00.

If you think you've got the stomach for it, come get soused at *Windows on Hollywood* over an order of "City Walk Escargot" or "Gnocchi Frederick's" while rotating 23 floors above the Walk of Fame. Just remember, should you be overcome with nausea and need to make a mad dash to the porcelain altar, the restroom door may not be where it was twenty minutes ago!

Windows on Hollywood
Holiday Inn
1755 East Highland Ave.
Hollywood
(213) 462-7181

Appreciating the fine art at *Circus Liquor*

The first time I saw you, you crazy clown, I fell in love. I stopped and stared and tried to take you all in...but I couldn't. You were twinkling like a star, so bright and full of life—bigger than life, in fact. And that smile. Your magic, tragic smile. I met you in the parking lot.

Is That A Bottle Of Night Train In Your Pocket

Or Are You Just Happy To See Me?

And in awe, I knelt down and stared at my newfound love; then I stood, turned and walked away. Our love could never be, for I'm just a kid from the right side of the tracks, and you...you are nothing more than a giant neon liquor store sign in the form of a happy-go-lucky clown. But oh, what a sign!

Circus Liquor. It's a pretty good liquor store as far as such establishments go, but nothing to write home about. Sure, it's also a "Jr. Market," which, by virtue of its name, may one day aspire to be just like Dad. But the store pales in comparison to the glorious sign out front, which is the real reason to make the Mecca to this blighted, nethermost patch of North Hollywood. For this mammoth argon-fired glass-and-steel Pierrot is more than just a sign. It's a symbol for that primordial party animal in us all, the one that likes to strap on the red rubber nose every now and then and get downright stinkin' silly.

If *Circus Liquor* puts you in the mood for other forms of clown-themed entertainment, may we suggest a quick jaunt over the hill to **Jumbo's Clown Room**, where topless dancers perform their art in a circus-like atmosphere? And after that, drop by **Phillipe, The Original** and enjoy a French Dip sandwich in the booth lounge in the rear, where the walls are lined with nostalgic black-and-white photographic prints of life under the Big Top.

—ARL

Circus Liquor
5600 Vineland Avenue
North Hollywood
(818) 769-1500

Jumbo's Clown Room
5153 Hollywood Blvd.
Los Angeles
(213) 666-1187

Phillipe, The Original
1001 North Alameda St.
Los Angeles
(213) 628-3781

The Firefly
Cocktails for Pyros

Not long ago, when I was still in training to become a professional barfly, I had a favorite drinking hole I would frequent whenever I longed for the scent of burning human hair. That place was **The Firefly**, which once could be found on Vine St., just south of Hollywood Blvd.

The bar was simple enough, a long straight affair that was backed with a mirror and the typical late 50s red naugahyde decor. There were tables that lined the north wall of the shotgun-shack-shaped room, but most of the seats could be found at the bar, and if you sat in one and looked up at the mottled acoustic drop-ceiling, you'd notice this strange smoky dark line that ran the length of the bar. This dark streak was there for one simple reason: at *The Firefly*, they lived up to their name—they set the bar on fire. And not just on special nights. Every night, and especially towards closing time, the barback would seemingly transmogrify into an endless wall of flame.

The bartenders—twin brothers who appeared to be in their mid-thirties—were the perpetrators of the pyrotechnics, and with a half-dozen drinks in you, it was always quite a sight to watch the siblings (dressed in identical clothing) set fire to the bar. Here's how it worked: The twins would peel up the thick rubber nubby strips that fit into the barback well (the barback is the shallow inset trough that runs along length of the bar on the bartender's side and is where he mixes his drinks). Then they would take out the Zippo lighter fluid and dispense a very generous amount of the flammable liquid along said barback, beginning to end. Then, without a great deal of fanfare, they would ignite the combustible concoction from the end of the bar closest to the front door, thus setting in motion a chain-reaction of flame and fume that, if you were not prepared for it, would singe your eyebrows, eyelashes, and whatever other hair you had on the front of your face. Worse, if you were really in your cups and unfamiliar with *The Firefly*'s unusual practice, you might have truly questioned your sanity after witnessing in your drunken peripheral vision a wall of fire zip past your nose at a distance of no more than two feet. Then, of course, there was that odd, sickly scent of burning human hair that I mentioned before.

As one might expect, *The Firefly* was a popular target of the Fire Marshall's, and I recall that on the day I paid a visit and found the place chained up and closed forever, I couldn't help but wonder if the twins had incurred one citation too many. Over time, when the place did not reopen and it finally sank in to my alcohol-addled brain that I'd never imbibe and witness the ignition again, I truly felt a sense of loss. If anyone else in America knows of another such bar, please let me know. *The Firefly*, as far as my life experience goes, was truly a one-of-a-kind oddity—and for a time, L.A.'s finest cocktail lounge by sheer virtue of its intrinsic incendiary insanity.

—ARL

**The Firefly
(Deceased)**
Vine just south of Hollywood
R.I.P.

A Drinker's Six-Pack

In Which One of the Authors Examines a Half Dozen of the City's Not-So-Obscure Watering Holes

"An alcoholic is someone you don't like who drinks as much as you do."

—Dylan Thomas

Given the time and the appropriate amount of alcohol, I'd have filled this book with too many long-winded, insufferable paeans to every cocktail lounge between Valencia and Long Beach. Lucky for you, dear reader, that my drinking habits no longer resemble those of Nicholas Cage in *Leaving Las Vegas*— lucky for me, too, otherwise the publisher would have torn up our contract and laughed in my face as my partner slowly tightened his grip around my neck.

Instead, for your fast-paced, free-wheeling enjoyment, here is a sober yet informative selection of six of the more infamous bars in L.A. that actually fulfill their herculean reputations without being obnoxiously nouveau—an amazing feat in and of itself in this city of fleeting fifteen-minute fame. Best of all, you'll find these critiques written up in terse, coherent prose that serves as testament to the efficacy of O'Doul's over Old Crow.

You may think that in order to tie one on at **The Polo Lounge** you need to be a bonafide celebrity or celebrity-monger (otherwise known as an agent). I know I used to labor under this misconception until I walked into the hotel one sultry summer afternoon, strolled into *The Polo Lounge*, and ordered a beer without being thrown out on my ass. I was amazed, and decided to hang out as long as I could, assuming that as soon as the bar became packed with Hollywood muck-a-mucks, I'd then find myself suddenly being led out the service door to the back alley. Again, I could only muster astonishment as my table remained my own personal fiefdom, despite the fact that a number of people who looked like they were very important were standing uncomfortably by the bar. I'm not paranoid about being treated like a second-class citizen in Beverly Hills, either: Once I was on my way to being seated at a booth at *Kate Mantilini's* when suddenly the hostess was waved back to the front of the restaurant by the frantic host, leaving me standing in the aisle only to be mistaken for a busboy by the porcine patrons who angrily shook their empty bread baskets at me and demanded to have their tables cleared. The hostess returned a few moments later and told me I'd have to wait for another booth or sit at the counter. Why? Because *Judge Reinhold* had just popped in without a reservation and wanted a booth of his own. *My* booth. Forget the fact that I'd already spent close to a half hour cooling my jets and sucking on a stale imported beer while I waited for my own booth. That didn't seem to matter once a famished, booth-mongering, B-level movie star showed up. The look of star-struck wonderment on the hostess's face indicated that she expected me to graciously give up my booth to the puckish mega-celeb, as if poor stupid plebs like me live our whole lives just waiting for the day when we can sacrifice our dinner hour for a higher cause. She was wrong, of course.

This incident occurred around the time of the *Beverly Hills Cop* movies, a time when people actually knew who Judge Reinhold was, which may explain why an otherwise rational management practically wet their pants and promptly downgraded my already dubious status to that just directly above a piece of dogshit that gets stuck to the bottom of your Topsiders. My attitude that evening—and now—was "Fuck 'em." So hey, my hat's off to *The Polo Lounge* for letting cretinous common folk such as myself rub cocktail olives with the rich and famous without humiliating us by insisting we get up and sit in the corner behind a potted plant whenever Efrem Zimbalist, Jr. comes in and demands our seat.

The Polo Lounge at The Beverly Hills Hotel
9641 Sunset Blvd.
Beverly Hills

It ain't the *Polo Lounge*, but this place *is* older than Mick Jagger and smells like it, too. Worse, on a hot summer day, **The Formosa** interior reaches temperatures close to that of the hotbox that Alec Guinness endured time and again in *Bridge Over the River Quai*. Lastly, the food leaves much to be desired—so much so, in fact, that I heartily advise you make your dinner of the liquid variety if you decide to drop in.

The Formosa Cafe
7156 Santa Monica Blvd.
Hollywood

And by all means, do drop in—don't let the admonishments of the prior paragraph scare you off, because *The Formosa* is a slice of L.A. history that definitely deserves your undivided drinking attention. From the customized concrete car-stops in the parking lot that still bear the names of the frequent star patrons from years gone by, to the extensive collection of Elvis Presley liquor decanters that line the darkened bar, *The Formosa* is a veritable time machine that will transport you to an era when AIDS was a word that followed BAND, when smoking cigars was a working man's pleasure and not an obnoxious trend fueled by callow fad-followers, when the cocktail ruled supreme and Alcoholics Anonymous was just a blurred twinkle in Bill W.'s bloodshot eyes. That's not to say that you won't be subjected to hip West Hollywood types who revel in the retro-cool lifestyle, but enough martinis can even make this obnoxious crowd seem somehow palatable...unlike the food, unfortunately. Who knows, you may even luck out and catch Shannen Doherty charming the patrons by making a complete ass of herself.

Some things never change.

Sharon Tate, Jay Sebring and their doomed entourage enjoyed their last supper at **El Coyote**. It wasn't the shitty Mexican food that did them in, however; it was Tex Watson and the rest of the LSD-crazed, blood-thirsty bunch dispatched by Manson to slaughter the incredibly fortunate Terry Melcher—who had moved out of the Polanski/Tate house some months before. Of course, this isn't meant to imply that you, too, will be stabbed and beaten to death by smelly hippies if you eat at *El Coyote*, but you'll wish you were if you drink too many of their cheap, potent, famous margaritas.

If an overdose of these tequila concoctions don't make you puke, the interior design of *El Coyote* may do the trick. Mismatched wrought iron accesories, bad art on the walls, crushed glass and tile chandeliers...it's enough to make Liberace's head spin—if he were still alive. To be honest, I've never really understood the appeal of this place—despite the reputation of the margaritas and trendy crowd—but if the long wait for a table is any indication of quality, they must be doing something right.

Then again, there's often a line outside the *Hard Rock Cafe*, the *McDonald's* of store-bought cool, so take *El Coyote* for what it's worth.

El Coyote
7312 Beverly Blvd.
Los Angeles

Musso & Frank Grill
6667 Hollywood Blvd.
Hollywood

Whenever I was in the mood for a good martini—a real martini—I went to one of two places in Hollywood. One was the bar in the *Nickodell* restaurant, which unfortunately forever closed its doors some years ago. The second watering hole, **Musso & Frank Grill**, is still alive and kicking, and serving up the classiest martinis east of the *Oak Room* at New York's *Plaza Hotel*. When it comes to James Bond's favorite drink, *Musso & Frank's* ranks head and shoulders above any other in town, including the fond memory of *Nickodell*'s offering, which was pretty damn good. But since this penultimate cocktail is merely a simple concoction of gin and vermouth, it relies on quality ingredients and sophisticated presentation to set it apart from the crowd. *Musso & Frank* uses your choice of first-rate gins and the best vermouth, but it's really the way they serve the drink that makes you feel like a king. Whether you prefer your martini shaken or stirred, it will be presented to you in an appropriately lemon-peeled vessel, and accompanied by a classic glass decanter containing the remainder of your drink, nestled in a cozy glass bowl of ice to keep it cool. This set-up alone would be worth the trip to *Musso & Frank*, but the contents are equally as impressive. If it was good enough for Dashiell Hammett and Nathanael West, it's undoubtedly good enough for you. Maybe too good, in fact.

Here's the first restaurant/bar on the list that also happens to serve excellent food—if German fare is your bag. If it is, I wholeheartedly recommend the beef *rouladen* to soak up the inordinate amount of beer you will undoubtedly imbibe. If it isn't, then the *rouladen* will surely make you a convert. Unlike wine, beer is a beverage that does not benefit from age, and the German drafts at **The Red Lion** are as fresh as you'll find in the Southland. Dortmunder and Spaaten are two particularly rare brands to find on tap, though the *Red Lion* also offers up Beck's for those of you who've watched too much TV. And for a few dollars more, you can order your liter or half-liter of beer in a hefty, German-made clay stein that's yours to take home. Or if you're really thirsty, there's also a 2-liter glass boot (yes, a giant glass in the shape of a man's boot) which will kick your ass in more ways than one.

If you've never had an authentic German wheat beer, called *Wiezenbier* or *Weisse* depending on the region or origin, then you're in for a treat. Served with a slice of lemon, wheat beer is a welcome change to the relentless parade of imported pilseners and lagers, lights and darks, and the *Wiezenbier* at the *Red Lion* is particularly tasty and a delight in the torrid summer months. So if you like large quantities of great German beer, live accordion music, and busty Teutonic barmaids in traditional busty Teutonic barmaid garb, then *The Red Lion* is the perfect place to get shitfaced and sing "Roll Out Those Lazy Hazy Crazy Days of Summer." Nat King Cole would be proud.

The Red Lion
2366 Glendale Blvd.
Silverlake

Before visiting my accountant in Santa Monica for the yearly torture of figuring how much the IRS is going to steal from me, I like to drop in on **Bob Burns** and have a few stiff ones to soften the jolt. Like *The Red Lion*, *Bob Burns* not only boasts an outstanding bar, but also some hearty food that's worth jamming into your pie-hole. And they also offer some cool live jazz for your listening pleasure. Still, it's the dark, sophisticated, no-nonsense bar that always gives me solace, one glass at a time.

Located adjacent to Santa Monica's revamped *Promenade*, *Bob Burns* is one of the City by the Sea's more endearing fixtures—and one of the few that hasn't undergone a trendy facelift at the hands of overzealous Geary-esque designers. Inside the decor is still comfy and unpretentious, featuring old-fashioned amenities like cushy, expansive booths and high-backed tuck-and-roll chairs upholstered in real leather. Another long-standing and unchanged *Burns'* feature is Smitty, otherwise known as Hewlett Smith, the blind piano player who has been tinkling the ivories there since the final year of the Kennedy administration.

The drinks at *Bob Burns* are of the straight-ahead cocktail variety. You won't find any fluorescent-colored Polynesian mutations here or a micro-brew still behind the bar, but the martinis are overwhelmingly satisfactory, and just happen to be the favorite drink of the trendy youngsters who have rediscovered *Bob Burns*—along with cigars, bell-bottoms, and polyester print shirts. For those of you who don't know how to drink a real martini or happen to be of Russian descent, the bar is well-stocked with just about every variation of vodka other than Ralph's generic blue label.

Bob Burns has another location at the *Promenade* shopping center in Woodland Hills, and though the drinks and dining are much the same, the decor is sadly not as arcane as the Santa Monica location. If you can tolerate the occasional TV stars, industry schmucks, and hyperbolic hipsters who frequent *Bob Burns* in Santa Monica, an evening there can be a pleasant way to while away the hours.

Just don't ask Smitty to play "I Can See Clearly Now."

—ARL

"I only drink to make other people seem interesting."

—George Jean Nathan

Getting shit-faced, Polynesian-style, at the *Tiki Ti*

The **Tiki Ti** opened its doors in 1959—during the golden age of the tiki bar—and has remained a Silverlake institution ever since. Those who have sampled its charms willingly drive from across town just for the opportunity to nurse a Zombie, a Princess Pupuli or a Dr. Funk amidst the *Tiki Ti*'s inimitable milieu. While *Trader Vic's* and *Bahooka* offer remotely similar environments, the *Tiki Ti* is in a class by itself. If the *Enchanted Tiki Room* at Disneyland had an adjacent speakeasy or dirty backroom, our guess is that it would look just like the *Tiki Ti*.

Dr. Funk Is In The House

Blowfish lanterns and Christmas lights illuminate the diminutive room, with its original Polynesian decor still intact. A handful of cocktail tables and a couple of dark, cozy nooks supplement the counter seating, with glowing tiki-shaped drink menus mounted to the walls, a surfboard hanging overhead, and various forms of taxidermied sealife punching up some of the rooms emptier corners. Rattan stools line the short counter, behind which bubbles a lava rock waterfall randomly spray-painted with fluorescent oranges and greens—the surrounding area is loaded down with South Seas novelties, tikiana, and bottles of booze, looking much like a shrine to the Tahitian god of alcoholism. Some bars are more conducive to jovial drunkenness than others, and there's something about the *Tiki Ti*—call it the X factor—that can turn even the staunchest puritan into a lighthearted lush.

The crowd here is varied and diverse; a skin-headed dyke with pierced eyebrows might warm a barstool across from a sixty year-old Mexican gardener, but the later you show up, the more likely you are to see the place packed to the gills with the decidedly hip. Still, to its credit, the scene is never too conscious of itself.

It's easy to pass by the *Tiki Ti*, even if you're watching for it. From the outside, the Lilliputian watering hole looks more like a Polynesian outhouse—and it's further dwarfed by the looming shadow of the monstrous Circuit City across the street. Though small in stature, the *Tiki Ti* is a steadfast giant in the world of unduly garnished phosphorescent cocktails.

Beware: the fruity concoctions of the *Tiki Ti* are notorious for packing a sucker punch, and if you're not careful you'll get knocked on your ass faster than you can say "designated driver."

Tiki Ti
4427 Sunset Blvd.
Los Angeles
(213) 669-9381

OUT-AND-ABOUT

Las Vegas meets ... just a stone's throw from Disneyland

Eden Roc Motel
1830 South West Street
Anaheim

How to enjoy *Disneyland* on the rocks

"We at Disneyland do not approve of the use of alcohol."

'll never forget those words, spoken by a security guard who had just busted my buddies and me in the Disneyland parking lot. Our crime? Drinking beer in our car. Despite the fact that none of us had finished so much as a single beer, we were forbidden from entering the park and banished from the parking lot. Rather harsh punishment and hypocritical words when you consider that a secret restaurant and bar pours drinks within puking distance of the Pirates of the Caribbean.

Club 33 is the only place in Disneyland where alcohol is served. Unfortunately, you can't buy a drink there unless you're a member—and with the cost of Remy Martin cognac at *$90 for a single shot*, perhaps it's for the better that you aren't one of the lucky 400 suckers who cough up the $2,250 a year in dues (on top of a $7,500 individual membership fee). Located at 33 Royal Street, between the Blue Bayou restaurant (which deigns to serve plebeians) and the Christmas Shop, the entrance to *Club 33* is an unimposing, unmarked white door. The brass intercom is the only hint that something hoity-toity is going on inside. Look for it the next time you visit Disneyland—it's a great spot to panhandle.

Is That A Mickey Mouse Swizzle Stick In Your Pocket Or Are You Just Happy To See Me?

Even if you could afford the exorbitant membership fee, the waiting time to join is approximately two to three years, so don't think you can just walk in flashing ten grand in cash and order an Old Milwaukee. But don't despair. Drinking proles will take heart in the knowledge that libation can be had at Disneyland without sneaking a slug from an airline-size bottle of Chivas (though this is without a doubt the best way to bring your own booze into the park). Again, you'll have to endure a wait, but it'll be shorter than trying to get into *Club 33*. If you don't mind standing in line for the Monorail and leaving the park for a little while, you'll find that the futuristic train will deliver you to the **Disneyland Hotel**, at which you will find more than one bar to service your needs. When you're sufficiently greased, the Monorail is your designated driver back into the park. This is a foolproof—albeit circuitous—method of putting a little more magic into the Magic Kingdom, while still playing by their rules. And you know, there's nothing quite like beating the system at its own game.

—ARL

Club 33
(Members Only)
33 Royal Street
New Orleans Square,
Disneyland

Disneyland Hotel
1150 Cerritos Avenue
Anaheim

chapter four

Press- ing the Flesh

For the life of us, we can't figure out why they call Las Vegas "Sin City." If anything, a town that intentionally ugly, with a history so salacious it makes Gommorah look like Santa's Village, deserves a moniker more in the realm of "Straight to Hell City." As far as we're concerned, L.A. is the rightful owner of the name "Sin City." After all, we're the porno capital of the western world, cranking out enough adult videos each month to fill the Grand Canyon. We've got the preponderance of über-hookers who cater to the stars, whether it be servicing Hugh Grant in a rent-a-car in broad daylight, or being forced to drink the late Don Simpson's used toilet water at his palatial house of horrors. We have Hollywood studios puking up so-called entertainment like "Striptease" and "Showgirls" and pretending it's supposed to be something other than chub-inducing trash for sexually immature misogynists. We have talent agencies dedicated solely to providing porn stars for the insatiable sexual maw of the hypocritical American public. We have the Playboy mansion and its female fixtures. We have Larry Flynt and his prosthetic penis. We have Heidi Fleiss and her humble Santa Monica boutique. We have sex stores that sell foreskin extenders, extra large enema bags, and dildos as large as Lou Ferrigno's arm. We have clubs dedicated to size queens and their well-hung quarry, hotels with voyeuristic elevators, and an X-rated version of Mann's Chinese Theater—complete with cement imprints out front. We even have a hardcore nudist colony run by a paraplegic. Some cities talk about helping the handicapped, but here in L.A., they help themselves.

And we're damn proud of it—all of it!
So Las Vegas, you can go to Hell where you belong.
We're the real "Sin City," and we have the credentials to prove it.

If you have any doubts, just read on....

Discovering the Sexual Treasures of

The Pleasure Chest

n a nation as sexually stuffy as the United States, it's somewhat refreshing to stroll into a store like **The Pleasure Chest** and see customers from all walks of life browsing and buying sex toys and apparel with shameless impunity. Perhaps a store that bills itself as "The World's Largest & Finest Erotic Department Store" wouldn't play in Peoria, but it certainly makes a pretty penny adjacent to West Hollywood, the heart of L.A.'s gay community. Though *The Pleasure Chest* is obviously geared to accommodate its surrounding neighborhood, it also goes out of its way to make the heterosexual customer happy in more ways than one by offering plenty of neat and naughty merchandise for "breeders."

Is That A Foreskin Extender In Your Pocket Or Are You Just Happy To See Me?

Beyond this, a trip to *The Pleasure Chest* is, in itself, an education in alternative lifestyles. One would never imagine that so many varieties of enema bags and nozzles even existed, much less were used as instruments of pleasure. The same is true for their selection of handcuffs, catheters, foreskin extenders, rectal inflators, nipple clips, disposable speculums, and other items you'd expect to encounter in either a doctor's office or a dungeon.

Besides offering a stunning selection of adult videos, dildos, vibrators, lubes, and other so-called "marital aids," *The Pleasure Chest* also features such unique fetish accouterments as full-on Highway Patrol and Police Uniforms, ball stretchers, studded leather cock rings, colon tubing(!), leather chaps, penis pumps, paddles (leather and wooden), riding crops, human leashes (available in both two-foot and five-foot lengths), "buddy connectors," bull whips, hoods, gags, blindfolds, and enough other mondo gear to make you either perverted for life or thankful for the missionary position for the very first time.

If any of these items are beyond the realm of your comprehension or experience, *The Pleasure Chest* has a variety of books to educate and entertain. Those interested in the world of "safe and fun s/m lovemaking" will want to check out *Learning the Ropes*. Or perhaps you've been aching to learn all there is to learn about the art of spanking and being spanked; for you there's *The Bottoming Book*, or *How to Get Terrible Things Done to You By Wonderful People*. Lovers of the aesthetic can take their pick from the oversized beefcake classics of Tom of Finland to the—ahem—*seminal* drawings of the delightfully demented John Willie (of "Bizarre" Magazine fame).

Still, all this may seem daunting—or downright unappetizing—to some of you, and in that case, perhaps the store's myriad of humorous novelties may yet arouse your curiosity—if not satisfy your Christmas gift list altogether. Whether you're in the mood for a Big Tit Coffee Mug, a wind-up jolly jumping pussy, a six-foot inflatable penis, or that classic kid's game, Pin the Boobs on the Babe, you'll encounter all these and more at this Wal-Mart of wantonness.

Though *The Pleasure Chest* will send you a brochure that also doubles as a catalogue, you really can't fully appreciate the vast scope of this tastefully subdued sex supermarket unless you pay a visit in person. And if you can't make the trek to West Hollywood, then be sure to visit their new "cyberstore" online at www.thepleasurechest.com. Those of you not yet acquainted with late 20th century technology can still use the telephone to take advantage of their toll-free mail order service at 1-800-753-4536. With one convenient call, you can rest easy knowing that your edible bra or Lucite nipple suction cup is winging its way to you.

In discrete packaging, of course.

The Pleasure Chest
7733 Santa Monica Boulevard
Los Angeles
(213) 650-1022

Browsing at *Le Sex Shoppe*

With many convenient locations throughout the metroplex to serve all your prurient interests, **Le Sex Shoppe** (LSS) is to adults what *Toys 'R Us* is to kids: Fantasyland, pure and simple. Where else could you go to find such a varied selection of magazines, books, vibrators, inflatable partners, and of course, the obligatory peep booths, without having to walk through an embarrassingly garish

Is That A Pair Of Ben-Wa Balls In Your Pocket Or Are You Just Happy To See Me?

facade of unholy signs that scream out XXX and NUDE GIRLS in glaring neon lights!? Unless you're completely sober and looking for it, you could easily pass the *Le Sex Shoppe* on, say, Van Nuys Boulevard (just north of Ventura Boulevard), and never have an inkling of what was really going on beyond the subtly smoked glass door. Yes, there is a big pink awning out front, but the tasteful proprietors of *LSS* have somehow managed to make even that monstrosity seem somehow...not so monstrous. Could be a bubble gum shoppe for all you know. Across the street, families do their weekly shopping at a large grocery store. A popular deli and a cutesy 50s diner are but a stone's throw from the front door of this particular *LSS*, and surrounding neighborhoods are hardly downscale—especially due south.

It all seems so charming, really, that it makes one wonder if some upper-middle-class families might even have a stop at *Le Sex Shoppe* to add to their daily errand list:

1) **Get turkey franks, bread, and soda at store**

2) **Pick up dry-cleaning at Chan's**

3) **Get new issue of "Golden Shower Chicken Slaves"** at *Le Sex Shoppe*

Of course, no such title exists—at least, not at *Le Sex Shoppe*. This fine establishment adheres to community standards and doesn't trade in any mags or videos that would appeal to pederasts, copraphiliacs, or Catholic Priests.

Le Sex Shoppe

4539 Van Nuys Blvd.
Sherman Oaks
(818) 501-9609

4877 Lankershim Blvd.
North Hollywood
(818) 760-9529

21625 Sherman Way
Canoga Park
(818) 992-9801

6315 Hollywood Blvd.
Hollywood
(213) 464-9435

12323 Ventura Blvd.
Studio City
(818) 760-9352

45 E. Colorado Blvd.
Pasadena
(818) 683-9468

Call your local information operator
for more convenient locations in your area!

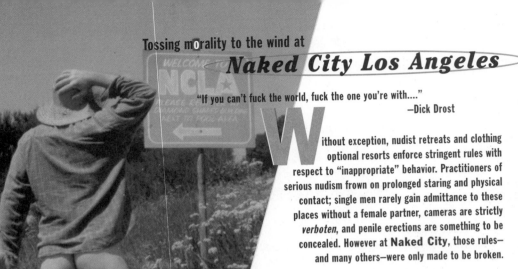

Tossing morality to the wind at
Naked City Los Angeles

"If you can't fuck the world, fuck the one you're with...."
—Dick Drost

Without exception, nudist retreats and clothing optional resorts enforce stringent rules with respect to "inappropriate" behavior. Practitioners of serious nudism frown on prolonged staring and physical contact; single men rarely gain admittance to these places without a female partner, cameras are strictly *verboten*, and penile erections are something to be concealed. However at **Naked City**, those rules—and many others—were only made to be broken.

Uptight nudists steer clear—*or you might get caught in the line of spewing ejaculate!* The proprietors of *Naked City* welcome a poolside fuck-frolic or a stag male guest roaming the grounds boner-to-the-wind with a camera hanging around his neck, because here, it's sex with a capital X! In business since 1981, *Naked City* exists as the sole adults only, clothing optional "vacation spot" catering to swingers in all of Southern California.

The scene at *Naked City* is like a melange of Russ Meyer movies on bad acid. The grounds span twenty-two acres of dry, rocky desert hilltops dotted with abandoned trailers and crumbling car ports. A dirt road leads through the compound to the tip of Mammary Mountain, the *Naked City* check-in point. The dusty parking lot at the mountain's edge is quietly active with couples and single men getting their clothes off, slathering themselves with sunblock and locking up their cars. Adjacent to the lot is the clubhouse through which *Naked City* becomes accessible. Bearing striking resemblance to a grounded alien space vessel, it's this mirrored, diamond-shaped building that sets the mood for the *Naked City* experience. Out front, an American flag waves high above *Naked City*'s white stretch limousine, which sports a license plate reading "NUDE." A buzz at the intercom system will prompt one of the *Naked City* employees—all nude women—to invite you in.

Inside, a low-rent *Love American Style*-meets-*Plato's Retreat* decor abounds; a stripper's catwalk of bright blue astroturf runs diagonally through the center of the main room and up to the ceiling. Mirror-tiled walls create a cubist's nightmare out of the towering bank of video monitors simultaneously screening a non-stop blitzkrieg of XXX films. Color snapshot photo collages of the lewdest and crudest moments from *Naked City*'s past are trimmed with yards of chaser lights pulsating in rapid-fire succession. Silver sequined floorlength curtains sweep over doorways, reflecting the red and blue lightbulbs glowing in their shiny chrome fixtures. Red shag covers the floors. In a corner, a nubile and naked eighteen-year-old secretary with long blond hair (winner of *Naked City*'s "Ms. Nude California" title, I would later learn) sits toiling away at her laptop computer. She is buried up to her nipples in a heap of papers and overstuffed file folders as she tends to some *Naked City* bookkeeping. In an instant, she glances up from her work, shooting her gaze to the stack of television screens running the adult feature *Trampire*. She watches as the title character slowly goes down on her male co-star, prompting the barely legal Ms. Nude California to enthusiastically squeal, "Bite it! *Make blood come out!!*"

"Welcome to *Naked City*..." a voice calls from a round bed fitted with a silver sequined dust ruffle positioned just next to the front door. Lumped in the center, a frail looking paraplegic lies loosely wrapped in white bedsheets with his head perched on a high pillow. Two tanline-free women are sprawled at either side of his tiny frame. His arms rest palms-up, outstretched and lifeless. His face is flushed with a pinkish glow and his skin glistens lightly with perspiration. Most of his shoulder-length dark hair is pulled up away from his neck and hangs over the back edge of his pillow support. Looking like a demented Time/Life operator, he wears a telephone headset held tightly to his ear, with the mouthpiece positioned close to his half-parted lips. Like a weak, underfed sparrow, his eyelids gently hang half closed, exposing only the whites of his eyes, intermittently falling completely shut for several minutes at a time. His breathing is slow and shallow and it appears as though his heartbeat is slowly giving way to the intense desert heat. I expect at any moment for a nude priest to walk in and give him his last rites. Instead, a few more naked swingers enter the clubhouse to sign in, and he quickly—almost miraculously—perks up to greet them.

This is the infamous Dick Drost, owner and proprietor of *Naked City*. A bizarre hybrid of Hugh Hefner, Andy Warhol and Stephen Hawking, Drost proves to be an extremely sweet man with an endearing sense of humor, quick to put nervous guests at ease with a bottomless reserve of lines like "We accept Visa, Mastercard and Masturbate..." He rules his kingdom from his round mattress—literally charming the pants off everyone who enters—forever flanked by a bevy of naked young girls. And who says the handicapped are underprivileged?

The scene on the bed completes an intensely staggering sight, although visitors don't seem to pay much mind. Nude men walk casually through the room, making their way to a threshold marked "XXXXXXXX," and stepping in past its silver curtains to the video room. Furnished with several chairs, a double bed and a hot tub, patrons "lounge" beneath the silver foil ceiling in this private area, illuminated mainly by the glow from the X-rated video being played from the large TV screen.

"No G-strings attached..." claims the *N.C.L.A.* mailer. It also credits *Naked City* with "Great Mouthwatering Buffets," "Perfumed Breezes," "Molten Native Sunsets," "The Complimentary Bon-ape-tit (sic) Snack Bar," "The Peek-a-boo-tique Giftshop," "Rustic Hiking Trails" and a "Palm-Fringed Sparkling Pool." Though such promises measure up in content equivalent to those made on the cardboard packaging of a Sea Monkey kit, *Naked City* does pull through—just barely—with the hype: the rustic trails are the dirt roads leading around the property, the Bon-ape-tit Snack Bar is the motel-sized refrigerator inside the clubhouse stocked with soda (with a coffee maker and a small display of chips and pretzels arranged neatly on its top). The Peek-a-boo-tique Gift Shop is nothing but Dick Drost's mail order catalogue consisting mostly of *Naked City* events on video—and not a bad selection at that. The pool does in fact have a couple of palm trees growing next to it, but "sparkling" is really a subjective term—you get the idea. As one *Naked City* regular euphemistically explained while sunning poolside, "As you can see, Dick takes some artistic license with those flyers..."

Naked City sponsors several special events throughout the year, among them the "Ms. Nude California" and "Ms. Nude World" pageants, which allow cameras at an additional $30 fee. Popular too is the "Nude Olympixxx" ("Lots of breast strokes and broad jumps," says Drost), featuring many original games not practiced by the ancient Greeks, like "Nude Chocolate Pudding Wrestling."

HAPPY N-U-D-E YEAR FROM "NAKED CITY"!!!

D!CK DROST POSES WITH SEXXXY MS NUDE HOLLYWOOD
EROTIC MS NUDE AMERICA & KITTY FOXX 1-800-XXX-NCLA

"One time the girls really got into it and pudding went flying everywhere...I had pudding all over my wheelchair, it was a mess," Dick laments with a grin. If only Leni Riefensthal could document *these* Olympic games. (Chocoholics take note: don't bring a spoon, the pudding immediately goes sour under the blistering desert sun).

The *Naked City* regular calendar of events carries an everchanging lineup, like the "Jack-off and Jill-off Chili Cook-off," the "Select and Connect Wesson Oil Sunday Splash," the "Pretty Pussy and Damndest Dick Contest," and "June Is Bustin' Out All Over Day," where visitors who tip the scales at 210+ pounds are admitted free. Dick is never at a loss for new and creative ideas, and really topped himself with the "Foxx Hunt." In this case, it was porn star Kitty Foxx, often billed as "The World's Sexiest Senior," who served as the Foxx to be hunted. She ran and hid somewhere on the grounds, and when Drost gave the signal, a pack of naked, horny men were let loose after her. "Whoever finds her, gets her," Dick chuckles.

Your chances of scoring big at *Naked City* are slightly increased due to the fact that everyone here has already taken off their clothes (though technically "clothing optional" few, if any, opt for clothing), conveniently eliminating one time-consuming step from the process of bedding down a total stranger. And the lay of the land? Surprisingly attractive for a swing establishment located deep into the hills of Riverside County.

At once filthy, frightening and peculiarly fun, the *Naked City* experience isn't an easy one to shake off—try as you might. Dick Drost and his sunkissed comrades will revisit you in your dreams and fill your thoughts during long rush-hour standstills months after you've traveled down the series of pitted, narrow dirt roads leading away from the high desert skin-show and back to pleasingly familiar freeways. Like an unwelcomed rite of passage, *Naked City* will push you beyond a place in human consciousness to which you'll never again return. Even those hiding a past littered with a string of sloppy one night stands and sleazy self-compromise will somehow feel less pure after a visit to the peak of Mammary Mountain.

–MM

FROM LOS ANGELES:
Take the 60 freeway east to the 215 freeway south to highway 74 east in Hemet. Travel on 74 east for about five miles into Homeland, and turn left on Juniper Flats. Follow Juniper Flats about three miles (it turns to the left) to Quail Canyon. Turn right on Quail Canyon and follow the road to a large gate with a red and white triangular reflector. Turn left at the gate and veer right on Bahler. Go up Mammary Mountain for about one and a half miles (you'll see a series of boulders spray-painted in fluorescent colors—always an indication of a top-notch establishment). You'll see a "NAKED CITY" sign directing you down a road to the parking lot. Check in immediately at the clubhouse.

As one would expect, the ratio of men to women is consistently unbalanced, at about five to one, and the admission rates reflect this: a day pass for a single man runs $30, a male-female couple $10, a single woman $1. Yearly membership rates for single men $500, couples $175, and single women $50. Special discounts are offered occasionally, check with *Naked City* before you arrive. For a current calendar of events send a SASE with your request.

N.C.L.A.
Box 2000
Homeland, CA
92548-2000
Phone: (909) 926-BANG
Fax: (909) 926-1737

9th Annual Night of the Stars

Hob-Knobbing with the Knob-Gobblers at

Night of the Stars

Every porn fan's dream is to spend an evening (at the very least) mingling with their favorite filmic fornicators, imagining what their idols must look like with their clothes off. While this may seem like an unlikely fantasy for most, it is, in fact, a reality that can yearly be fulfilled at what is dubiously dubbed as "Night of the Stars."

Sponsored by the Free Speech Coalition—a loosely knit group of adult entertainment manufacturers as concerned with the First Amendment as they are with their own well-being—*Night of the Stars* is an annual self-congratulatory celebration of porndom and all that goes with it. Awards with prestigious-sounding names like the "Joel T. Warner Good Guy Award" are doled out like sausage samples at a supermarket opening, but the bottom line is that this is a night for the so-called stars to see and be seen. And unlike so many other entertainment industry events, this puppy is open to the prurient public—at a substantial cost, of course. Then again, how much would you pay for a ticket to the Oscars just to get a chance to rub elbows with—and possibly get punched out by—the likes of say, Steven Seagal? Now just imagine the thrill of getting the opportunity to squeeze the amazingly globular butt cheeks of Ms. Nina Hartley? The implications are nothing less than crotch-boggling!

Save the Last Dance for Peter North

Night of the Stars is usually held each year in mid-July at a local L.A. hotel, complete with dinner, dancing, and entertainment (no, not a live donkey show). For industry insiders it is just another glad-handing event, an opportunity for self-aggrandizement and self-promotion, but for the layman (no pun intended) it's virtually a night in Nirvana itself.

While the spur-of-the-moment, extra-curricular activities at *Night of the Stars* have been somewhat curtailed over the years (read: no more naked girls performing cunnilingus on each other in the middle of the dance floor), you can still expect to get an eyeful of cleavage and other carnal delights just the same.

Should you dare to be indulgent in such sinful repartee, you can get your tickets to the event by contacting The Free Speech Coalition for further info, dates, and ticket prices. Don't expect to get in for a mere pittance, but then again, how much *would* you pay just to see Janine sashay by in a form-fitting sequined dress slit up the back to display the crack of her ass? For some porn addicts there is no price too high—so open up your wallet and bleed...after all, it's in the name of Free Speech—and there's no additional charge for popping a chubby as long as you keep it in your pants. Who knows, a trip to the urinals may result in an encounter with Mr. Mega-Wad himself, Peter North, who may even share some of his world-famous hair-grooming tips with you. And that alone should be well worth the exorbitant price of admission.

Call the Free Speech Coalition to find out just how much your groovy evening of wacky fun will set you back. But keep in mind that your ticket may be tax-deductible, which is more than you can say for a shopping cart full of dildos and inflatable sex partners from *Le Sex Shoppe*.

Although these stars may be of the falling variety, you'll be sure to find at least one or two porn icons to chat up—and perhaps feel up—when you attend *Night of the Stars*.

Just remember to play safely—and *bone* appetit!

Night of the Stars
Sponsored by
The Free Speech Coalition
(818) 348-9373

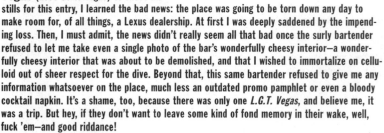

Remembering **L.G.T. Vegas**
Viva L.G.T. Las Vegas!

By the time you read this, one of the Valley's seedier landmarks will have been unceremoniously ushered into the pages of architectural history. When I visited **L.G.T. Vegas** (Let's Go To Vegas) to shoot the stills for this entry, I learned the bad news: the place was going to be torn down any day to make room for, of all things, a Lexus dealership. At first I was deeply saddened by the impending loss. Then, I must admit, the news didn't really seem all that bad once the surly bartender refused to let me take even a single photo of the bar's wonderfully cheesy interior—a wonderfully cheesy interior that was about to be demolished, and that I wished to immortalize on celluloid out of sheer respect for the dive. Beyond that, this same bartender refused to give me any information whatsoever on the place, much less an outdated promo pamphlet or even a bloody cocktail napkin. It's a shame, too, because there was only one *L.G.T. Vegas*, and believe me, it was a trip. But hey, if they don't want to leave some kind of fond memory in their wake, well, fuck 'em—and good riddance!

L.G.T. Vegas aspired to magically transport its clientele from the North San Fernando Valley to the glitz and glamor of Glitter Gulch—without the drunks even having to leave their seats. This miracle was accomplished via a subtle combination of the aforementioned interior—a tribute to Naugahyde, dark velvet, and frantically blinking lights—as well as plenty of non-paying slot machines and electronic casino games, and, of course, high-quality live entertainment like a Tony Orlando and Dawn lookalike act.

The real Las Vegas itself is a blight on the face of America, a town so stinking with rotten luck that not all the oxygen pumped into all the casinos can eliminate the overwhelming bad vibes. So why on earth would anyone want to subject themselves to even an evening at this scaled-down, B-rate imitation of our nation's modern-day Gommorah? Perhaps within the answer lies the explanation of why *L.G.T. Vegas* is now a memory, replaced by a surface of flat black tar and a phalanx of overpriced Japanese luxury sedans.

Which, perhaps, is just what *L.G.T Vegas* deserved, especially after treating one of your authors with such unmitigated rudeness. Let this be a lesson to you all. *L.G.T. Vegas* once stood at 1100 N. Sepulveda. The only people who'll miss it most will probably outlive the place, anyway, forcing them to take their money to the mother of all deep-dark holes and throw it all in a Vegas trash can.

–ARL

Celebrity worshipping at the *Tomkat Theater*

ids today don't know what they're missing. They'll never have the experience of dialing a clunky rotary phone and getting a busy signal, or hearing that coitus interruptus *ka-chunk* in the middle of a favorite song played on an 8-track tape cartridge. For them, there's no such thing as music without video, or home without a home P.C. What do they think O.J. did before June 12, 1994? Do they know that 7-Eleven used to *serve* you a Slurpee, or that a person had to actually walk *into* a bank to withdraw cash? And what about pornography? Where do these kids think dirty old men and horny teenagers used to go for full length, X-rated features? The video store? HA! No such thing! *Viva* **The Pussycat Theater!!**

Sadly, the once ubiquitous *Pussycat* chain is now a dying breed. Having lived eight-and-a-half of her nine lives, she's now just an old flea-bitten, mange-riddled arthritic feline laying to rest in the shadow of the adult home video industry. There was no such thing as fast-forwarding through the dialogue sequences, or rewinding to see that cum shot one more time. At the *Pussycat*, it was over when it was over, and it was the only time in movie-going history that previews for coming attractions were actually entertaining.

Pounding The Pavement

Through the 80s most of the *Pussycat*s closed down or changed hands and became "legit" movie theaters. The old *Pussycat* location on Santa Monica Boulevard, however, is a noteworthy exception for two reasons. One, it has had an interesting metamorphosis; cleverly reinventing itself as the *Tomkat*, it now runs gay male porn exclusively. Second, and more importantly, it's the *Grauman's* of skin flicks, featuring the hand and foot prints of pre-safe sex porn notables like John Holmes (Betty Grable put her leg in concrete for Sid Grauman. Jimmy Durante, his nose. Alas, all John Holmes gave for posterity were the soles of his shoes), Linda Lovelace, Marilyn Chambers and Harry Reems. The *Tomkat* has carried on the tradition, enshrining a handful of gay fuck-film big wheels, but unfortunately a grainy low-grade concrete was used, rendering several signatures virtually illegible.

This little-known, only-in-Los Angeles attraction is easily missed unless you're on foot, and unfortunately the city's sole curbside homage to porn luminaries goes virtually unnoticed by the only foot traffic this stretch of Santa Monica Boulevard gets—portly Russian women and feculent street hustlers.

The Tomkat Theater
(formerly The Pussycat)
7734 Santa Monica Blvd.
Hollywood
(213) 650-9551

The Pussycat Theater
1508 North Western Ave.
(at Sunset)
Hollywood

1442 2nd Street
(at Broadway)
Santa Monica

Catching the Goings-on Outside

All American Burger

Once while I was at the intersection of Sunset and Crescent Heights waiting for the light to turn green, two male tourists driving a rental car in the lane next to me motioned that I roll my window down. They were wrestling with a large road map, and were in need of directions to a famed Hollywood attraction that was conspicuously absent from their AAA guidebook. In an accent that smacked of the late Tennessee Ernie Ford, the driver asked, "Wot port 'a Sunset Boleevord du th' hukkers hang owt at?" These poor slobs were obviously unaware of two very important facts: #1, Never end a sentence with a preposition, and #2, The city of Los Angeles has made it ridiculously simple to locate its working girls; just look for the street signs that read "NO TURNS 11:00 P.M. TO 7:00 A.M. NIGHTLY" and you're sure to find yourself a hotbed of curbside hanky-panky very nearby!

Sunset Boulevard stands out as the only hooker drag in town that was given an endorsement—albeit unwittingly—by a major movie star. However, Hugh Grant's seal of approval was a tragic catch-22 for Hollywood's red-light district. On one hand it was free publicity on a stellar scale, making Hollywood's poon-tang promenade internationally visible, thereby generating loads of potential overtime for the throngs of spandexed, high-heeled harlots who punch their imaginary timeclock on this eight-block stretch of Sunset Blvd. On the other hand, the police cracked down considerably on this sex-for-pay playground for the very same reasons, making it nearly impossible for these gals to take advantage of all those prospective Johns fumbling with their road maps.

Enough time has passed since the Hugh Grant debacle, and business is for the most part back to normal—much to the dismay of nearby homeowners. In spite of all the terrible things one could say about Hugh Grant's conduct as a John, he does go straight to the top when it comes to cruising for sex; these are high-class streetwalkers working Sunset, reportedly charging an astronomical $40 to $60 for a simple lunch-hour blow-job. The inflated fees—I presume—are for overhead; these girls *dress*. The fashion parade on Sunset Boulevard is like a Frederick's of Hollywood trunk show. While nearly toppling over in white vinyl skyscraper stilettos, these fashion whores sport a variety of *pret-a-porter* day-glo spandex creations, proving that there's something to be said for puritanical body shame.

Although the sex professionals of Sunset could probably make a better career choice, their spirit is admirable. Through the month of December, many of these girls bring to back-seat sex what Martha Stewart brings to a holiday buffet—and I'm not talking about Miss Piggy. They're the most festive hookers in town, donning Santa Claus hats and sexy Mrs. Claus-esque miniskirts. Now *that's* getting into the Christmas spirit! You'd think after their thirtieth or fortieth blow-job of the day that they'd be ready to say bah-humbug and throw in the towel! But no—after wiping off and straightening their furry red cap, it's back out onto the street they go, spreading Christmas cheer and a myriad of STDs. Honestly, which whore would you rather receive service from: the one that looks like Santa's helper, or the one in Levi cutoffs and a tube top, standing barefoot in the parking lot out front of a liquor store?

The **All American Burger**, located on the corner of Sunset and Spaulding, is to curbside solicitation what the *Brown Derby* was to the movie industry—a watering hole for the trade. During the lunch rush you could conceivably place an order, step outside to the pay phone and meet your "date," hop in your car and pull around the corner, soil your auto upholstery, and pull back into the parking lot in time to hear your order number called—all before your onion rings get cold! Even better, a window seat at *All American Burger* offers a safer alternative. You can watch all the action transpire on the streets from your table—live vicariously through some strange John and let him risk arrest while you nibble some fries. And though you may have to fight a hungry hooker for a place to sit, *All American Burger* is unrivaled for the best burger and fries this side of the *Apple Pan*, and the prices can't be beat—after all, can sixty filthy construction workers and five bitter whores all be wrong?

What many don't know is that Hugh Grant isn't the only celebrity to frequent these streets. Locals are hip to that unduly muscled hunk who favors sex-for-pay over the throngs of horny housewives who adore him, and the semi-famous husband of that very famous TV star who was rumored to cruise for hookers to bring home for three-ways. And the pig who became a household word due to a lascivious sex-crime of his own hasn't shyed away from these streets either. In fact, autograph seekers take note: you're likely to find more of your favorite male stars here than at *Spago*.

—MM

A Bacon Cheeseburger Or A Blow-Job?

All American Burger
7660 West Sunset Blvd.
Hollywood
(213) 874-5779

Sunset Blvd. Prostitution
7800-7200 blocks of
Sunset Blvd., between
Fairfax and La Brea

Mustang Books & Video

art of the fun in visiting a dirty book store is the feeling that you're doing something bad. Although *The Pleasure Chest* and *Drake's* offer a nearly unrivaled selection of goods, it's become so fashionably alternative to shop these places that many customers go there simply to see-and-be-seen. What's happening to our society?! Can't a person act sleazy anymore without being looked up to?

Is That A Penis In Your Pussy Pants Or Are You Just Happy To See Me?

There are four really great reasons to patronize **Mustang Books & Video**: #1, The excellent selection of pornographic entertainment. #2, It's not hip, and you will feel somewhat sleazy shopping there. #3, The location is so far away from any place anyone you've ever known would ever be, that the chances of running into someone you've met at, say, your Weight Watchers meeting, are remarkably low. #4, After you've stocked up on gang bang videos and sex toys, there's a Christian Book Center located right across the street for those wrestling with religious guilt.

Mustang is quite unique in that they offer the one commodity unavailable in most porn shops, the commodity that anyone who has ever entered a dirty book store desperately wants and seems to have some difficulty in finding—*sex partners!* And we're not talking about a 1:00 A.M. cruise in the magazine section or an inflatable doll. On the wall just next to the hallway leading to the maze of private video booths, there hangs a large bulletin board covered with index cards and lurid Polaroided body parts. Each index card features a handwritten personal ad, some with accompanying photos. To make it a little easier, ads are broken down into the categories "Straight," "TV & TS," "Gay," and "Bondage." Even if you're not on the prowl for recreational sex, the bulletin board makes for great reading. The ads run the gamut from titillating to terrifying; an attractive, thirty-year-old junior high school teacher itchin' for group sex, a buff fireman willing to "perform" in his fire gear, some poor soul who "Wants Penis Removed," and dozens more. There's something extra revealing about a sex classified that's been *hand*written. Judging only by the handwriting, see if you can tell the difference between the seemingly harmless fireman and someone who may very well be a psychopathic serial rapist. In addition to penmanship, spelling too seems to be a lost art among those looking for no-strings-attached sex. Would you choose to get naked and intimate with someone looking for "laddies" who "injoy" huge "coch"? How about a guy hungry for wet "pusse"? Would you like to watch him "masserbate"?

The variety of magazines, videos and books (straight, gay, and fetish) are rivaled only by the selection of novelties and toys. Ferret away some no-fail stocking stuffers like penis toothpick holders, wind-up hopping vaginas, or motorized toys like the "Happy Jerk-off Clown" months before the Christmas rush. Tired of Scrabble? Try "Bride Bingo" or "Fart, the Game." At *Mustang*, sex toys come in peculiar varieties too. What would you get the horny astrologer who has everything? How about a set of zodiac dildos?! Steven Spielberg might be interested to know that *Mustang* carries a line of "Jurassic" vibrators—an alternative ride to that of Universal Studios. Save yourself a trip to Sweden—or worse, Mexico—with a pair of "Dick Pants," the second-skin briefs that can turn a she into a he. Just pull on the tight rubber pants and presto—no more penis envy! The aforementioned guy who wanted his pecker removed may want to invest a few bucks in a pair of "Pussy Pants"—the vaginal alternative to the gender-enhancing latex undergarments—before he does anything too drastic. Besides, they'll always provide a safe place for him to keep his wallet if he ever travels to Spain.

You're welcome to help yourself to a cup of hot coffee as you browse, and though it's an odd place for it, there's a candy machine that dispenses exactly one handful of Boston Baked Beans or Sweetarts just outside the coin-operated video booths, conveniently leaving one hand free to...insert coins.

The best part about *Mustang Books & Video* is the "Try Me Then Buy Me" vibrator display—a piece that could easily command thousands in a SoHo art gallery.

Ride 'em cowboy!

Mustang Books & Video
959-961 North Central Ave.
Upland
(909) 981-0227

Also nearby:
The Toy Box
(Comparable to *Mustang* in size; the only other store to feature bulletin board classifieds!)
1995 West Arrow Route
Upland
(909) 920-1135

T&A Video/ Tropical Lei
(Mediocre store that also features nude dancers)
240 Foothill Blvd.
Upland
(909) 985-1575

OUT-AND-ABOUT

Nothing hits the spot after a big, greasy southern-fried meal like a prodigious dose of ginseng root. You probably wouldn't expect to find an extensive selection of Korean pharmaceutical products at a chicken 'n ribs joint—but this is the San Fernando Valley, and anything's possible!

To our knowledge, Smokey Joe's Barbecue is the only western-style coffee shop in the world that features a ginseng display counter.

Smokey Joe's Barbecue
12851 Riverside Drive
North Hollywood

Enjoying L.A.'s Premier Moving Peep Show at

The Bonaventure

Going Down!

The futuristic exterior of the **Bonaventure Hotel** in downtown L.A. has served as the backdrop for a wealth of sci-fi flicks and other Tinseltown offal, while the equally modern interior has also seen its share of Hollywood action. In fact, full-size posters near the valet parking cashier and cheesy brass plaques outside the elevators even tell you what movies were shot there (*Lethal Weapon 2* and *In the Line of Fire* are but two of the timeless classics bandied about). You may recognize the *Bonaventure* for the cylindrical glass elevators that run up and down the outside of the mirrored monstrosity, and which are perhaps the hotel's most endearing feature. Indeed, a jaunt in one of these unique lifts is like being in *Willy Wonka and the Chocolate Factory* as you shoot from the lobby through the roof and into the smog-encrusted sky. Here you can enjoy a breathtaking view of our glorious city...and a damn good look into the rooms as you pass them by! And that's what really makes the *Bonaventure* such an, uh, interesting place.

Keep in mind that voyeurism on the *Bonaventure* elevators is a hit or miss experience. Sometimes you'll find that the guests are either being discrete and have drawn their blinds, or are downright boring and not even engaged in a sexual act. But when the drapes are open, the libidos are high, and discretion has been thrown to the wind—then look out!

This fascinating free peep show was an innocent discovery on my part. I was at the hotel for drinks one evening, minding my own business as I rode the elevator to the revolving lounge on the top floor, looking out at the huge neon "Jesus Saves" sign (now gone) when I happened to glance over into one of the passing rooms. It was then that I got an eyeful of a naked man sitting on the edge of his bed and a young woman in garters and stockings kneeling before him. And she wasn't bobbing for apples. Needless to say, I was late for my drinking engagement that night, riding that same elevator up and down. And, like some perverted tour guide, I was quick to point out the copulating couple to any unfortunate soul who happened upon my lascivious lift. Surprisingly, not all were charmed with my ersatz attempt at sexual enlightenment, and quickly got off the elevator long before they had reached their intended destinations.

Since I'm not a professional peeping-Tony and have better things to do than ride an elevator all night long in the hope of seeing a middle-aged businessman and a hooker, I must confess that I haven't made a habit of returning to the *Bonaventure* for such cheap thrills—though I'm always on the lookout whenever I do have the occasion to visit. Of course, this doesn't mean you're some kind of pervert if you make the elevators a regular part of your sex life.

It just means you're bored.

Whatever you do, don't forget the Dramamine.

—ARL

The Bonadventure Hotel Elevators

404 S. Figueroa St.
Downtown Los Angeles

Swingin' low with *The Hung Jury*

Are you a guy with a king-size schlong looking for a size queen to share it with? Check out *The Hung Jury*—the only club of its kind, specifically designed for "Women Who Think Big."

The Hung Jury was founded by Jim Boyd whose credo is that, without question, penis size is important to women. A bit fanatical, Boyd goes so far as to assert that all women have an innate desire for large cocks and any woman who proclaims otherwise has been brainwashed by "size doesn't matter propaganda." Apparently, the people who share his beliefs are great in number. He formed *The Hung Jury* in 1977, and the club has grown to over 2000 members strong nationwide and even boasts a British agent. At present, the club consists of about 50% single men, 30% women and 20% couples.

Membership requirements are strict and adhered to. Boyd puts all new members through a stringent screening process to ensure legitimacy and sincerity. All members must be at least eighteen years of age, and male members' members must measure a minimum of a full eight inches when erect (Note: This means 8" when measuring the underside of the cock, from the base of the balls to the head, which adds more length than the more accepted and accurate mode of measuring from the pubes to the head. Beware!). Sex must be absolutely consensual and the club expects the men to be polite and respectful of the women with whom they perform "jury duty." For their records *The Hung Jury* requires phone numbers from all club members and nude, boner-fied, full body photos of the men for verification of size. Anyone joining under false pretenses or lying about penile expanse will be dropped without refund—and it ain't cheap to join, but remember you are paying by the inch here.

Four issues of their contact publication "Measuring Up" runs $49 bucks which includes a 100-word personal ad. Photo ads cost $59 for four issues, and letter forwarding costs you $1 per letter. *The Hung Jury* requests that all letters are answered as a matter of courtesy. "Measuring Up" features scores of ads from donkey-dicked dudes and cock hungry gals and couples from all over the country, all races, ages and interests. "Measuring Up" also features club news, informative penis literature and 1-900# personals.

Although the club is almost exclusively heterosexual, both bisexual men and women are permitted to join. Most members are seeking nothing more than recreational sex but many are looking for committed relationships. In fact, *The Hung Jury* has been responsible for over 200 marriages. Like most contact services, the members run from the piquant to the unpalatable but no one seems to be complaining; after all, foot-long cocks don't grow on trees, you know.

No Hampsters Allowed

And *photos! photos! photos!* You've never seen so many huge dicks and fun luvin' chicks crammed into one newsletter. And as if they haven't done enough, *The Hung Jury* also offers a special service for the men: a Mistress of Measurements! For a $35.00 initiation fee, a Mistress of Measurements will pay a personal visit to you at your home, with a girlfriend and camera in tow. Upon her arrival you'll be required to strip naked and exhibit your 8"+ hard-on. Then out she whips her tape measure to confirm that you do in fact meet membership standards. A brief photography session follows (you provide the Polaroid film), and after completion of her technical duties one measurement maven claims that she'll also "fuck you dry if you turn me on." Another Mistress of Measurements and her female friends hold *THJ* measurement/sex parties for aspiring male jurors.

The Hung Jury will gladly send you a sampling of over 100 ads from men, women and couples pulled from their most recent issue of "Measuring Up," in addition to measure-ment instructions and membership information. Send $10 and a letter-size SASE to:

THJ
Post Office Box 1443
Studio City
91614

Discovering new career opportunities at

World Modeling Talent Agency

"I don't think pornography is very harmful, but it is terribly, terribly boring."

—Noel Coward

A mong L.A.'s many dubious distinctions, perhaps the most titillating is the fact that the San Fernando Valley is the nation's capital of porno production. Situated amidst the tract homes, shopping malls, and weapons contractors are the handful of companies that churn out the bulk of the adult videos so many Americans are quick to deny they've ever seen, yet have hidden in the nethermost corners of their closets. Not surprisingly, the Southland also serves as a breeding ground for the disillusioned, cynical, gum-chewing hardbodied babes who find it far easier to fuck on film than put in a full day at *Baskin-Robbins*. Likewise, the seductive porchlight of Hollywood attracts too many moths: corn-fed cuties who come here seeking fame, and, flying too close to the flame, end up burning out in the servitude of prostitution or substituting their dreams of super-stardom with the less glamorous compromise of porno celebrity.

Yet, contrary to popular belief, porn actresses are not forced into their careers at gunpoint, nor are they kidnapped and brainwashed in order to be bought and sold on the white slavery market. As incredible as it may sound, the gals who vie for X-rated stardom do so of their own volition, and the competition for fame is fierce. With the ultimate and most elusive prize being a long-term contract with one of the larger companies, most of the actresses must battle it out for each and every role. And though the casting couch

Is That An Erect Penis In Your Pocket

Or Are You Just Happy To See Me?

has its place in porndom, it's not half as worn out and sticky-stained as it is in so-called "legitimate" Hollywood, where "innocent" wanna-bes are chewed-up and spit out by demonically abusive producers like the late Don Simpson. The fact of the matter is that the ranks of Hollywood's most elite callgirls and the roster of top porn stars are not mutually exclusive. Just ask Heidi Fleiss.

While the phrase "talent agency" may be an oxymoron when used in reference to the porn industry, the **World Modeling Talent Agency** is L.A.'s largest and most infamous avenue into the world of porn stardom. And though some may call him a pimp in agent's clothing (yet another oxymoron), proprietor Jim South has received enough black eyes and broken limbs from fuming husbands, boyfriends, and fathers to deserve the respect of the Sherman Oaks Chamber of Commerce.

A pomaded, mustachioed Southern gentleman who looks like a cross between a used car salesman and Howard Sprague from "The Andy Griffith Show," South does his business from a humble suite of second floor offices on Van Nuys Blvd. *World Modeling* is the nexus of L.A.'s porn scene, overseen by the man with the shining brown mound of hair and surrounded by what seems to be used dorm furniture and glossy color nudes of his biggest clients. It is here that one gets a true feeling for the plush splendor that is the XXX business.

Mr. South handles both male and female clients, though the latter make up the bulk of his revenue. Giving new meaning to the term "cattle call," *World* often holds such *en masse* auditions in his cramped domain, which in the sweltering heat of summer can often be a daunting scene for anyone with even the slightest case of claustrophobia. If you happen to attend one of these notorious cattle calls—either as producer or talent—you will have a good idea of what a wild night on New Orleans's crowded Bourbon Street is like, albeit *sans* the primordial aroma of barf, piss, and booze. No, the scent at *World* is much more sophisticated: a noxious, emetic melange of too many colognes and perfumes, punctuated by the faint undertone of sweat, which at times can make one long for the fragrant fracas of Bourbon Street after all.

Jim South

From the perspective of the casting agent, the audition process goes a little something like this: You sit in one of the handful of small rooms that surround South's main office, which is packed to the gills with stars both new and old. One by one, they make their way into your room for the interview process, which consists of asking the performers' their vital statistics, who they will and will not perform with, and what sex acts they are willing to perform. The interview usually concludes with a Polaroid session in which the performer is photographed in the nude for future reference.

World Modeling Talent Agency
4523 Van Nuys Boulevard
Sherman Oaks
(818) 986-4316

World Modeling is also a prime provider for the models who appear in skin mags, so whether you're simply looking to pose nude for *Skank* magazine, or if your life's ambition is to have sexual intercourse with the gigantic hedgehog that is Ron Jeremy, one visit to *World Modeling* may be the answer to your dreams.

Or the beginning of your worst nightmare.

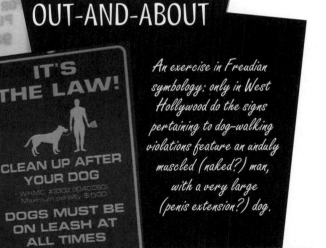

OUT-AND-ABOUT

IT'S THE LAW!

CLEAN UP AFTER YOUR DOG

WHMC #3302 (10400601)
Maximum penalty $500

DOGS MUST BE ON LEASH AT ALL TIMES

An exercise in Freudian symbology: only in West Hollywood do the signs pertaining to dog-walking violations feature an unduly muscled (naked?) man, with a very large (penis extension?) dog.

Is That A German Shepherd In Your Pocket Or Are You Just Happy To See Me?

Thought there was no other way for you to show your support for the porn business other than to frequent your local video store seven days a week to rent repetitious, ridiculously titled skinflicks that are embarrassing as heck to bring up to the front counter? Or perhaps you prefer to demonstrate your firm belief in the First Amendment by flogging your equally firm log to the likes of "Buttman Goes to Ruby Ridge" with the living room drapes wide open? On the other hand, you may be like most Americans who wish they could stand up for their constitutional rights but lack the guts to do so, opting instead to hide your porno tapes in the back of the coat closet while you deny you've ever watched anything raunchier than "Married with Children." Gutless wonder or not, you'll be pleased to know that a mere $25 dollars will not only symbolize your generous support for the smut business, but also entitle you to all sorts of neat fringe benefits, like discounts on X-rated items, invites to skin-oriented shows, and even the opportunity to be an extra in a blue movie. All you have to do is become a member of **F.O.X.E.** (pronounced "Fox," not Foxy), a clever acronym for "Fans of X-rated Entertainment."

F.O.X.E. is the brainchild of Bill Margold, an X-rated veteran who has worked in front of and behind the camera since 1969, an opinionated yet humble man whose business card is headed with the quote, "God created man. William Margold created himself." (Wonder how his parents feel about such a scientifically impossible claim?). With his deep, booming voice and brazenly confident manner to match, Bill may come off as somewhat abrasive to some, but his oversized heart is definitely in the right place, especially when it comes to giving of himself to his beloved porn biz and its stars, whom he lovingly refers to as "the kids."

In Bill's words, *F.O.X.E.* is "dedicated purely to getting the fans off their asses and supporting the industry." Or put more succinctly, *F.O.X.E.* exists for the purpose "of getting fans involved and admitting that if society can't fess-up to jacking-off then they shouldn't be upset when congress cuts off its dick." Perhaps those are harsh words on Bill's part, but in this age of impending right-wing castration at the hands of the Christian Coalition and their righteous ilk, such virulent verbiage rings true in a frightening way.

Your $25 membership fee, which basically covers operating costs and Margold's modest salary, will entitle you to the *F.O.X.E.* newsletter—"FOXE Tails"—as well as the opportunity to take part in the Adult Video Consumer Report, which the *F.O.X.E.* promotional materials claim will be the basis for a major adult entertainment awards show. And if humanitarianism is more your bag than witnessing the interaction of the human reproductive system at close range, you'll be pleased to know that some of the money from *F.O.X.E.*'s paltry coffers goes to another of Margold's inventions, **P.A.W.**— "Protecting Adult Welfare."

With a motto like "Reach Out and Get Touched By Someone," it would be easy to mistake *P.A.W.* for a phone sex service, or worse, an organization for frottage freaks, but in fact this service is dedicated to helping porn people with problems. 24 hours a day, seven days a week, *P.A.W.* offers an open ear and a kind voice to anyone in "the business" who may be struggling with depression, a drug problem, stress, sexual abuse, low self-esteem, relationship difficulties, a bad case of crabs or whatever else might drag a pornster down. Unlike your generic hotlines, *P.A.W.* is manned by a staff of voluntary counselors who are well-versed in the ins-and-outs (so to speak) of a particularly demanding and misunderstood industry. *P.A.W.* also offers peer counseling sessions, specialized enlightenment seminars and practical experience services. Unlike *F.O.X.E.*, *P.A.W.* is a non-profit organization and exists solely on money from *F.O.X.E.* as well as any donations that may trickle in. Feel free to join the trickle if the spirit moves you. Perhaps if *P.A.W.* had been around a few years ago, X-rated superstar Savannah would have picked up the phone and not a pistol when she smashed her Corvette. Her suicide, along with the needless self-inflicted deaths of others in the porn biz, was one of the main reasons Margold decided to try and make a difference.

While many Americans may poo-poo such an organization—as well as anything having to do with porno—*P.A.W.* is truly a noble effort, albeit from a man who many in the skin biz would not put at the top of their Christmas list, much less call for spiritual counsel in their darkest hour. But when the chips are down because you're worried about your health and don't know where to turn, how many individuals can you count on to take you to a doctor, get you proper treatment, and then pay the bill for you? Nope, not Tom Cruise, smart guy. Bill Margold and *P.A.W.*, pure and simple.

So if you enjoy a good dirty movie now and then, or are simply a fan of the Bill of Rights, why not cough up a small donation for *P.A.W.* or join *F.O.X.E.*? You don't have to scream out your love for porn at the local mall, but you can make a difference to the people who help you vicariously realize your unfulfilled fantasies by parting with a few of your hard-earned bucks. Who knows—you may even sleep a little better at night...after watching your favorite scene from "Three Men and a Babysitter," of course.

Just remember: a libido is a terrible thing to waste.

F.O.X.E.
8231 DeLongpre Avenue,
Suite 1
West Hollywood
90046
P.A.W.
1 (800) 506-4XXX

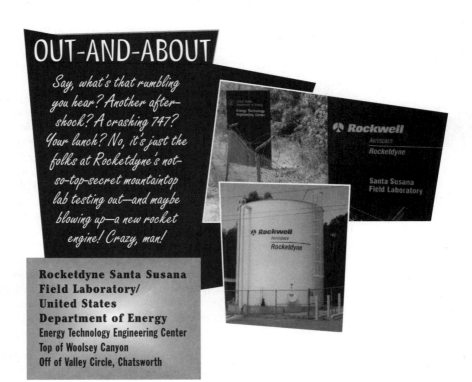

OUT-AND-ABOUT

Say, what's that rumbling you hear? Another aftershock? A crashing 747? Your lunch? No, it's just the folks at Rocketdyne's not-so-top-secret mountaintop lab testing out—and maybe blowing up—a new rocket engine! Crazy, man!

Rocketdyne Santa Susana Field Laboratory/ United States Department of Energy
Energy Technology Engineering Center
Top of Woolsey Canyon
Off of Valley Circle, Chatsworth

HardArt Phallic Replicating Service

HardArt offers the single greatest gift idea on planet earth: imagine the surprise (or horror) on the face of your loved one when presented with an exact, life-size replica of your own erect penis—fashioned into an incense burner, canopic-esque jar, or rubber dildo!!

Such is the business of Bill Hall and Jerry Lands of *HardArt*, quite possibly the country's most unique cottage industry. Clients have been putting their penises in *HardArt's* capable hands for nearly five years, and in turn, *HardArt* has produced an imaginative and ever-evolving line of custom-replicated penis products. Wow the guests of your next dinner party with an incense burner made in your own aroused image; watch as they trace the trail of fragrant smoke as it softly billows from the urethra of "your" dick! Next time your partner whines for sex and you're too pooped to pop, toss them your rubber likeness and consider the job done (stay hard forever no matter how drunk you get!). You'll surely be the hit of the office if you keep a stash of paper clips in "your" testicles. Both decorative (their cock-headed gargoyle goes a long way in sprucing up a drab IKEA bookshelf) and undeniably functional (like the aforementioned dildo or incense burner), the wares of *HardArt* are impeccably designed and surprisingly affordable. You can take home one of their simple "phallic sculptures" for a mere $50, or invest a little more for a "Romanesque Eagle Plaque," priced at $200. All other styles dangle somewhere in between.

Certainly, there's more to all this than simply placing an order by phone. There is the casting process to consider, and it isn't quite as effortless as that of a dental mold. Those who are predictably erection-shy or suffer from acute modesty will not fare well here. For most, it's not every day that we're required to get it up in front of two strange men—of which Bill and Jerry are keenly aware—and this is one of the first orders of business they tend to with a preliminary rundown. They take this time to answer any questions, address any concerns, and clarify what exactly their service consists of and what it is that you can (and can't) expect. Sexual orientation need not factor into your *HardArt* experience.

Is That A Phallic Replication In Your Pocket
Or Are You Just Happy To See Me?

Since it's necessary that the process be somewhat hands-on, clients are often understandably ill-at-ease—but after working closely with several hundred erect penises, Bill and Jerry have the process down to a science. They're masters at making nervous clients remarkably comfortable without being creepy. You're encouraged to bring any material that will most effectively assist you in your self-fluffing process—be it a smut-rag, video, or your favorite sex partner. Best of all, you aren't expected to perform like a seasoned porn actor or stud-for-hire so there's no rush, and you're given as much time as you need. Once you're "prepped" and ready to get dunked, timing is everything. Bill starts furiously mixing the quick-setting casting goo (similar to that used in a dentist's office) and Jerry helps to get you positioned onto their "glory table"—basically a massage table with a sizable opening in the center through which hang your "goods" (gravity works to your benefit here). Immediately your member is slipped into the mix (much like being slipped into a wet mouth) and from then on it's pretty smooth sailing; the setting time only takes about three minutes. If you want your mold "complete" you'll have to shave your balls, but since most men are reluctant to take a razor blade to their scrotum, many opt for the shaft-only variations.

For those yearning for a phallic replication to call their own, but find the *HardArt* casting process a bit daunting—good news! At no additional cost, *HardArt* can accommodate even the most bashful clients with their "Home StarterPak"; an easy, step-by-step do-it-yourself kit that allows you to complete the first stage of the replication process in the privacy of your own home. You then send your initial mold back to *HardArt*, and they do the rest. In four to six weeks, *viola!* A self-aggrandizing *objet d'art* is delivered right to your door.

HardArt is busily fine-tuning new additions to their ever-expanding product line: including a Video/Dildo Combo, so that you can play with your favorite porn star's replicated dick as you view his on-screen performance. They also have plans to jump on the CD-ROM bandwagon with a similar concept, and look forward to making their replicating service available to a female clientele, introducing a labia product line (ashtrays? pencil sharpeners?), as well as bazooms and posteriors, in the near future. As *HardArt* is obviously aware, the possibilities are endless, and thus far the competition is hardly stiff—they've got their market cornered. And since the business of genital replication probably won't catch on like the *Mrs. Fields Cookies* chain, it's likely to stay that way.

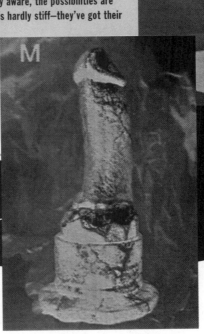

HardArt
Phallic
Replicating
Service
(213) 667-1501

OUT-AND-ABOUT

It's not like you see a giant revolving bottle of barbecue sauce every day. Or do you?

Chris & Pitts
9243 South Lakewood Blvd.
Downey

Seeing sounds and hearing colors at
The Madonna Inn

Inn-Credible!

here must be something in the air of California's Central Coast that turns otherwise ordinary people into frenzied interior decorators. First, William Randolph Hearst built his monstrous and unduly ostentatious kitsch-palace in the hills of San Simeon, then, decades later, Phyllis and Alex Madonna broke ground in San Luis Obispo to make way for the sensational Madonna Inn. This can be no coincidence.

Sometimes fate is kind enough to bring two great creative forces together, producing a brilliant partnership to benefit the rest of humanity. What else but that special magic in the universe could have given us the inspired teams of Jean Arp and Sophie Taeuber, Federico Fellini and Giulietta Masina, Jeff Koons and Ciccolina, Shields and Yarnell, Bob Mackie and Cher, or Liberace and Scott Thorson? Phyllis and Alex Madonna are one of those unique partnerships, and *The Madonna Inn* is their contribution to the world. Alex Madonna is the brains behind the architectural design and construction, and it was his idea to make each room different from the next ("...that way we can't make the same mistake twice"). His wife Phyllis is responsible for the inimitable interior, a job she undertook without any prior decorating experience. She's a natural. *The Madonna Inn* opened its doors on Christmas Eve 1958 with a total of twelve rooms, and invited their first round of visitors to stay free of charge. By 1960, the *Inn* had tripled in size and layout soon began on the main building and restaurants. Today—it's like the *Sagrada Familia* of San Luis Obispo—the construction continues.

If you haven't spent at least two nights of your life at *The Madonna Inn*, you simply haven't lived. Not only is *The Madonna Inn* a mind-boggling spectacle of design, it also happens to be a top-notch hotel with all the amenities of many places double the price and with half the flare. It's a crime not to take advantage of *The Madonna Inn's* "backyard" location to Los Angeles; there is no more perfect place in which to escape for a lost weekend of romance and/or debauchery—or to just get lost, figuratively speaking.

Enticing names like "Jungle Rock," "The Crystal Room," "Ren Dez Vouz" (three adjoining rooms named "Ren," "Dez" and "Vouz"), "Travelers Yacht," "Cayucos Queen," "Barrel of Fun," and "Cloud 9" are engraved into plaques hanging on the doors or above the thresholds of the *Madonna's* 109 rooms. To say that no two are alike is a gross understatement. Using parts of her brain that most interior decorators access only while in deep r.e.m., Mrs. Madonna isn't afraid to push the envelope of interior design by incorporating elements like six-ton boulders, gilded chandeliers, glitter-flecked cottage cheese ceilings, flocked wallpaper, high-gloss enamel, and velveteen drapery, to create a surreal—often blissfully disorienting—high-style playground for her bedazzled guests. Eye-watering color schemes of bright candy apple red, radiant robin's egg blue, vibrant kelly green, blinding canary yellow and dizzying shades of blistering pinks and abusive fuchsias may be a bit startling at first, but you'd be surprised how quickly you'll become accustomed to Mrs. Madonna's other-worldly color palate and her liberal use of

leopard skin, cherubs, and cascading rock waterfall showers and basins. Unfortunately Mrs. Madonna's *überdecor* is often lost on the plebeian, quick to dismiss her unique sensibility simply as "gaudy" or "kitsch." However, a true aesthete with a keen and highly developed eye for color, texture and composition understands Mrs. Madonna's work as no less than brilliant. Make no mistake: in addition to being an accomplished accordion player, Phyllis Madonna is one of the greatest living artists of our time.

If you're going to stay at *The Madonna Inn*, do it right. While every room packs a punch, it's the larger suites that will bring you to your knees in a full-scale, no-holds-barred, grand mal wig-out. Many of these suites not only have spacious bedrooms, they also boast sizable sitting areas or separate living rooms, fireplaces, and private balconies with panoramic views of the pastoral San Luis Obispo countryside. These suites are also ideal for partner-swapping and group sex if that's your bag, as many of them are multi-bedded with little or no dividing walls between sleeping areas. It's also these larger suites that feature the celebrated stone grotto waterfall showers, large enough to accommodate several oversexed adults.

In addition to the mind-bending accommodations, the *Inn* also features a coffee shop (with pink sugar at every table), a ballroom (with a swing band playing Tuesday through Saturday nights), and several gift shops—none of which have been denied the peerless *Madonna Inn* milieu. The Gold Rush Room is their formal restaurant, done entirely in bright reds and pinks, with circular pink vinyl booths (vinyl is a popular material at *The Madonna Inn*), a marble balustrade from Hearst Castle, and a central lighting scheme beyond compare: a twenty-eight-foot gold "tree" dripping with gilded grapes, cherubs and sparkling candelabra. The edges of the booths are girded with potted faux-cherry blossoms and ferns, all strung with thousands of twinkling white lights. A doll way too big to be cute sways back and forth on a mechanical swing hanging from the oak branches above the cashier's stand (her costume changes with each holiday). Adjacent to the dining room is the ultra-plush lobby and Silver Bar, with its pink vinyl heart-shaped chairs and white marble cocktail tables positioned around a mammoth flagstone fireplace (prehistoric bones jut out of the adjoining rock masonry) that appears to defy all laws of physics. Be sure not to miss the downstairs men's room just off the wine cellar; it's noted for the cascading stone waterfall urinal. Not since the days of Manhattan's infamous sex club, The Toilet, has pissing been this much fun!

The Madonna Inn is more than just a feast for the eyes, as proven by the pastries and homemade candies in the Coffee Shop and Bakery. You won't be able to resist loading up a bag packed with peanut butter cups the size of actual cupcakes, fudge, brownies, slabs of pie or mile-high slices of black forest cake to take back to your room. *The Madonna Inn* is all about earthly delights.

Don't make the mistake of showing up without a reservation, and with the assumption you'll be able to score a popular suite like the Caveman Room. The best rooms—*especially* the Caveman—book up sometimes as long as three months in advance. Call first and speak to the reservations desk, they're really good at offering room recommendations, just be specific about what you want (a rock waterfall shower is very important). Also important to keep in mind: when making a reservation inquiry, do not ask questions like *"What have you got that's really, really cheesy and awful?"* or *"Which suite is the tackiest?"*—the staff will pretend that they don't

know what you're talking about and you won't get the information you want. Instead, use more complimentary and euphemistic terms like *"lavish,"* *"exotic,"* *"opulent,"* or *"most unusual theme."* There's a photo album featuring all 109 rooms available at the reservations desk for your perusal in case you should decide to upgrade once you've arrived (and you will after seeing some of the pictures). Their very best suites are in the $140-200 range (worth every cent) and if you're staying more than one night it's perfectly acceptable to ask for a different room each night to get the most out of your visit.

The hour following checkout time presents a golden opportunity to peek into all the other rooms while they're being cleaned (the staff doesn't mind lookiloos, just be polite and don't make a pest of yourself), and you absolutely must make one last trip to the lobby and stock up on their outstanding selection of postcards. A stay at *The Madonna Inn* is always over too soon, but look at it this way: with 109 different rooms and future expansions already in the works, you won't be at a loss for weekend plans for at least the next two years.

The Madonna Inn
100 Madonna Road
San Luis Obispo
(800) 543-9666
(805) 543-3000

Sampling the Brand Spankin' New Products of *Shadow Lane*

Sung to the tune of "Penny Lane":

"On Shadow Lane, the Master Spanks Another Customer..."

ave you ever wondered what kind of people get their kinky kicks slapping someone's bare ass or getting their own butts spanked until their cheeks turn a pinkish-crimson hue? While that's not exactly our favorite form of sexual arousal, it sure intrigued us once we discovered **Shadow Lane**. One look at the *Shadow Lane* catalogue of products—featuring "Spanking Erotica for the Sophisticated Enthusiast"—and it's plain to see that there exists an entire subculture of men and women who thrive on the fine art of over-the-knee discipline in all its many fine forms. And if *Shadow Lane* is any indication, this is a group of well-educated and stylish folks whose so-called perversion, if somewhat painful, is far from crass. In fact, it's sometimes downright high-brow.

To be sure, the *Shadow Lane* catalogue is one of the most well-designed collections of fetish material that we've ever come across. Although the entire booklet and accompanying pamphlets are printed completely in black-and-white, the photo layouts and ad copy are consistently well-balanced, witty and well-wrought. Although well within the confines of S&M and B&D, the *Shadow Lane* collection is a far cry from the black-hooded, nipple-clamped, tied-to-a-cross-in-a-dank-basement variety of fetish material that typically characterizes the genre.

The videos and photosets from *Shadow Lane* are content-specific to an almost fanatical degree, indicating that the spanking enthusiast has certain tastes and requirements that must be met. Attention to detail is the trademark of each piece and accompanying description, like this one from "Tony Disciplines Tanya":

"...This sweetly suggestive 10-piece color photo set depicts the spanking and shows Tanya in position to receive an enema, while on all fours as well as kneeling on a chair. With the skirt of her exquisite silk-satin nightie folded back and her ravishing bottom bared and divided, the beautiful face of our compliant pet reveals the fearful anticipation that any young lady will experience upon being told she is to receive a thorough cleansing."

Note the subtlety contained therein: There is only the mention of an enema; the actual "cleansing" is never actually administered. Tanya's position is specifically mentioned, as is her clothing and its placement. And then there are those tantalizing, polysyllabic adjectives like "exquisite," "ravishing," and "compliant." To compare this description with the typical porno movie synopsis is like comparing T.S. Eliot to Howard Stern.

Other descriptions often emphasize the intelligence of the players involved, the brattiness of the young ladies and the wrath their misbehavior incurs, and the unseemly romantic conclusion to almost every spanking, usually in the form of a warm kiss. Penetration is strictly *verboten* in these tapes and pics, and even total nudity is practically unseen in the collection, with the emphasis more on pulled-down panties, pushed-up skirts, and other partially clothed scenarios. The variety of titles and themes must be seen to be believed, and even then, the big picture seems somehow unbelievable.

Such incredulity stems from the sheer magnitude and organization of *Shadow Lane*'s many products. Not only can you choose from the aforementioned truckload o' tapes and photos, but *Shadow Lane* also features a wealth of audio tapes, works of fiction with a spanking theme, spanking publications with titles like *Stand Corrected*, *Spank Hard*, and *Over the Knee*, and a daunting selection of spanking accessories from the new Red Irish Leather Paddle to the custom-made Teak Spanking Paddle. Fans of caning will find two models to choose from, and you can even show your true colors—no, not black and blue—with the tasteful *Shadow Lane* lapel pin. If you're looking for that perfect someone to take a riding crop to your buns (or vice-versa), then you can always place a personal in *Shadow Lane*'s flagship magazine, *Scene 1*. Finally, for those who like to press the flesh en masse, *Shadow Lane*'s annual weekend party of spanking mischief is a must-attend affair.

Who knows, it might even change the way you think about corporal punishment as a recreational sport. Unless, of course, you've already been through Catholic school.

Send catalogue request to:

Shadow Lane
P.O. Box 1910
Studio City, CA
91614
(818) 985-9151

chapter five

AFTERLIFE, THEN WHAT?

Mention L.A. and some folks think happy thoughts about year-round sunshine, movie stars, and Beach Boys' tunes. These are the same people who can watch Regis and Kathy Lee without getting nauseous, and we'll put them in the "glass is half full" category. On the "half empty" side, you have those to whom L.A. conjures up images of smoggy air, coke-snorting star-fuckers, and unrelentingly abrasive gansta rap. And, of course, imminent death. After all, Los Angeles is the happy hunting ground where mass murderers and serial killers come to settle down, where natural disasters like earthquakes and fires are a way of life (and death), and where disillusioned wanna-be superstars commit suicide in their cheap Hollywood apartments only to be half-devoured by their pets before their bodies are discovered.

Other than proud Angelenos, who can honestly boast that they live in a town where Manson groupies erroneously killed pregnant Sharon Tate and her guests, where the late, great John Holmes ratted out his cocaine buddies and then led their murderers to their lair where he was forced to watch the slaughter, and where a Mexicana airliner screamed down from blue skies and exploded into the peaceful suburb of El Cerritos? We're the home of the Night Stalker, the Freeway Killers, and the longest, most famous murder trial to ever light up the world's TV screens. The garish center-piece of this banquet table of death is affectionately known as "The Industry," a factory of tiny minds which single-handedly perpetuates the mythical glory of violence in big-budget gore epics and TV trash that masquerades as entertainment.

Let's face it, this facade of paradise is now known more for its drive-by shootings than its drive-thru fast food stands. And why not? Death and violence is the Yang to L.A.'s sunny-side Yin. Here in the City of Angels, "Have a Happy Day" is just another phrase for nothing left to lose. And if you spend enough time scrutinizing the dark minutae of our bright and cheery metropolis, you'll soon come to realize that the glass is indeed half empty, not half full— no matter how much you may dig the banal, happy face rantings of Regis and Kathy Lee.

Here then, for your morbid perusal, is a guide to some of our city's more deathly attractions, from a pet cemetery to the resting places of the stars, from the L.A. Coroner's Gift Shop to Spahn Ranch, and off into the great beyond....

Go in peace.

Perusing the Dead Pets at the

Los Angeles Pet Memorial Park

Some people think that burying your deceased pet is a ridiculous ritual, if not downright sacri-
legious. These people have obviously never owned an animal they really cared for (and vice-
versa), were denied that precious guinea pig when they were in third grade and now hold a
grudge, or are simply missing that chunk of human emotion called "compassion." Next to my
lovely wife and dear mother, my best friend on this planet is a fat hairy cat named Dr. Gene
Scott. "The Doctor" and I have been through a lot together in 12 years, and, like any loved one,
he cannot be replaced despite the prevalence of pet shops and breeders of similar Himalayans.

So when I took a trip to the **Los Angeles Pet Memorial Park** in
Calabasas, my mind was not only on business (i.e., this book), but also on finding a final
resting place for my feline friend, Dr. Gene. After all, this was the pet cemetery of the
stars, containing the graves of pets once loved by Hollywood luminaries ranging from
Gloria "I'm Ready for My Close-Up, Mr. De Mille" Swanson to Aaron "Love Boat 90210"
Spelling. Hopalong Cassidy's horse is buried here, along with Petey, the ring-eyed, four-
legged mascot of the "L'il Rascals."

Whatever You Do, Just Don't Say "Blinky"

I found the well-hidden boneyard easily enough—thanks to some good directions—
and was amused to see a real fire hydrant located just outside the perimeter fence.
As I imagined all the ghost dogs taking leaks on the yellow metal hydrant, and perused
with morbid curiosity the giant refrigerator and gurney just outside the main office,
I had no idea that my innocent visit would soon turn into a tense, mystery-laden
encounter centered around something as seemingly innocent as a dead store-bought
hen named "Blinky."

"Blinky" was a typical Foster Farms chicken, not unlike the countless other dead,
plucked hens cooling in meat sections across Southern California. What made "Blinky"
different from her peers was that she didn't turn up as a main course on someone's dinner
table, but instead was the main event of a memorial service and burial at the *L.A. Pet
Park* in 1978—thanks to Canoga Park conceptual artist Jeffrey Vallance. As he describes
the event in the "Pranks" edition of the San Francisco publication *ReSearch*, Vallance
bought the chicken at the Ralph's in Canoga Park, then took it to the park where it was
placed in a powder blue coffin with pink satin lining—along with a paper towel since Blinky
was beginning to thaw and leak—then carried out to the grave by some pallbearers (How
many men do you need to carry a single dead chicken, anyway?). Blinky was lowered into
the ground, the ceremony ended, and—ever the artist—Vallance retreated to the nearby
Howard Johnson's for the Chicken Special. Case closed, or so you would think.

Cut to 1996, and I'm standing in the humble air-conditioned trailer that functions
as the cemetery's office, showroom, and God-knows-what-else. Everything is going great
until I mention to Sandy, the park's rep, that I'd like to see Blinky's grave. When I mention
Vallance's name, she visibly stiffens. Suddenly the kind-hearted lady who just moments
ago was showing me cat caskets and quoting burial fees is now obviously perturbed as
she flips through the grave files in search of Blinky's resting place. With a chilly and suspi-
cious demeanor, she asks me all sorts of questions about Vallance (Doesn't he run some
kind of a group? Does he still live around here?) to which I have no answers. Referring to
her map of the cemetery, Sandy then leads me to a tiny plot less than a hundred yards
from her office where, sure enough, a granite marker reads:

1976-1978
BLINKY
THE FRIENDLY HEN
JEFFREY VALLANCE

Then Sandy pops the big question, the one that's obviously been bothering her all along: Was I part of a group that visited the cemetery a few years ago? When I tell her this is, in fact, my first visit, she proceeds to spin a grim tale about a bunch of "weird, rude people" who showed up one Sunday after the *L.A. Weekly* had run some kind of mention of Vallance, Blinky, and the park. "They said and did some really nasty things," she said, "awful things that disturbed the patrons who were here visiting their pets." When I pressed her for details, she begged off, saying she wasn't there at the time and only heard the complaints come Monday. She also made it clear that she didn't know whether Vallance himself was part of the offending entourage. But one thing was clear: Sandy was still pissed off by whatever went down that Sunday, and as far as she was concerned I had *something* to do with it since I knew about Blinky. When I kindly requested her permission to take a photo of the casket room, she replied with a terse, "Absolutely not," then lit up a long cigarette. Needless to say, I had burned a bridge with my curiosity about Blinky, and now I'd never get a shot of the surreal animal casket room thanks to the cranks who did whatever they did that Sunday afternoon a few years ago.

Fortunately, before my Blinky *faux pas*, I did manage to cop a folder of materials for the park. This slick package was packed with helpful pamphlets like "The Proper Good-Bye," "Are You Coping?," and "Death of Your Four-Legged Friend"—which obviously excludes owners of birds, chimps, and kangaroos. I also found out that the cost of burying my cat would be somewhere in the neighborhood of $450, not including the marker of my choice. This figure did seem a bit high, considering the fact that the cat casket looked more like a couple of plastic litter boxes, the top turned upside down, and the bottom lined with satin, but the fee did include the back-breaking task of digging the grave, lowering the litter-box coffin (and cat) into it, filling it again with dirt, and installing a permanent vase for flowers—or catnip, as the case may be. But who can put a price tag on the opportunity to take one last glance at your beloved companion in the park's peaceful "Slumber Viewing Room"? For an additional charge, you can also add an engraved granite marker that looks as nice as anything any human deserves, if not better.

Although the park is open to the public (like any cemetery), if you plan to visit, please don't come in a large group and make obscene comments to the grieving patrons while you desecrate the grounds. Instead why not take in all the beauty of this peaceful, well-maintained park, and let yourself be touched by the love and dedication of those who have attempted to give their late house pets a little bit of dignity in death—and perhaps just a touch of immortality?

But whatever you do, don't ask about "Blinky." That damn chicken is nothing but a troublemaker.

—ARL

OUT-AND-ABOUT

A face only Burbank Blvd. could love: a cyclone fence trimmed with barbed-wire is the only thing between you and this nightmarish (and anatomically correct) mascot of 10726 Burbank.

Is That A Mangled, Rusted Piece Of Steel In Your Pocket Or Are You Just Happy To See Me?

It's A Long Drive To Bel Air...

First off, there is no **Spahn Ranch**. The legendary Manson Family hangout was torched in the early 70s and the charred remains eventually bulldozed to the ground. Still, over the past two decades, visitors who made the trek out to the Santa Susana Pass could traipse among the archeological leftovers of Charlie's regime (i.e., trash), pose at the cave formation that was a regular backdrop in Family portraits, and carve their own initials on the large rock where "CM" and his band of unwashed, death-dealing cronies did the likewise.

Adventurous fans of the moribund can still do the same, but now the stakes are a bit higher: a large fence festooned with "No Trespassing" signs has been erected around the area, which has allegedly been purchased by Ronald Reagan's son, which, if so, seems somehow perversely appropriate. There are no guards on patrol, however, so fence-hoppers rarely get popped by the cops. But there have been sporadic crimes in the area—including the murders of some necking teens—which add a whole new sense of danger to your quest. On the other side of the fence, look for the sign that says "Retz Ranch" and then head down the dirt road to the gulch where a summer of hippy insanity became pop murder history. Whether you choose to carry a sidearm or not is your prerogative.

Or, better yet, you can stay legal altogether and visit **The Church at Rocky Peak**, built across the street from the deceased *Spahn Ranch*, on the site where Manson allegedly staged mock-crucifixions (with Manson as Christ, of course). As if to somehow balance what must be a million years of bad karma, *The Church at Rocky Peak* is the Yang to *Spahn*'s Yin. When we visited the church, we met a helpful staffer who seemed amusingly inured to constant queries about the church's Satanic ex-neighbor, and was pleasantly helpful in pointing out where the ranch once stood, and shared some of the more colorful tales of the area (including the murders

of the love birds). *The Church at Rocky Peak* is the perfect place to go after you've trespassed on private property to pay homage to a site where a bunch of smelly, dysfunctional scumbags once festered in the desert heat until they actually came to believe that the neo-cretin who led them was actually Jesus Christ. A quick prayer won't bring back pregnant Sharon Tate and her entourage, or Rosemary and Leno LaBianca, or anyone else the gang murdered, but it may just dust off some of the evil aura you will have undoubtedly collected during your visit.

Maybe.

To get to the old **Spahn Ranch**, take the Ronald Reagan Freeway (118) to Topanga Canyon and head south. Make a left at the light for Santa Susana Pass and keep going until you see the sign for **The Church at Rocky Peak** (on your right) and *Retz Ranch* (on the other side of the fence on your left). *The Church at Rocky Peak* is located at 22601 Santa Susana Pass Road, Chatsworth.

Visit his grave—but do not speak his name.

**Los Angeles Pet
Memorial Park**
see page 94

*Gitalong little 'gator—
an early form of L.A. transportation*

The California Alligator Farm
see page 168

No one can beat the
Big Boy's meat.

Bob's Big Boy
see page 35

Yesterday's inn of tomorrow: gone today.

Stovall's Best Western
see page 151

L.A.'s historic glory-hole district in its glory years.

**The Los Angeles Conservancy
Walking Tours**
see page 140

*A blowfish will
illuminate the path of
enlightenment.*

Amok Books
see page 46

Someone's in the kitchen with Sirhan.

The Ambassador Hotel
see page 157

Is that Joel Grey or one of Bob Baker's marionettes?

Bob Baker's Marionette Theater
see page 158

Here's Lucy...dead.

Forest Lawn Hollywood Hills
see page 107

Next! Grave diggin' at the Holy Cross Cemetery.

see page 104

Visit Yosemite without leaving downtown
Los Angeles; the wildlife sanctuary
of Clifton's Cafeteria.

see page 16

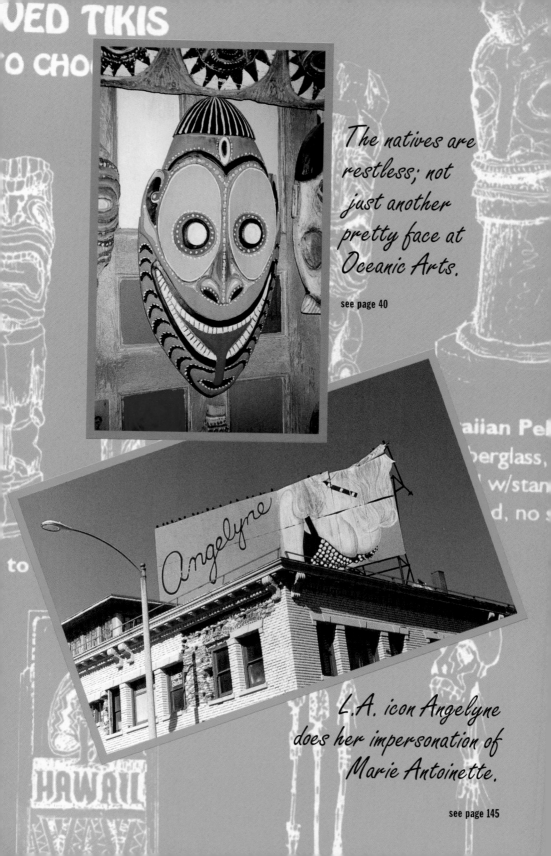

VED TIKIS
O CHO

The natives are restless; not just another pretty face at Oceanic Arts.

see page 40

aiian Pe
berglass,
w/stan
d, no

to

L.A. icon Angelyne does her impersonation of Marie Antoinette.

see page 145

HAWAII

Take a Freudian drive through
La Puente's big brown hole.

The Donut Hole
see page 169

Roy Rogers' favorite
dog is gone now, but
his memory lives on
in this stuffed
canine carcass.

The Roy Rogers and Dale Evans Museum
see page 128

A tisket, a tasket, it's Michael J. Fox's Hollywood Wax Museum tinfoil basket.

see page 164

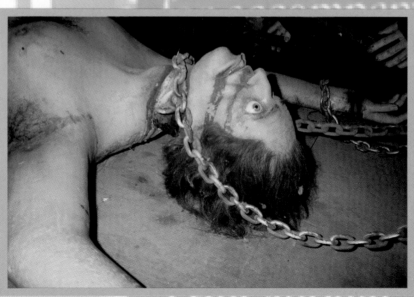

Fun for the whole family.

Hollywood Wax Museum

see page 164

Too tall to live...

...too weird to die.

**The Chicken Boy Catalogue
for a Perfect World™**
see page 186

He sees when you are surfing, he knows when you're awake...

Santa Claus Lane
see page 169

It's hip to be square.

The Double 'R Squares
see page 146

A pig behind bars!
Will ironies never cease?!

Farmer John's

Arno Jordan, a scenic slaughterhouse savant.

see page 138

Dinner and a crotch-shot, two bits.

Wild Bill's Wild West Dinner Extravaganza.
see page 148

Grab a falling star and squeeze.

Night of the Stars
see page 73

Inn-credible:
plush accommodations
for the color-blind.

The Madonna Inn
see page 88

High art, Hollywood style: The Sherman and Peabody
sidewalk mural at The Dudley Do-Right Emporium

see page 44

Kitten Natividad:
Hotter than a
Mexican's lunch.

The Kitten Club
see page 184

Old strippers never
die—they just move
to the desert and
open a museum.

Exotic World
see page 122

No, that's not another one
of L.A.'s homeless, it's
the patron saint of tooth
decay: the Lollipop Lady
of Santa's Village.

Santa's Village
see page 120

Gifts from Before the Grave:

Skeletons in the Closet,

The L.A. Coroner Gift Shop

f you've been searching for that perfect gift that says, "I wish you were dead," look no further than the L.A. Coroner's Office. Back in 1993 they devised the morbidly

Is That A Body Bag In Your Pocket Or Are You Just Happy To See Me?

wonderful fundraising idea of selling personalized toe-tag keychains to the public, and from there the idea blossomed into a full range of souvenirs from one of L.A.'s more colorful and fun-filled municipal departments.

Admittedly, the folks at the coroner's office aren't in the marketing business, which is why they may have dreamed up the lame pseudo-mascot dubbed "Sherlock Bones," a skeleton-in-a-trenchcoat with a Sherlock Holmes hat on his head and a magnifying glass in his hand. Sherlock is a hokey attempt to personalize the rather cold business of dissecting dead humans, and in doing so, misses the mark completely. Anyone with the warped mindframe to order gifts from the coroner's office doesn't want a tee shirt emblazoned with a goofy skeleton. He's expecting the outline of a dead body—which fortunately is exactly what is featured on a number of other pathological party gifts like beach towels, boxer shorts, wrist watches, refrigerator magnets, baseball caps, sweats, scrubs, tee shirts, wall clocks, playing cards, and...the list goes on and on. These wonderfully tasteless treats beat the silly Sherlock Bones shirts, mugs, and bags by a mile. Best of all, they even offer children's sized tee shirts for that Wednesday and/or Pugsley in your family.

Funds raised from **Skeletons in the Closet** go to the Youthful Drunk Driver Visitation Program, an alternative sentencing option available through the court system for mischievous tykes who have been nabbed operating a vehicle under the influence, and for drug, alcohol, and weapons-related offenders on the teen side. According to the department, the results of young punks looking at the mangled remains of their unlucky peers have been positive, and have put many back on the road to righteousness—or on a bee-line for the nearest toilet, at the very least.

You're welcome to drop in to their humble office-cum-giftshop, or write or call for their surprisingly hip and well-designed brochure. Either way, you'll discover that the folks at the coroner's office are anything but a bunch of stiffs, and best of all, your holiday gift-giving woes will be over once and for all. The toe-tag keychains make great stocking stuffer gifts for all your drinkin'-and-drivin' buddies!

Skeletons in the Closet

Los Angeles Department of Coroner

1104 Mission Road

Los Angeles

(213) 343-0760

The Dark Side of ***Disneyland***

Sung to the tune of "It's a Small World After All":
"It's a world of murder, a world of pain
It's a world where the Matterhorn will crush your brain
You can drown or get crushed, lose an eyeball or such
It's a dead world after all!"

Some of L.A.'s most popular tourist traps are also great places to get killed. And while a few of these spots are painfully obvious—like Hollywood Boulevard and Santa Monica Beach after dark—others may not seem so blatantly dangerous. Take **Disneyland** for example.

Through the eyes of a six-year-old child, *Disneyland* can truly be a Magic Kingdom. But for many others, the self-proclaimed "Happiest Place on Earth" can often turn out to be Hell on Earth. To be sure, the maniacally cheery staff, the claustrophobic crowds, the endless serpentine lines, and the in-your-face merchandizing of overpriced souvenir trinkets can all combine to turn any happy-go-lucky tourist into a potential Charles Whitman, cocked and loaded atop the Matterhorn. And those not inspired to go on a sniper frenzy may just as easily be pushed to the brink of becoming the next Unabomber.

Indeed, *Disneyland* has had its share of bomb threats over the years, presumably from park "guests" (Disney parlance for "customer") who endured the insanely saccharine theme to "It's a Small World" one time too many. And the summer of 1971 was a particularly active season for such antics. Yet amidst all the bogus phone calls that summer threatening to blow the Magic Kingdom to Kingdom Come, a real live bomb was actually found on the tracks of the PeopleMover where it passed through the AT&T building. Packed in a simple shoebox, the device was defused before it went off. Still, the mere threat of a bomb exploding at such oft-targeted attractions as the Matterhorn, the Submarine Voyage, the Skyway and It's a Small World cost the park untold bucks in clearing, closing, and fully investigating each incident. Fortunately, no bomb has ever exploded at *Disneyland*.

Merely getting to the park can sometimes prove to be a fatal experience. How many potential guests never made it to the gates due to a car crash en route? We'll never know. What we do know is that two of the worst civilian helicopter crashes in U.S. history occurred while the *Disney*/LAX helicopter service was shuttling guests to and from the Happiest Place on Earth—and in the same year, no less. It was May, 1968, and as the summer of love was just shifting into gear, a chopper carrying 23 guests back to LAX came apart in mid-air, showering debris on the ground below. There were no survivors. In less than three months, another *Disney*-copter—this one bound for the park with 21 passengers on board—came crashing down on a Compton playground. Again, no one on board lived through the ordeal.

Even if you manage to make it to the parking lot, you may still not be safe. In 1985, a seven-year-old girl was crushed beneath the wheels of a tour bus as she and her uncle were looking for their car. A year later, in 1986, a woman was robbed at knifepoint by a mental patient who wandered away from his tour group with thoughts other than simply riding Space Mountain. He stole her purse, two cameras, and her car. He was arrested a few hours later when he used the same car during a robbery of an Anaheim *McDonald's*.

When you think of gangs in Southern California, you usually think of African-Americans or Hispanics. But Asian gangs are also prevalent in the Southland, especially in Orange County, and tensions were high between Tongan and Samoan rivals one night in 1987. The conflict began just after closing, when a hat worn by an eighteen-year-old Samoan named Keleti Naea incited some nasty comments from the Tongans. Verbal battle escalated into a fistfight when Salesi Tai, a Tongan, pulled out a .22-caliber pistol. The fight was broken up before any shots could be fired, but as the gangs moved on into the parking lot, Naea and some of his buddies confronted Tai, who whipped out the gun and

fired. He missed his targets, but wounded a fourteen-year-old boy some 150 feet away. The Samoans jumped Tai, who dropped his gun. Naea grabbed the pistol and emptied it, hitting Tai in the side and back. Tai was rushed to a hospital but died soon after from loss of blood, a day before his sixteenth birthday. Naea was later apprehended, and is currently serving seventeen years to life in prison for the second degree murder of Tai.

Coincidentally, that same night, in another part of the parking lot, a sixteen-year-old boy was abducted at gunpoint by two men as he was retrieving the family car to pick up his folks. With a gun to his head, the boy was forced to drive to nearby Santa Ana, where he was dumped off, unharmed.

The most notorious murder within the confines of the Happiest Place on Earth took place on March 7, 1981, when eighteen-year-old Mel Yorba made the biggest mistake of his life by pinching the butt of the wrong girl. Her boyfriend, a 28-year-old unemployed dry-waller named James O'Driscoll, chased the kid and his buddies through the park, caught up with them and grabbed the wrong guy. When his girlfriend told him so, O'Driscoll let the teen go—and Yorba stepped up and slugged O'Driscoll in the face, dropping him to the pavement. Yorba and his friends moved on, but O'Driscoll wasn't finished with them yet. After his girlfriend pointed out Yorba as the bottom-pincher, O'Driscoll grabbed him by the shirt, only to receive another blow to his face. Then Yorba lunged at O'Driscoll and the two went at it. The fight was short-lived, though, and so was Yorba, because O'Driscoll was wielding an eight-inch knife, and somehow Yorba was stabbed twice—in the chest and stomach—during their scuffle. O'Driscoll took off and was later apprehended after trying to sneak out of the park. The knife was found in the moat that surrounds the Sleeping Beauty Castle.

Four security officers arrived at the scene of the crime shortly after a nurse who was visiting the park began to apply pressure to Yorba's wounds. Instead of assisting the nurse, the guards worked at keeping away others who tried to help Yorba. Some twenty minutes later, a park nurse finally showed up and made the fateful decision to take Yorba to a hospital two-and-a-half miles away in a Disneyland First Aid Van—not an ambulance.

The trip took eleven minutes, and when he arrived at the hospital, Yorba was declared dead. The van in which he was taken had no emergency lights, no siren, and with the exception of oxygen, no lifesaving equipment to speak of. As if to guarantee that Yorba's ride to the hospital would be his last, the van followed all speed limits and stopped at all red lights and stop signs. Had an ambulance been called, it could have brought the wounded teen to another hospital with a suitable trauma center a mere mile further—and, with its sirens and lights, in less time than it took the van to reach the first hospital. In addition, para-medics could have worked on Yorba during the ride. Then again, had an ambulance been called, who knows how many guests would have been perturbed and subsequently endured a less than idyllic evening at the park?

Yorba's family took *Disneyland* to court, and while the surgeons who operated on Yorba testified that his wounds were mortal, the clincher came when it was revealed that *Disneyland* did, in fact, have a written policy calling for paramedics to be summoned in life-threatening situations—of which the *Disney* nurse testified she was completely unaware. The jurors ruled that *Disney* was negligent in not following in its own policy and ordered the park to pay $600,000 to Yorba's parents. Ever-vigilant, *Disney* demanded an appeal. The Yorba family, faced with an expensive legal bill in order to pursue such an appeal, accepted a smaller, undisclosed settlement from the kind-hearted, sympathetic folks at *Disney*.

Four days after the Yorba family filed their wrongful death suit, a similar suit was filed by a woman whose husband had gone into cardiac arrest in New Orleans Square. He, too, was taken via the *Disney* van instead of an ambulance to Palm Harbor hospital, where he died. One week after this suit was filed, another park guest suffered convulsions, collapsed, and was taken to the hospital in a white, unmarked company van. She, too, passed away at Palm Harbor Hospital of natural causes. The next day, *Disney* finally announced that it would hire a full-time ambulance service to handle medical emergencies. All it took was at least three dead people and the spectre of a scandal in the form of a torrent of wrongful death suits.

Perhaps the worst imaginable *Disney*-related death, however, is one in which you are done in by an attraction meant to cause howls of excitement, not screams of expectant death. Take the Matterhorn, for example. From the park's opening in 1955 to May of 1964, *Disneyland*'s safety record was squeaky clean. But six months after shots rang out in Dealey Plaza, *Disney*'s own Camelot came crashing down when 15-year-old Mark Maples stood up at the summit of the Matterhorn rollercoaster and did his own impression of Tinkerbell as he flew right out of the sled. He landed on the track below, unconscious, with his skull fractured and suffering internal injuries. He never awoke, and died four days later.

Maples' Matterhorn demise wasn't half as grisly as the fate that befell 47-year-old Dollie Young in January of 1984. Young was seated in the rear of the "bullet" sled with her child, and somehow during the course of the ride, her safety belt became unbuckled and she was tossed out. As she tumbled along the track, Young tried to regain her footing, but was struck by another sled, which crushed her under its wheels and dragged her body a full car-length before coming to a stop. Only her feet could be seen sticking out from under the heavy sled. She was pronounced dead at the scene.

The flip-side of the fast-moving Matterhorn was the PeopleMover, which sped along a track at a whopping two miles an hour. The ride was removed in 1995 as part of *Disneyland*'s renovation of Tomorrowland, but not before it had claimed two lives over the years. The PeopleMover's first victim came along in 1967: seventeen-year-old teen named Ricky Lee Yama and his pals were jumping from one slow-moving car to another when Yama lost his footing and slipped beneath the wheels of the oncoming tortoise-paced car. He was crushed, his head split in two, and the ride needed to be shut down and taken apart in order to remove his mangled body.

On a Grad Nite thirteen unlucky years later, Gerardo Gonzales repeated Yama's stunt and suffered a similar fate. Unlike Yama, however, his body was dragged beneath the ride for hundreds of feet before the PeopleMover was finally shut down. This second incident prompted some park employees to refer to the ride as the People*Re*Mover.

Yama's gruesome demise pales in comparison to the ugly accident that snuffed out the life of Thomas Cleveland on another Grad Nite, this one in 1966. Cleveland, nineteen, had snuck into the park by climbing over a fence and onto the monorail track, which he followed into the park. A guard spotted the errant teen and warned him of an oncoming train. Instead of jumping off the track, Cleveland laid down on a plastic canopy that covers a walkway. Unfortunately, the clearance between the canopy and the bottom of the train is about two inches. After being sucked up under the train and smeared along 40 feet of track, Cleveland's body—or what was left of it—had to be hosed from the bottom of the train. Quite a price to pay for free admission.

Disneyland is no stranger to drownings, either. In 1973, an eighteen-year-old New Yorker named Bogden Delaurot and his ten-year-old brother eluded the closing of Tom Sawyer Island in an attempt to spend the night there. Later in the night, when they became bored, the duo decided to swim back to the park—only Bogden's little brother couldn't swim. Bogden attempted to carry him on his back, and that was his fatal mistake. He drowned about halfway to the shore, and his little brother was lucky enough to be picked up by a passing boat. Bogden's body was found the next day.

In 1983, an Albuquerque native named Philip Straughan was celebrating his high school graduation and eighteenth birthday on yet another fateful Grad Nite when he and a buddy "borrowed" a maintenance boat and took off for a late-night joyride on the Rivers of America. Both of the kids had been drinking, which probably contributed to their sloppy navigating. When the boat hit a rock, Straughan was thrown from the boat and drowned in four feet of water.

Even *Disneyland* employees aren't safe from the vagaries of fate, as exemplified by the 1974 death of Deborah Gail Stone, who was crushed between the moving walls of the seemingly docile attraction called America Sings. Stone was only eighteen and new to the park when she took the position as hostess of the hokey musical attraction show that featured a circle of six theaters that moved around a fixed central stage. During the interval between shows, Stone somehow got caught between the rotating architectures, and never lived to greet another audience.

Aside from the aforementioned murders and tragic accidents, *Disneyland* has also played host to a number of natural deaths. From the grandfather who croaked on the Matterhorn and keeled over on his two granddaughters, to the 300-pound Hawaiian woman who died during Pirates of the Caribbean and couldn't be lifted from her boat, most of these natural deaths have been the result of heart attacks. Yet with the sheer number of bipeds who pass through the park each year, it's astounding that there aren't more people dropping like flies every day at the Magic Kingdom.

To all these morbid reports of *Disney*Deaths, the faithful will be quick to point out that an individual is far more likely to get killed in a car accident than at *Disneyland*. And they'd be right. Yet the fact of the matter is that auto wrecks are a dime a dozen. We see them all the time. But the mere thought of someone flying out of the Matterhorn or getting creamed by the Monorail or crushed by the PeopleMover is far more fascinating than rubbernecking another gory fender-bender. So next time you visit the Magic Kingdom, maybe you'll not only keep an eye peeled for falling bodies, but also be just a little bit more careful yourself.

After all, you never know when this small world will become one person smaller.

> *"Avast there, lubbers! There be rough water ahead! Sit close together and keep your ruddy hands in board. Dead men tell no tales! Har!"*
>
> —*Warning as you enter Pirates of the Caribbean*

(*Disneyland, Fantasyland, Magic Kingdom, New Orleans Square, Walt Disney,* and *PeopleMover* are registered trademarks of the Walt Disney Co., Inc.)

Disneyland
On Harbor Blvd.,
between Katella Ave.
and Ball Road
Anaheim
(714) 999-4565
(automated information)
(714) 781-4560
(human contact)

Post mortem autograph hunting at the

Celebrity Grave Sites

Cemetery hopping is an ideal activity for the morbidly star-struck; parking is free, there are no admission fees, no drink minimum, and best of all, no lines! Stalking dead celebrities can be problematic though. Since memorial parks haven't yet figured out how to sort their occupants alphabetically, the process of locating deceased stars is much like a macabre Easter egg hunt. Though this process can be somewhat maddening, we've tried to make it a little easier with our gravesite guide to anybody who's anybody who's dead.

Grave Diggin'

Hollywood Memorial Park Cemetery
6000 Santa Monica Blvd.
Los Angeles

This place is a perfect old-Hollywood graveyard. It's just rundown enough to be haunting, with dead lawns and slightly overgrown shrubbery obscuring some of the headstones. Since it's located on an unsavory section of Santa Monica Blvd., it's not unusual to run into the occasional psycho-vagrant muttering to himself in a cold dark corner of the mausoleum, or silently following you around the park like a hungry zombie. Add to this the surreal juxtaposition of **The Hollywood Memorial Park** and *Paramount Studios*; the south end of the cemetery grounds literally run right up against the north edge of studios, with no dividing wall to separate the properties.

Rudolph Valentino (1) is here in the Cathedral Mausoleum. The sexually ambiguous silent film actor died at the age of 31 from peritonitis, and was temporarily laid to rest in this wall crypt while a large-scale monument was to be built in his honor. For one reason or another, the big monument never materialized, and Valentino still rests in his "temporary" hole-in-the-wall. He's in crypt #1205 at the left end of the southeast corridor.

Cathedral Mausoleum

Barbara La Marr (2) was a drug-addicted, anorexic slut more than a half-century before it became vogue. During her brief tenure as a movie star in the 20s, she had six husbands, countless lovers, and died of an overdose before she hit the big 3-0. These were the good ol' days before the Betty Ford Clinic, when a junkie just dropped dead and was done with it—sparing the public from lengthy accounts of their "recovery" saga by way of talk show appearances, movies of the week, and inevitable autobiographies. At the opposite end of the mausoleum close to the floor sit the ashes of *Voyage to the Bottom of the Sea* co-star **Peter Lorre** (3), nee Laslo Löwenstein, who died of a stroke in 1964. Dancer **Eleanor Powell** (4) was put to rest here in 1982 after she lost a battle with cancer. The famous tap dancer would have been thrilled to know that her final resting place has marble floors and great acoustics—one can only fantasize about her ghost strapping on a pair of character shoes and pummeling the stone hallways with a fervid, postmortem tap routine after the mausoleum gates are locked.

Abbey of Palms Mausoleum

He may be dead, but it's not too late to sit on **Tyrone Power's** (5) face since his unique headstone also doubles as a bench. The gravemarker belonging to the voice of Bugs Bunny, Porky Pig and Yosemite Sam, et al. is inscribed with the familiar "That's All Folks" —except this time **Mel Blanc** (6) really means it. While she was alive, actress **Joan Hackett** (7) was known to hang a sign on her dressing room door that read "Go Away, I'm Asleep." Her crypt reads the same.

It's a long way to San Simeon: look for the DOURAS crypt alongside the lake—this is the current home of **Marion Davies** (8), nee Douras, actress and famed mistress of William Randolph Hearst (who bankrolled her movie career). Her tomb is a large white affair that also contains what's left of her son-in-law, actor **Arthur** "Dagwood Bumstead" **Lake** (8). Be the twelve-millionth person to deliver the line "I'm ready for my close-up, Mr. DeMille," at the foot of **Cecil B. DeMille's** (9) double crypt, which he shares with his wife Constance. Apparently **Douglas Fairbanks, Sr.** (10) threw humility to the wind when laying plans for his large-scale shrine—the sunken garden gravesite of Pick-Fair proportions sits just next to the Cathedral Mausoleum.

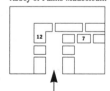

102 L.A. BIZARRO!

The gang's all here! **Carl "Alfalfa" Switzer** (11) of *Our Gang* fame was shot to death, that much we know. Different reports give different explanations for the murder, and whether it was over A: a $50 debt, B: a drug deal, or C: a reward for a lost hunting dog remains unconfirmed. Alfalfa's on-screen love interest who later became the voice of the Chicken of the Sea Mermaid, **Darla Hood** (12), also died an early death at 48 (though not from a gunshot wound) and is within kiss-blowing distance from her freckle-faced, cowlicked colleague in the Abbey of Palms Mausoleum at the other end of the park. A different breed of gangster, **Bugsy Siegel** (13), Hollywood's hob-nobbing mobster, lies to rest in the Beth Olam Mausoleum in the far southwest corner of the park. In addition to his careers as heroin dealer, bootlegger and hitman, Bugsy gave us the *Flamingo Hotel* in Las Vegas—the first hotel and casino of its kind, setting a precedent for the Las Vegas to come. He was gunned down while reading a newspaper in his living room and his killers were never caught. Seeing that we ultimately have Bugsy to thank for the hideous theme-park Las Vegas of today—what with *The Luxor, Excalibur,* and *Treasure Island*—it's too bad they didn't nail him sooner.

Another point of interest at *The Hollywood Memorial Park* is the lakeside burial site of **Jayne Mansfield** (14)—especially since her mangled corpse actually lies three thousand miles away in Pen Argyl, Pennsylvania. Put there recently by her fan club, the headstone used to bear a small portrait of her on porcelain that has since been chipped away—probably by some idiot who thought he was getting a piece of the real thing. Only in Hollywood do celebrities have facsimile tombs—but don't let that idea leak to the freaks that gave us Grauman's Chinese Theater in Florida, or we'll soon have celebrity cemeteries popping up in every city across the country like *Planet Hollywood*.

Before there was O.J. Simpson, there was Fatty Arbuckle, and before there was Nicole, there was **Virginia Rappe** (15). Virginia was a small-time actress with a reputation for sleeping around. Nicole was a small-time model with a reputation for sleeping around. Fatty was a beloved American comic; O.J. was a beloved American football player. Virginia died as a result of stab wounds from a sharp bottle, and her alleged killer was acquitted after a lengthy trial. Nicole died as a result of stab wounds from a sharp knife, and her alleged killer was acquitted after a lengthy trial. Fatty's prosecution couldn't produce a bloody bottle. O.J.'s prosecution couldn't produce a bloody knife. As a result of the scandal, Paramount dumped Arbuckle. As a result of the scandal, Hertz dumped O.J. Fatty became the most hated celebrity in America, and when people saw him on the street they whistled the tune, "I'm Coming, Virginia." O.J. became the most hated celebrity in America, and when people see him on the street they yell, "MURDERER!" Lincoln's assassin shot him from a theater and fled to a library; Kennedy's assassin shot him from a library and fled to a theater.

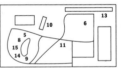

Hollywood Memorial Park Cemetary (grounds)

This diminutive boneyard is an easy one to miss if you don't know where you're going. It's hidden behind a cluster of large commercial buildings and parking structures just south of Wilshire Blvd.—the last place you'd expect to find a cemetery. Turn south off Wilshire onto Glendon and make the first possible left into a driveway (look for the small sign that reads **"Pierce Brothers Westwood Village Memorial Park and Mortuary."** Follow that short road into the park—a "dead end" of sorts.

Here you'll find an eclectic mix of ill-fated celebrities. You'll also find an eclectic mix of fans of ill-fated celebrities—*Westwood Village Memorial Park* is a popular haunt, so to speak. Busloads of camcorder-toting tourists trample the grounds daily, mostly to pay a visit to its most famous resident, **Marilyn Monroe** (1).

Heather "They're He-re" **O'Rourke** (2) of *Poltergeist* fame is here, too (she died during surgery in 1988), and the girl who played her sister in the first *Poltergeist* film, **Dominique Dunn** (3), is just a few yards away (she was strangled to death by her boyfriend). It's like the *Rebel Without a Cause* syndrome. And speaking of *Rebel Without a Cause*, two of the film's stars rest here—although **Jim Backus** (4) may not be as remembered for his role in *Rebel* as he is for Thurston Howell III or Mr. Magoo. The grave marker of **Natalie Wood** (5) lies towards the center of the lawn next to a potted cypress tree.

One might not expect **Truman Capote** (6) to be buried in Westwood, but he is. He ended up here after the urn containing his ashes was stolen—along with a bunch of jewelry—from the home of his dear friend Joanne Carson (Johnny's ex). The ashes were returned but the jewelry was not. "The Sanctuary of Tranquility" seems like the last place on earth to find a drummer, but that's where **Buddy Rich** (7) is entombed, bottom row, second from the front on the right side. Look for **Burt Lancaster** (8) near the edge of the curb in front of the Sanctuary of Love on the opposite side of the road, and **Minnie Ripperton** (9), roughly the fourth marker from the same curb down near the Sanctuary of Remembrance. **Donna Reed** (10) can be found just a few rows back from Natalie Wood.

Playboy centerfold **Dorothy Stratten** (11) was raped, tortured, and killed by her estranged husband Paul Snider before he blew his brains out. At the time of her murder, she had been seeing director Peter Bogdanovich. See her Playboy layout, watch *Star 80*, do some lines, visit her grave. She's roughly four rows up from the edge of the east (rear) curb, in the center section.

Frank Zappa, Roy Orbison and the most innocuous of the Gabor sisters, **Eva Gabor**, are all here in unmarked graves. You'll just have to stand in the middle of the park and send good vibes. See if a divining rod styled into an Eva Gabor Wig won't lead you to the *Green Acres* star. Or just look for Merv.

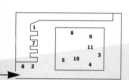

Holy Cross Cemetery and Mausoleum

5835 West Slauson Ave.
Culver City

It's impossible not to fall in love with **The Holy Cross Cemetery**; their grounds are open a full hour longer than most, they have an extremely helpful and courteous staff, and their mausoleum features pay phones and restrooms!

Although *Holy Cross* is fairly enormous, most of its big names are concentrated in one general area. Make a beeline to the hilltop rock grotto. The lawn in front of the shrine is home to **Bela Lugosi** (1), third row back from the front of the grotto, who was buried in his Dracula cape (but don't get any ideas). **Rita Hayworth's** (2) final years were fraught with a very unglamorous battle against Alzheimer's disease. She lies just to the right of the grotto with a simple headstone. Further down front you'll find **Bing Crosby** (3), forever dreaming of a White Christmas since he's buried on a grassy green hill in Culver City. **Walter Brennan** (4) is a few rows down from Crosby towards the street edge of the lawn.

To the left of the shrine on the upper level is **Charles Boyer** (5). Boyer killed himself with an overdose of seconal, two days after the death of his wife. Charles' son must have inherited the suicide gene from pop, because he snuffed himself too. They're all here. In the same section, the park's most photographed headstone sits just a few rows from Boyer's, that of **Sharon Tate** (6) and her unborn baby. On the opposite side of the grotto lies **Jackie Coogan** (7). *The Addams Family*'s Uncle Fester festers six feet under on tier 57, grave 47, in section F.

Up the hill in the restroom-and-pay-phone-equipped mausoleum you'll find **Ray Bolger** (8), **Mario Lanza** (9), and **Joan Davis** (10). Down the hill, in the "Precious Blood Section M" rests Auntie Mame, **Rosalind Russell** (11). She's a cinch to spot, at the foot of a gigantic white cross on an otherwise green hillside—too bad all celebrity markers aren't this easy to find.

HOLY CROSS CEMETERY AND MAUSOLEUM

Also starring:

John Candy

Jimmy Durante

Jack Haley

Fred MacMurray

Louella Parsons

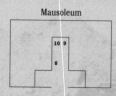

Mausoleum

The name may not ring a bell, but it's a familiar sight to thousands of rush-hour commuters packed bumper to bumper on the forever-sluggish 405 freeway near LAX.

The domed pavilion with trailing waterfall visible from the freeway—and the centerpiece of the cemetery—is a self-designed monument to **Al Jolson** (1). Jolson put considerable forethought into his vainglorious death shrine—a structure so large it seems to scream "HEY LOOK AT ME, I'M DEAD!" It even features a bronze sculpture of himself on bended knee.

Just outside the mausoleum to the right of the entrance sits the crypt of television game show guru **Mark Goodson** (2). The man that brought us *Match Game*, *The Price Is Right* and *Family Feud*, as well as just about every other game show you could possibly think of, has a crypt bearing an engraving of his name inside a television screen-shaped frame. *I Was a Teenaged Werewolf* star **Michael Landon** (3) has his own room in the mausoleum. Although the Landon Room is locked and only accessible to family members, you can still easily see his crypt from outside the glass door. Take the front entrance to the mausoleum and head straight through the center courtyard area and out to the family rooms on the left; the Landon Room is opposite a side entrance to the mausoleum. The *Hillside* cemetery is shaping up like a Ponderosa Ranch for the dead, with **Lorne Green** (4) just a few yards away. His headstone even bears the name of his *Bonanza* character, Ben Cartwright. Greene's marker is on the left lawn of the mausoleum, opposite a psychedelic glass window (a real treat at sunset!!).

Inside, you'll find a large black burial vault containing what remains of **Jack Benny** (5). Benny is located right at the end of the Hall of Graciousness. He died from cancer in 1974. He was 39.

**HILLSIDE
MEMORIAL PARK**

Also Starring:

Eddie Cantor

David Janssen

Vic Morrow

Dick Shawn

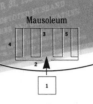

Forest Lawn cemeteries are plain fucking weird. This boneyard chain fancies itself more like a happy park or a cultural center, rather than the death racket it *really* is (note that there are no standing headstones in order to avoid the graveyard aesthetic). *Forest Lawn* offers visitors churches, sculpture gardens, "art" museums, musical performances, historical exhibits, and even live shows like *A Visit With Michelangelo* ("portrayed by a professional actor"). Some parks even feature special holiday events for kids! *In a cemetery!* Spacey, fairy music is piped in almost everywhere—even outdoors—and the environment here is so controlled, so contrived, and so laden with security, the overall effect ends up being the antitheses of what *Forest Lawn* so desperately aims for; *this is the creepiest cemetery of them all!*

Celeb grave-hopping at **Forest Lawn Glendale** is problematic for many reasons. First, the place is too damn big—the Yosemite of memorial parks. Second, all the employees are cocksuckers (figuratively speaking), guarding the place like there's gold doubloons buried here, not cadavers. The doors to The Great Mausoleum are all locked, with buzzers and speakers at each entrance like a goddamn Beverly Hills jewelry store. There's always someone manning the main entrance a la Studio 54, and if you're lucky enough to get inside, you'll find entire hallways declared off-limits for "property owners only." What we want to know is what the hell are they so adamant about guarding?! These are *dead bodies sealed behind solid marble* for Christ's sake! If they see you with a camera or anything that resembles this book, they will probably cite some bullshit about "company policy" and "invite" you to buzz off. Jeez, and we thought cemeteries were the one place a person could go to be left alone. You'll never encounter a more hostile, paranoid, trouble-making pack of losers than at *Forest Lawn Glendale*.

Bring a small bunch of flowers (*real* flowers, since *Forest Lawn* prohibits the placement of fake flowers). This is always a good decoy, and the objectionable staff will be less likely to hassle you if they think you're there in a state of genuine bereavement, rather than to have your picture taken in front of the Jean Harlow tomb. If you're going to try to take pictures (indoor photography is *verboten*—another senseless rule) *keep your camera concealed* and use

The Great Mausoleum

Freedom Mausoleum (top floor)

Freedom Mausoleum (bottom floor)

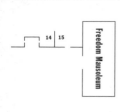

very fast film, without a flash, and only when no one's looking. Or, use a flash and snap like mad, feigning ignorance should you get caught—but be prepared for immediate ejection.

Gaining entry to the Great Mausoleum is tricky, not impossible, and you'll need to think ahead and be prepared to do some fast talking. First, park and walk up to the Gardenia entrance at the far, narrow end of the lot. Look through the locked glass door and locate a name, any name, on one of the visible wall crypts. Commit the name to memory, including the year of death. This name is going to be your dear departed aunt, uncle or cousin to whom you are paying a visit should they give you the third degree at the entry point (and they probably will). Keep in mind that celebrity lookiloos are about as welcome at *Forest Lawn* as David Allen Smith at a Girl Scout rally—but don't let them intimidate you! This park is open to the public and you're not breaking any laws.

Plan B is somewhat easier. One of *Forest Lawn Glendale*'s ridiculous attractions is "The Last Supper Window." This is a stained glass window of the Leonardo da Vinci painting, with an accompanying narration. The "show" runs every hour on the half, and the window is located *inside* the Great Mausoleum. You can slip in at show time. Sooner or later some security guard may be breathing down your neck, so be sure to brush up on your self-defense before paying *Forest Lawn Glendale* a visit!

The Great Mausoleum holds some of the parks biggest names. **Clark Gable** (1) and **Carole Lombard** (2) are to the left center of the Sanctuary of Trust. Carole was killed when her plane crashed outside of Las Vegas in 1942 on her way home from an appearance at a war bond drive. At the time of her death she and Gable had been married for three years. She was only 34, but had already hammered out the fine details of her own interment. A foremost concern was which dress she'd be wearing, and specifically stated in her will that only a white gown by Hollywood costume designer Irene would do.

Jean Harlow (3) was only twenty-six when she died of uremic poisoning reportedly caused by her failed kidneys, which had been damaged as a result of the alleged beatings she received from her suicidal husband Paul Bern. Due to her mother's belief in Christian Science, doctors were prohibited from caring for Jean and she soon died. William Powell, her fiancé at the time of her death, spared no expense on her burial. An estimated $25,000 was spent on the imported marble used to tile the Jean Harlow Room near the end of the Sanctuary of Benediction. The ashes of silent film actress **Theda Bara** (4), née Theodosia Goodman, a Jewish girl from the midwest groomed by her studio into an exotic "vamp," are enshrined on the left in the Columbarian of Memory. Down the hill on the left side of the Great Mausoleum rests evangelist **Sister Aimee Semple McPherson** (5) who killed herself with an overdose of sleeping pills (too bad Jim Jones didn't follow her example). Rumor has it that she was buried with a live telephone at her side. Number unlisted.

The Freedom Mausoleum is considerably easier to crack because its doors remain unlocked and for the most part, unmanned. In the Sanctuary of Heritage you'll find **George Burns** and **Gracie Allen** (6), **Nat "King" Cole** (7), **Alan Ladd** (8), **Jeanette MacDonald** (9), and **Clara Bow** (10). Downstairs, **Larry Fine** (11) of the Three Stooges sits just one hall away from **Chico Marx** (12) of the Marx Brothers. Silent film giant **Frances X. Bushman** (13), is located at the far end of the mausoleum in the Sanctuary of Gratitude.

FOREST LAWN MEMORIAL PARK GLENDALE

Also Starring:

Joan Blondell
Humphrey Bogart
Lon Chaney
Walt Disney
W.C. Fields
Mary Pickford
Spencer Tracy
Ed Wynn

Outside the Freedom Mausoleum lies **Sammy Davis Jr.** (14) in the right section of the Gardens of Honor. Sometimes the door to this section is locked and only accessible to "golden key" holders (What the fuck is this, The Playboy Club?). **Errol Flynn** (15) lies closer to the mausoleum entrance in the Garden of Everlasting Peace. Flynn's marker is just beneath a bronze sculpture of a semi-nude woman, against the wall opposite the entrance.

Forest Lawn Glendale probably prides themselves on their stick-up-the-ass attitude and tighter-than-a-tomb security, but it's just a graveyard after all, not the *Bel Air Bay Club* for crying out loud. Who the hell do they think they are? Show up with a camera and give 'em hell.

Though a kissing cousin of the *Glendale Forest Lawn*, the vibe at the Hollywood Hills location is considerably lighter. There are no indoor mausoleums here, hence no doormen with delusions of grandeur. It's loaded down with just as much nonfunereal-nonsense though, like "The Birth of Liberty Mosaic" ("...the largest historical mural in the United States"), reproductions of George and Martha Washington's clothing, a reproduction of Michelangelo's "Moses," a reproduction of Henry Wadsworth Longfellow's study, and a reproduction of Boston's Christ Church. Forest Lawn is big on reproductions.

One might expect the gravesite of **Lucille Ball** (1) to be somewhat grandiose. But instead of some sky-high marble monument with trickling fountains, bronze statuary, or an imported marble headstone in the shape of a television screen, Lucy opted for a small urn, tucked discreetly away inside the Columbarium of Radiant Dawn (Where *do* they come up with these names?!). A teensy little wall marker reads simply "MORTON Lucille Ball 1911-1989." No "Queen Of Comedy" epitaph, no miniature Emmy statuettes, no shiny brass stars. Maybe she wasn't the world's greatest mom, maybe she did drink a lot, and maybe she was a ball-buster, but as demonstrated by this modest interment, she obviously had class. If you have a tough time locating this one, just look for the spot on the wall completely obstructed by flowers; it's probably Lucy's.

The burial vault of **Wladziu Valentino Liberace** (2) is surprisingly tame for a man who made a habit of spraying glitter in his hair, wearing floor-length furs, and driving rhinestoned automobiles. The world's most ironic closet-case died of AIDS in 1987, while insisting his weight loss was due to a watermelon diet. He's entombed with his mother, and brother George Liberace, towards the inside center of the Court of Remembrance, on the right. Viral myocarditis took the life of singer **Andy Gibb** (3). Although Andy suffered from the heart disease for years, it was the effects of a $1000-a-day cocaine habit and his penchant for vodka that ultimately did him in. He died of heart failure five days after his 30th birthday. Just outside lies **Bette Davis** (4) in a large crypt to the left of the main entrance. Her epitaph reads, "SHE DID IT THE HARD WAY."

At the right end of the Sanctuary of Light you'll find one-note actor **George Raft** (5) side by side with one-bullet comic **Freddie Prinze** (6). Across the park near the sixty-foot monument to the American Revolution lies comedian **Stan Laurel** (7). He's on the second level to the right, behind the Washington statue, and within pie-throwing distance of the walkway. His nameplate is mounted on the wall and easy to spot.

Generally, all cemeteries keep their grounds open 9 to 5, and mausoleums are usually locked up a half-hour before the park closes. Keep your radios off, drive slowly, don't step on any headstones, and don't bring your dog.

Picnic baskets are also discouraged.

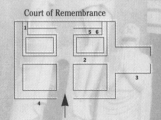

Court of Remembrance

Court of Liberty

FOREST LAWN
HOLLYWOOD HILLS
Also Starring:
Scatman Crothers
Marty Feldman
Buster Keaton
Ernie Kovacs
Fritz Lang
Marjorie Main
Jack Webb

Reevaluating the price of superstardom on

The Hollyweird Death Tour

Hollywood's a pretty weird place to live, sometimes an even stranger place to die. Like the producers, casting agents and other demi-gods who whimsically bestow stardom upon the latest meat puppets, the hand of death moves indiscriminately in Tinseltown—casting the famous, the not-so-famous, and the downright forgotten in their final roles.

Is That A Suicide Note In Your Pocket Or Are You Just Happy To See Me?

The 80s began with a bang as boyish killers like Mark David Chapman and John "Small Caliber" Hinkley came out with both guns blazing. They represent the two archetypal celebrity loons: star-obsessed fruitbats who 1) can't go on living until they've off'd their imaginary doppelganger (as in the case of Chapman and John Lennon) or 2) taken some potshots at a celeb for revenge and/or attention. What better way to impress an ambivalent Academy Award-winning actress like Jody Foster than to kill the President of the United States? On the celebrity assassination scale, that's a whole lotta love.

Being a nation of sheep, it was only a matter of time before this hot new fad caught on—and trickled down. Big stars, little stars, it doesn't really matter anymore. Nowadays, with a little odd fortune, just about anyone can acquire a special admirer. Obscure actress Theresa Saldana grabbed the spotlight repeatedly not with rave notices, but with raving pleas to keep her bug-eyed assailant from carving her up again. A lunatic with a thing for the late Michael Landon sent a Paramount security guard on his own "Highway to Heaven" when he stormed the gates of the studio in search of the one-time "Bonanza" star. Tiny Michael J. Fox was terrorized by a jealous, chinless couch-sloth until he persuaded the court to issue a restraining order. From Madonna to Suzanne Somers, Bob Saget to the Barbi Twins, seems like just about everyone has had their dance with maniacal stalkers and obsessed fans.

Of course, homicidal admirerers are just the latest trend in a town that's seen fads come and go like so many B starlets. Death still comes in all shapes and sizes in Dreamland, most of them nightmares. You have your suicidal types, your drug fiends, your indiscriminate murder victims, your bizarre unsolved crimes. Yeah, being famous isn't all it's cracked up to be. But we're getting ahead of ourselves here. After all, as Karen Carpenter would say, "We've only just begun" our fabulous **Hollyweird Death Tour.**

It's a bright sunny day on the Sunset Strip. As we round the bend you can see the *Chateau Marmont* (8221 Sunset Blvd.) nestled behind some trees over there at the base of the Hollywood Hills. It was there, in the hotel's cozy bungalow #2, on March 5, 1982, that John Belushi choked to death on his own barf while overdosing on a speedball of heroin and coke.

Unlike Belushi, who required a woman named Cathy Smith to do his needlework for him, Lenny Bruce could handle a syringe all by himself. And he did it quite often, it would seem, by the marks found on his arms when medics who discovered him dead and naked in the bathroom of his home in the hills above the Chateau (8825 Hollywood Blvd.). Lenny had been numbing himself with morphine when he got a little greedy...or suicidal. It was 1966, and Lenny was 41 years old.

A short sidetrack south brings us to the front step of 120 North Sweetzer, former home of actress Rebecca Schaeffer. Schaeffer was doing quite well with appearances in movies like *Radio Days, Down and Out in Beverly Hills* and her co-starring sitcom role in *My Sister Sam*. Well enough to attract the attention of a disturbed 19-year-old loner from Arizona named John Bardo.

Bardo had seen Rebecca on the tube and fell in love with her, scrawling out lengthy love letters. The missives weren't violent, or sexual, or even illiterate. They showed no sign of the insanity that gripped their author. He told her he was "a sensitive guy." Rebecca made the mistake of replying. Once. Oh, she didn't sit down and spill her guts or anything like that—John only received an 8x10 glossy with a few stock words of encouragement and an autograph. But that was incentive enough to make his mecca to Rebecca. And waste her.

Just before Bardo left his quiet Tuscon neighborhood, he wrote a letter to his sister in Knoxville, Tennessee. His intentions were fairly clear: "I have an obsession with the unattainable and I have to eliminate (something) that I cannot attain."

On Monday evening, July 17, 1989, Bardo took a Greyhound bus from Tuscon to Los Angeles. He had previously paid a Tuscon detective agency to provide him with Schaeffer's address. They did.

At 10:15 on the morning of the 18th, Bardo rang the front bell of Schaeffer's building. She had been up for a little bit, having laid her clothes out for a later meeting with Frances Ford Coppola. She came down to the front door, dressed only in her bathrobe.

Neighbors heard a gunshot, two screams, then silence. Bardo had fired one shot into Schaeffer's chest, not quite killing her instantly. Bardo quickly fled the scene, but later turned himself in, and told the police where he'd stashed the items he'd been carrying at the time of the murder. Among them was a copy of *The Catcher in the Rye*, the same book that Mark David Chapman was packing when he gunned down John Lennon.

Ironic that Sal Mineo was rehearsing a play called, *P.S. Your Cat Is Dead*, when he was knifed to death in the basement garage of his rented apartment (8563 Holloway Drive). Mineo, best known for his supporting role in "Rebel Without a Cause," was getting out of his car when he was assaulted by at least two unidentified men. Neighbors heard him scream, "My God! My God! Help Me!" Then there was a final scream and silence. It was two days before Valentine's Day, 1976. Mineo was 37, and died with the script of his upcoming play clenched in his fist. Bet his understudy was happy!

Just up the hill from Sal's pad you see an apartment building at 8787 Shoreham Drive. There, in 1969, Diane Linkletter—daughter of TV celeb Art Linkletter—leapt from her sixth-floor window to the pavement below, killing herself. Just before doing her "Flying Nun" impression, Diane had been confiding to a friend about some particularly mondo hallucinations she had experienced during a recent acid trip. She was beginning to question her own sanity. Whatever Diane saw on that trip was weird enough to make her want to check out, and when the friend reached out to grab her, she wound up with nothing but a handful of belt loops from the freaked-out chick's dress. John Waters immortalized the event in one of his earliest films, the little-seen short, *The Diane Linkletter Story*. To this day, Art still campaigns against drugs like it's going to bring her back, and admitted that he received great pleasure watching LSD guru Timothy Leary suffer a slow and painful death. Sometimes Art says the darndest things.

Driving up into the Hollywood Hills, we come to an unsuspecting split-level box at 8763 Wonderland Drive. What happened inside hardly resembled Alice's trip through the looking glass, however. The five murder victims were coke-tootin', house-robbin', drug-dealin' pals of the late porn star John Holmes, who had led them to the house of a rich club owner/coke dealer named Adel Nasrallah (AKA Eddie Nash) to rip him off. They did—and Nash, who also foolishly counted Holmes among his friends, figured out just who had screwed who. He forced Holmes at gunpoint to take him and a club-toting cronie to the Wonderland house, where they proceeded to usher the slumbering occupants into an even deeper sleep with bludgeonings so brutal that their faces were left unrecognizable. Holmes' palm print was found in a wall over one of the victims, indicating that the killers probably dragged the well-hung, whimpering coke addict up to face one of his old friends for one last look.

Pulling onto Woodrow Wilson Drive, we come to the spot where Inger Stevens killed herself in 1970 (8000 Woodrow Wilson Drive). Stevens, who played the swedish housekeeper in the TV series, "The Farmer's Daughter," was 35 when she took the big sleep. She had tried to commit suicide on another occasion. Practice makes perfect.

Down at the bottom of the hill, we find the former site of *The Landmark* (7047 Franklin Ave.), the hotel where Janis Joplin checked in but didn't check out. It was October of 1970, and Janis was in town recording what would be her last album, *Pearl*. The raggedy Texan was trying her damndest to clean up her act, but she was still fucked up on booze and speed and downers and heroin. On the 4th, she gave herself a massive injection of heroin and collapsed, cracking her skull open as she hit the floor. Suicide has never really been ruled out, due to the fact that any junkie worth her salt knows her maximum dosage. Janis had seen death on the horizon, though, and put aside a $2,500 fund for her funeral/party. The invitation read "Drinks are on Pearl." Appropriately, the Grateful Dead provided the music at her wake.

Heading up the hills to the famed "Hollywood" sign, we find a spot so tremendously popular for suicide that it has been fenced off with barbed wire. Peg Entwistle was a successful Broadway actress who came to Hollywood in the early 30s to try her luck in the movies. Despondent after being dropped from her RKO contract, Peg, being the true drama queen that she was, jumped from the top of the second "D" (the sign used to spell out H-O-L-L-Y-W-O-O-D-L-A-N-D) to an early—but remarkably stylish—death.

Speaking of obscure actors, Albert Dekker was a real strange cat, a character player from scores of flicks and best known for his role as Dr. Cyclops in the B-movie of the same name. He lived in these apartments on 1731 North Normandie. But what's interesting is the way he died there.

It was 1968 and the 62-year-old actor was obviously bored with life. So, in what turned out to be a final performance, Dekker decked himself out in his favorite silk lingerie, then scribbled his final words on his flesh with lipstick. The "suicide" that followed was truly unique in the annals of Hollywood self-destruction.

Dekker was found in his locked bathroom, hanging by his neck from a rope that was tied to the shower curtain rod. The rope was also tightly knotted to one of his arms and both legs. He wore handcuffs and had two hypodermic needles stuck in his body. His death was originally listed as a suicide, but a few days later the coroner said his death was an "accident," and indicated that there was no information to lead them to believe Dekker wanted to kill himself. What was he doing in there then, in that outrageous get-up? Perhaps Dekker subscribed to the treacherous masturbatory practice known as autoerotic asphyxiation or maybe he *did* just want to go out in style. Either way, Dr. Cyclops will never tell.

Cult film legend and disco icon Divine (nee Glen Milstead), was about to make his long-awaited crossover from cross-dressing into the mainstream, with a gig on a hit sitcom playing a male character. He was to begin his first day of rehearsals for *Married...With Children* the morning of his death at *The Regency Suites* (7940 Hollywood Blvd.). The 375-pound actor died peacefully in his sleep from an enlarged heart. It took six men to carry Divine's body from the hotel.

Rounding back towards Sunset again, we pass the apartment building that was once home to silent screen star Marie Prevost (6320 Afton Place). Even though Marie died way back in 1937, her story is still interesting today just because it's so damn disgusting.

Like so many silent screen stars, Marie found herself out of a job and out of luck when the talkies came around. The annoying Bronx accent didn't go with her classy looks. Marie took to the bottle with a vengeance, and it was the bottle that killed her. It was days before the body was found, and when the cops finally burst into her lonely room, they were treated to quite a sight: Marie's corpse had been half eaten by her devoted little dachshund, who still whimpered and whined at the foot of her bed. Whether he was trying to wake her up or the hunger just got to the poor fellow will never be determined. English pop star Nick Lowe eulogized Marie in his 1978 song that bore her name: "She was a winner/who became the doggie's dinner..."

Remember Auntie Em from *The Wizard of Oz*? Sure you do. But did you know that in 1962, Auntie Em got bored with life and decided to end it all? Right over there at 1735 Wilcox. Used to be called the Shelton Apartments back before they raised them to put the condos in. Clara Blandick was Auntie Em's real name, and on that glorious day when she decided to join Dorothy over the rainbow, she got all gussied-up, coiffed her hair, applied her makeup, and lay down on the couch. She covered herself with a blanket, then, being careful not to disturb her hairdo, she slipped a plastic bag down over her head. There really is no place like home.

The *Hotel Knickerbocker* (1714 North Ivar) has long been a colorful fixture in old-Hollywood legend. It was here that one of filmdom's top costume designers, Irene, checked in under an assumed name and slashed her wrists. Unfortunately for Irene, it was all for nought; not only was she still alive, but she had made a damn bloody mess of things. Plan B: leap from the window. Fortunately for Irene, she was on the fourteenth floor and plan B proved a success.

A hip-hop on the Santa Monica Freeway and we're back in beautiful Beverly Hills, home of the stars. Or better yet, home of the dead stars. Just across the way, on the other side of Wilshire Blvd., is the former funpad of wacky Chicano comedian Freddie Prinze (865-75 Comstock Ave.). Prinze, as you may recall, was the enormously successful star of Norman Lear's hit 70s sitcom, *Chico and the Man*. Freddie was only 22 in 1977, and should have been riding high on the success of his show; instead he was bummed out about a recent separation from his wife. Add to his despondent mood Prinze's belief that he was the reincarnation of his comedic hero Lenny Bruce, and you have all the ingredients for a grade A star suicide. Prinze, who often visited Bruce's old house on Sunset, told friends, "What a terrific life (it would be) to die young and be a legend." Prinze got his wish that year with a .22 caliber slug in his brain. Despite the fact that eyewitnesses saw Prinze draw the gun from under a couch cushion, put it to his head, and pull the trigger, a jury ruled in 1983 that the apparent suicide was an accident. Right.

Speaking of accidental suicides, it's still unclear whether actress Pier Angeli overdosed on purpose or just got sloppy back in 1971. The beautiful Italian actress had her share of starring roles in the 50s, but was perhaps best known as the girl who said "no" to James Dean's one and only marriage proposal. Instead, she married schmaltzy singer Vic Damone that same year, while Dean sat outside the church on his motorcycle and revved the engine full bore. Angeli's marriage was short-lived—as was James Dean and her career. She later appeared in a handful of forget-table foreign atrocities like *Octaman*, and at the age of 39 perhaps decided that a couple of fistfulls of barbituates beat playing second fiddle to some guy in a foam rubber octopus suit. She overdosed right here on the very fringe of Beverly Hills, at her apartment at 355 So. McCarty Street.

Back in 1958, Lana Turner was on her umpteeth lover, this time an underworld lout with a notoriously large cock named Johnny Stompanado. They lived together with Lana's delinquently precocious daughter Cheryl Crane, in a lovely mansion on 730 North Bedford Drive. There, Cheryl was often lulled to sleep by the dulcet tones of her mother being beaten by the Italian lug.

Cheryl was none too fond of Johnny, but he wasn't the first man in her mother's life to bring her grief. Most notable was Lana's previous lover, actor, and child molester Lex Barker, who saw fit to consummate his wedding not only with his wife, but with her young daughter as well—and on a regular basis. Johnny's violent outbursts were the last straw for Cheryl. One night in 1958 she slipped into his upstairs bedroom, stabbed him repeatedly, and it was "Goodnight, Johnny" forever. Understandably, Cheryl is now living a happy life as a lesbian, having spilled her guts in her tell-all book *Detour*. Now, with Lana's passing, maybe we'll get the *real* story about what happened that night.

Traveling just south of Sunset, down a tiny, narrow road called 5th Helena Drive, we see the frequent Kennedy pit-stop and former home of Marilyn Monroe. These days, the tiny bunga-low (12305 5th Helena Drive) is completely blocked from view by a large electric gate. Murder, suicide, accident? Only her hairdresser knows for sure. Moving up into the hills, we come to the

Rock Hudson home, the one in which he spent his final days (9402 Beverly Crest Drive). Hudson was only 59 when he helped to make AIDS a household word.

Lupe Velez, the feisty "Mexican Spitfire" of the 1930s, found herself broke, in debt, alone, and pregnant once the 1940s rolled around. Her sperm donor wasn't exactly thrilled over the prospect of fatherhood, and Lupe was growing increasingly despondent. Being Catholic, abortion was out of the question, so Lupe figured she only had one other alternative—and she wasn't thinking adoption. She slipped into a silver lamé gown, fluffed her flower arrangements, lit a bunch of candles, and gulped down an entire bottle of Seconal pills. Apparently it was Lupe's aim to die picture-perfectly in bed, face up, hands folded. What she didn't anticipate was that the overdose would induce violent wretching. When the maid arrived the following morning, a trail of vomit from Lupe's bed led her straight into the bathroom. It was there that Lupe met her maker, after passing out with her face in the toilet water. She had drowned (732 North Rodeo Drive).

Then there's Nick Adams' old place up 2126 Robel Ave. Nick had seen better days, having slipped from appearances in such films as *Rebel Without a Cause* and *Pillow Talk* to starring in *Godzilla vs. Monster Zero*. It was 1968—a good year for celebrity deaths—and Nick managed to OD under mysterious circumstances. Police found no pill bottles, syringes, paraphernalia—nothing. Nick didn't have a problem with booze or pot, so was it murder, suicide, or an accident? To this day, the cops still don't know how the massive dose of sedatives and drugs entered his system. Perhaps it was Monster Zero. Only Oliver Stone knows for sure.

Winding our way westward through the treacherous hills, we come to perhaps the most legendary address in Hollywood murder history; 10050 Cielo Drive. On August 9, 1969, the pregnant actress Sharon Tate was entertaining a small group of friends when they received some uninvited guests. Filthy, wild-eyed, and crazed on acid, Tex Watson and his knife-wielding wenches crawled in through the open windows and proceeded to make mass murder history. No need to rehash the well-worn gory details here. Suffice it to say the killers were, how should we put it, *over-enthusiastic*. Read *Helter Skelter*.

Just up the bend from the Tate house is the pad where George "Superman" Reeves—the chunky hero of the early TV series—was found in his bedroom, naked, with a gunshot wound to the head (1579 Benedict Canyon). The gun was found between his legs, so the coroner's office ruled his death a suicide. Reeves mother, however, smelled something foul and ordered her son's body to be put on ice until they could positively rule out murder. Eventually Reeves was cremated and his mother passed away.

Maybe mom knew best after all. Reeves had been tangled up in a ten-year affair with Toni Mannix, the wife of MGM studio exec Eddie Mannix. George was also a kept man; Toni not only regularly supplemented Reeves income, but she helped to set him up in his Benedict Canyon home. In 1958, George told Toni the affair was over; he had fallen in love with a young New York socialite named Lenore Lemmon. Toni was destroyed...and vengeful. She threatened to expose Superman's alleged bisexuality, and harassed the new couple with phone calls at all hours of the day and night—she was even suspected of having the brake fluid drained from Reeves' Jaguar to ensure a deadly car wreck. Reportedly, Reeves' death was at the hands of Toni, who instructed a hitman to use Reeves' own Luger (an earlier gift from Mannix) to waste the bulletproof superhero.

From the top of the hills, there's a great view of Pacific Palisades and the beach. And that lump out there in the Pacific? That's Santa Catalina Island. Both these places have their stories, but we'll take them one at a time.

Catalina's long been a romping ground for the stars, and once boasted its own casino. Chaplin brought babes here for erotic outings in the lush, goat-infested hills. And it was here, on the first day of December 1981, where Natalie Wood took her unexpected final dip into the briney just before midnight.

The fact surrounding Natalie's soggy departure are still unclear due to the zipped lips of Robert Wagner and Christopher Walken, key players in the "floating Wood" death mystery. Wagner was her husband; Walken, the co-star of her final film, *Brainstorm*. The Wagners and Walken had enjoyed a hearty meal on Catalina Island and then returned to their $250,000, 55-foot-yacht that Natalie and Bob had dubbed "Splendor," after her first big role in *Splendor in the Grass*. There was also a rubber dingy attached to the ship, aptly named after the least favorite of Wagner's films, *Prince Valiant*.

Bob and Chris got into an argument. The authorities still don't know just how serious it was, or what it may have been about, but the ruckus was enough to send Natalie, dressed only in a nightgown and a parka, scuttling over the side to the "Prince Valiant" for a little peace and quiet. Earlier in the evening when they were leaving for dinner, Natalie missed her step and almost fell in the water. With seven or eight glasses of champagne in her, she didn't fare much better in the pitch blackness.

Witnesses say they heard a woman crying, "Help! Somebody help me!" from the direction of the Splendor, but it seems the men were too embroiled in their secret argument to aid the damsel in distress. Wagner claimed he didn't realize she was gone for a couple of hours. They found her body about a mile away, floating facedown, just above Blue Cavern Point.

Back on the mainland up Pacific Coast Highway we come to the death garage of Thelma Todd, a popular comedic actress of the 20s and 30s, who appeared with Laurel and Hardy, The Marx Bros. and in a series of fairly forgettable comedies for Hal Roach.

By 1935, Todd had been receiving so many death threats that her maid's weekly chores included the bundling and delivery of Thelma's "fan mail" to the police station. In December that year, Todd was found dead, slumped over the wheel of her car inside the closed garage at 17531 Posetano Road. The death was ruled an accident—but because of her awkward placement, the blood at the scene, and the bruises that indicated some sort of struggle, murder was just as probable. And there was certainly no shortage of likely suspects.

Roland West—Thelma's married boyfriend and business partner—was a prime suspect for fifty years. Todd and West had opened *Thelma Todd's Sidewalk Cafe*, a beachfront restaurant just down the hill from her death garage. West wanted out of the partnership—he was receiving considerable pressure from Thelma's sometime plaything, gangster "Lucky" Luciano, to convert the unused third floor of the popular cafe into an underground gambling casino. West was also insanely jealous over an affair Thelma was having with a San Francisco businessman.

Another suspect was Charles Smith, the cafe's treasurer, whom both Todd and West suspected of juggling the books in cahoots with the underworld. Thelma had plans to check things out with a professional audit after the first of the year, which her death effectively prevented from ever happening.

Her former husband, Pat DiCicco, was supposedly the last man to see her alive. He was known for having a violent temper and had beaten Todd during their brief, volatile marriage. There was also "The Ace," a stranger who had hassled Todd with numerous death threats and extortion attempts.

Most likely of all was Luciano who had plenty of reasons to want Thelma dead. The two had been involved on and off for the last two years of Todd's life. Lucky was hell-bent on his casino idea, for which Thelma was to provide a high-rolling clientele. She flatly refused to cooperate, and may have sealed her own fate in doing so. As detailed in the book *Hot Toddy*, it was a hitman hired by Luciano who staged Todd's "suicide"—bringing an end to the long line of bad boys to populate Thelma Todd's messy life.

Speaking of the end of the line, this is it. Thanks for coming on our special *Hollyweird Death Tour*. The way things are going, we should have enough new celebrity deaths to do it all over again in no time.

See you then!

day
trippin

Let's face it:

Life in L.A. is about as stressful as showing up at a rap concert in a Klansman's outfit. So, after a week of running yourself ragged on the corporate hamster wheel, sometimes it's nice to pack up the car and get out of the city for a day. And L.A. has plenty of strange surrounding locales that offer you a variety of interesting and offbeat diversions for 24 hours or less. Roy Rogers and Dale Evans fans can take in the desert sights and check out the life and times of their favorite country-and-western duo at their very own museum. Further north along the coast, the world-famous Madonna Inn will challenge your rods and cones–along with whatever concept of interior design you may have. Nudists will find a wealth of beaches at which they can let it all hang out. Is your doctor stingy with his prescription pad? Then perhaps a jaunt down to Tijuana's many pharmacies is just what you need to relieve unwanted stress. Or you can relive the glory of Christmas year-round with a journey to Santa's Village. Maybe culture is your bag, and if it is, pack a sack lunch and head out to Exotic World for an eye-opening, first-person tour of the history of striptease dancing. Looking for an Adrenalin rush? Then how about jumping out of plane for the ultimate free-fall? And that's just a sampling of the day-tripping fun you can have without a little piece of blotter paper.

Best of all, these suggestions are completely legal...
for the most part.

Circumventing the F.D.A. at the
Tijuana Pharmacies

The problem with doctors is that they won't prescribe whatever drug you want. Of course, that's what drug dealers are for, but they tend to overcharge, and you never really know what you're getting. Add to this the off-chance that you may very well get caught in the crossfire of a deal gone bad, and it makes the whole ordeal that much more unsavory. Down in Tijuana, though, you can purchase just about any pharmaceutical drug your little heart desires, and not in some dark alley, either, but a from a real pharmacy—or farmacia. And who says Mexico is a backwards country?

Is That A Bottle Of Rohypnol In Your Pocket Or Are You Just Planning To Date Rape Me?

The fact is that many prescription drugs are readily available in Mexico without a prescription, and any border town with a farmacia has struck gold from the booming trade of Yanquis who make the trek to purchase cut-rate Prozac and other chemical staples. This news isn't hot off the press either; the phenomena has been making the media rounds for the past few years. Likewise, there's been a plethora of publicity generated by all the legislators and law enforcement officials who've been crying bloody murder about the so-called "date rape drug," Rohypnol (street name: Roofies), which is not legally available in the U.S., but can easily be had in Mexico. This media attention, of course, has only served to spread the scourge of date rape to countless more sicko losers who can't get laid by a woman as long as she's conscious. Is it just me, or have men always attempted to ply women with booze and other drugs in order to get into their precious, highly overrated pants? Rohypnol appears to be the latest boogie man in this never-ending horror story of the intransigent and indomitable male libido, bringing an even bigger and brighter spotlight on the "legit" drug commerce with our friends south of the border. Frankly, since more than one woman has fallen asleep on me in the midst of what I thought was a mutually gratifying experience, I've never really seen the need, nor the attraction, of a drug that turns your date into a temporary corpse—I only know of two groups who seem to prefer mating with women in such a state (necrophiliacs and frat boys).

Tijuana has always made for a great day trip, though you may end up spending the night there, intentionally or not, due to the myriad of sins that await you. Speaking from personal experience, you might want to avoid any behavior that will land you in the incredibly squalid Tijuana jail, since the Federales (Mexican police) are a rather capricious lot when it comes to law enforcement techniques. One minute they're laughing with you over some dirty joke you can't understand, and the next minute they're demanding a fine for some crime they've conjured up on the spot.

Let me relate a personal tale to illustrate the latter. I was once driving through Ensenada, a popular beach resort south of Tijuana, when I was pulled over by a Federale. It was late at night and I was hammered, but that didn't seem to be of any concern to the cop, who was wearing sunglasses at three in the morning. In fact, we both were. Our conversation went something like this:

"You ran a stop sign on the last block, Senor."

"I'm sorry, I didn't see any stop signs," I said, looking back to see that, indeed, there was no stop sign on the previous block.

When I pointed out this glaring fact to the policeman, he smiled like a character out of *Treasure of the Sierra Madre* and said to me, "Yes, I know, but there used to be one there."

He proceeded to ask me how much money I had on me, and when I told him, he was happy to inform me that the amount I was carrying was exactly that of the fine. Having already visited the Tijuana jail and knowing I had a car full of illicit substances, I gave him the money and he left me alone. Thank god I'm a good liar, or he would have cleaned me out completely.

That unpleasant encounter, combined with the ensuing indignity of having my car torn apart at the border by U.S. Customs Officials after waiting in a chaotic line of cars for three hours in the blazing summer heat has taught me this important lesson: I now leave my car on the U.S. side of the border and walk across the urine-scented overpass that takes me into the wonderland that is Mexico. May I recommend you do the same unless you have a lot of time on your hands and want to be harangued during your entire auto-wait by street vendors trying to sell you cheap blankets and ugly painted plaster facsimiles of Elvis Presley and Jesus Christ?

But I digress. The point here is that Tijuana is a gigantic candy store when it comes to shopping for cheap drugs and other recreational contraband. But beware that the process may not be as simple as it seems: Some farmacias may play dumb and attempt to con you into going down the street to grease the palm of a doctor—with whom they're in cahoots—before they will dole out the good stuff. Avoid these, because there are plenty of nice farmacias that will not only accommodate your requests, but even place the drugs in vitamin bottles or innocuous paper sacks that can easily fit inside the aforementioned plaster statues, much less your hip pocket.

They key to accessing one of these chemical wonderlands is finding the right taxi driver just after you cross the border. Most will only charge a few bucks to take you the short distance into town, and if you tip them well and make it clear you want to visit a farmacia without all the aforementioned doctor hassles, they will usually come through for you. Why? Because the cabbies get a kickback for taking you to the farmacia, and this award usually comes in the form of an appliance or color TV at the end of the year when the farmacias tally up just how many turistas the taxis delivered and how much the customers spent. Isn't that special?

Whether you're looking for Ampicillin or Xanax, you'll find it at an incredibly cheap price in Mexico. The reason? Both drugs are manufactured in Mexico. However, any drugs that aren't made in Mexico, particularly newer ones, may be very pricey or not available at all. Most of the so-called "Smart Drugs" that have become so popular in the U.S. over the past five years are an example of this discrepancy, and, for the most part, are cheaper to order from overseas firms specializing in such drugs.

Also, keep in mind that the friendly person helping you at the farmacia is not a doctor. You may ask for a certain drug and though the establishment doesn't carry it, the clerk may attempt to steer you to another one altogether—which may or may not be similar to your intended buy. Most of the better farmacias keep a dog-eared copy of the *Physician's Desk Reference* under the counter, so ask for it and look up whatever it is they're trying to sell you. If it doesn't remotely fit the bill, don't buy it. Or, if you happen to stumble upon some wonderful, obscure drug not known in these parts, please pass the info on to this author in care of the publisher.

Finally, a few tips on how to make it back across the border to the U.S. without getting popped by our friends at Customs (whose salaries we pay!):

Tip #1: Don't dress like a fucking freak—especially if you are driving across the border. On one trip, I looked like a Marine on leave, but my buddy Hector looked like, well, a fucking freak. He had hair down his back, and for the Customs folks, that was enough to make him a damn pre-vert as well as a Commie. So when I was sentenced to Secondary Inspection (where they "inspect" your car) in order to watch a team of U.S. Customs Officials—and their dog—tear out my door panels, rugs, dashboard, seats, and other hardware that does not just snap back in like a Lego set, I consoled myself with the thought that, "Hey at least they'll put it all back together when they're done playing The French Connection."

Silly me! After all those times I had flown back from Europe and passed through U.S. Customs just to witness the spectacle of my luggage being given worse treatment than the gorilla gave the Samsonite suitcase in those 70s TV spots, I should have known that these Customs cretins would take delight in not cleaning up the mess they so gleefully created. It may be a bitch to repack what was once a pristine suitcase, but to reassemble a car when I barely know how to check the oil is truly an unappreciated challenge. As with the Federales, there is no method to Customs' madness, so even if you look like Pat Boone, they still might take you in a room, put on rubber gloves, and peer up your butt with a flashlight.

Hey, what a scenario: Imagine Pat Boone with his pants around his ankles, a guy behind him with a flashlight in his teeth and his hands firmly spreading Pat's cheeks. "Hey Pat, what  you got up there? Your white bucks?!" Then everyone in the room has a good laugh, with the possible exception of poor Pat. Bottom line: You never know when your number will be up, so don't invite the Customs agent's wrath by looking like anyone other than Ward Cleaver.

Tip #2: Wear a disguise and bring back plenty of junk. I always find it helpful to buy some turista chachkies whenever I'm down there, just to throw the agents off. After all, if I'm packing Cuban cigars (which are usually too dry and unpalatable), a few bottles of Mescal and Kahlua, a silly hat, and a shirt that says something like: "Party 'til you puke at Senor Bullfrogs Cantina," I obviously am just another American idiot and not a crafty guy trying to take advantage of the F.D.A.'s loopholes. Which I am, of course.

Tip #3: Be careful what you bring back—and how much. It's a sticky issue, but the F.D.A. has been graceful enough to allow U.S. citizens to order and/or import up to a three-months' supply of prescription drugs that are sold over the counter in other countries. Although you are supposed to be using these drugs under your doctor's supervision, that's a lot like having to get a note from the Pope in order to buy condoms. So if you're purchasing anything questionable like downers, speed, or the like, then just get what you need for three months and don't be greedy. If you take 25 Valiums a day, then opt for a single month's supply, or better yet, consider rehab. You and the parole officer you'll never know will both thank you. Otherwise, if you overdo it and get busted, the Feds will think you're a dealer and not just a drug addict, which, of course, is far better in the eyes of the law.

If you are arrested, look at the bright side: Federal Prison is far better than the Tijuana Jail.

Tip #4: Avoid Illegal narcotics. Of course, you never intended to bring back a kilo of black tar heroin or a brick of coke, but if you come across the border with a wealth of Rohypnol, you may find yourself facing charges with similar punishment. As of this writing, bills have already been proposed in California, Florida, and other states to put Rohypnol in the same league as junk and blow. Wow, just imagine if Quaaludes had incurred such a ruthless clampdown during their heyday? There may have been no disco craze. No disco...period. It boggles the mind.

So there you go...all you need to know to find your way to prescription drug bargains beyond your wildest soporific dreams. Whether you happen to be one of those thrifty, stock-up-for-the-future types or simply a bonafide pill freak with an uptight American physician, take a daytrip down to Mexico, stock up, and then return home to amaze your friends and, if you must, your family.

Just watch it with the date rape, would you?

—ARL

Tijuana Pharmacies
Take the 5 or the 405 south and follow the signs to the border. Park on the U.S. side, then cross over and ask a cabbie to take you to a prescription-free pharmacy.

Remembering the Horror of the Northridge Earthquake
at the Site of the *Northridge Meadows Death Apartments*

Most of this book has to do with glib summaries of offbeat locales in the Los Angeles area. But when it comes to writing about the Northridge earthquake that shook the city on January 17th, 1994, at 4:31 A.M., there is no room for offhanded humor. There is a fine line between entertainment and bad taste—and God knows we've crossed it more than once in this book—but if you happen to notice the absence of any references to O.J. Simpson murder-related sites, they are purely intentional. The authors are as disgusted and burnt-out with the ex-football star's infamy as is the rest of America, so if you want directions to his Brentwood estate or Nicole's apartment, you'll have to look elsewhere. We didn't even include the Juice and his lethal legacy in our "death tour" entry, which may seem odd to some, but poetic justice to us.

Mother Nature Is A Murdering Bitch

However, the earthquake, though not funny by any means, does deserve mention. There is no need for a jury to determine whether or not Mother Nature was responsible for the mass destruction and death that befell our fair city that January morning. That's a given. And there is no better place to pay one's respects to the dead—as well as get an idea of the incredible force of the earthquake—than at the leveled site of the **Northridge Meadows** apartment complex that went from a three-floor structure to a two-story in a matter of seconds, crushing and killing 16 of the occupants on the first floor in their sleep. Oddly, this was the only building to endure such uniformly lethal damage.

For months after the quake, the security-patrolled apartments were a tourist attraction that drew curiosity seekers from all over the country who came to photograph, gawk and, one would assume, pray. Surrounded by a chain-link fence, the pancaked building was a pitiful sight, its broken windows and walls disgorging the contents of the long-gone occupants. Children's toys, broken lamps, and other household sundries lay alongside torn mattresses, soiled clothing, and crumpled cars that looked like the remnants of some killer twister. Within a year the complex was torn down and the debris hauled away. Now all that remains is the concrete foundation and the steps that once led up to the entrance. The fencing still stands, and though the macabre mess is gone, the effect is still as chilling. Vegetation has begun to creep over the grounds, a reminder that time cannot stand still. Like the *McDonald's* down in San Ysidro where James Huberty massacred 23 people, this razed site deserves some kind of plaque, a memorial to what transpired here. But in all likelihood, there will one day be a enterprising developer willing to put up another building—most likely a mini-mall—on this unholy ground, and erase all physical memory of the devastation and death of the *Northridge Meadows Apartments*. Some may say this is just as well, but we're not so sure. We think we Angelenos could use yet another morbid reminder that we build our homes on shaky ground, and that such cruel and random death at the hands of nature is just another amenity of living in the alleged City of Angels.

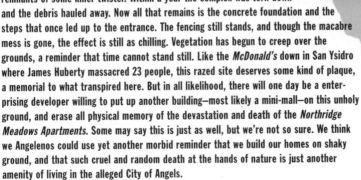

The Former Northridge Meadows Apartments
Reseda Blvd. on the west side of the street, just behind the shopping complex on Plummer

Santa's Village

I'll Be Closed For Christmas

Accessing different parts of our brain via *Santa's Village*

Piece together moments from the early Pia Zadora vehicle *Santa Claus Conquers the Martians*, select chapters from Terence McKenna's *Archaic Revival*, and throw in one of Lewis Carroll's most enigmatic wet dreams—maybe then you can begin to grasp the subtle glory of all that is **Santa's Village.**

Have you ever fantasized about sitting inside a giant Christmas Tree ornament spiraling at high speed around the circumference of a snow-tipped evergreen? Ever hope that you'd someday suck on Santa's North Pole but can't bear the thought of enduring weeks of fierce blizzards and dehydrated foods during the trek? Do you know what it feels like to take a ride on the back of an oversized bumble bee after stuffing your gut with pumpkin spice pastries dripping with gooey icing?

Run, don't walk, to Skyforest!

What's really odd about *Santa's Village* isn't just that it's an entire amusement park erected in honor of a pagan-cum-Christian holiday nestled in a forest clearing high in the San Bernardino Mountains. What's weird is the candy-coated surrealistic *ultra*-tapestry of Santa Claus idolatry and Christmas tree worship, four-foot-tall polka-dotted mushrooms, miniature horses that bite, a pumpkin-headed man, a lollipop lady, and—just in case the scene gets a little too heavy—a nondenominational chapel. It's this mind-expanding juxtaposition of elements like happy snowmen and flying dragons, or live peacocks and giant candy canes that pushes *Santa's Village* way beyond a "Rudolph the Red-Nosed Reindeer" mindset.

After passing through the portals of the *Santa's Village* Welcome House one almost needs to stop for a moment and refocus—or decide to run. The lay of the land takes shape much the same way the bottom of that rabbit hole must have hit Alice. Perfectly manicured pathways trimmed with 300-foot pine trees and psychedelic mushrooms crisscross through the grounds, leading visitors past freak-out focal points like a jack-in-the-box standing two stories high, or a hyper-surrealistic masterwork like the Crooked Tree House. Santa casually strolls the grounds with a reindeer or two on a leash, while the sounds of The Beach Boys' "Merry Christmas Baby" blares—along with an obscure mix of other holiday tunes—over the speakers perched high in the treetops throughout the park. Kids run laughing from the petting zoo—where they've just gotten their hands good and filthy with goat saliva—over to the Candy Kitchen for some homemade sweets. A spaced-out hippie gets into the holiday spirit as he sits beneath a box of popcorn twenty feet tall just across from the Pixie Pantry. With pupils dilated like two eyes made out of coal, he grooves to the *Santa's Village* color palate: a kaleidoscope of chartreuse, lemon yellow, acid green, sky blue, hot pink and orange popsicle. Young and old, Jew or Gentile, everyone is tuned in and

turned on at *Santa Village*. Maybe it's the calming effect of the forest setting that puts people in such fine feather. Maybe it's the magic of Christmas. Maybe it's the sugar.

Further into the woods, The Lollipop Lady—the *Santa's Village* patron saint of tooth decay—sits out front of the Good Witch Bakery: an enormous gingerbread house painted as garishly as the sets of "Hee Haw," finished with a thick layer of frothy pink frosting smeared over the rooftop, and detailed with chocolate cookies as big as tractor tires. Red, heart-shaped shutters adorn the windows, and puce-colored mushrooms grow out of its chimney tops. The Lollipop Lady, stuffed into a voluminous hoop skirt embellished with her namesake, waves a long candy wand streaming with multicolored ribbons. Looking like an aged Scarlett O'Hara with an insatiable sweet tooth, she sits in her makeshift throne luring passing children over to sample her wares, proving that there's still at least one place left where a person can accept candy from strangers. "We used to have a lollipop *tree*," she says, remembering the good 'ol days before sucrose deforestation, "but the kids would strip it bare. That's when I became The Lollipop Lady; now I hand them out one at a time."

Be sure not to miss any of the attractions, since the park is small enough that you won't have to sacrifice Cinderella's Pumpkin Coach Ride in order to visit Mrs. Claus' Spice Kitchen, and you'll never have to wait in long lines for anything except Santa's House. The Christmas elves at the control panels have no qualms about allowing you some extra time on a favorite ride—lines permitting—to the point that you'll be *begging* to get off the spinning Christmas tree or the body-bruising bobsled ride. Take a vacation from Christmas inside the Alice-in-Wonderland installation; a voice-over narration tells Alice's story as you zig-zag through corridors festooned with staggering dioramas of her life and times. The Wee Puppet Theater runs a revolving bill of puppet shows, the likes of which you probably haven't seen since preschool. Sit through one. It's wildly inspiring to see the same kids who have been weaned on Nintendo and CD-ROM technology transfixed by these somewhat primitive puppet plays, cheering the good guy and booing the bad. And don't be surprised if you too get a little swept away by the sheer spectacle and surprise special effects.

For better or worse, we live in an age of instant gratification; microwave ovens give us a hot meal in three minutes, overnight mail provides for us what fax machines can't, and *Santa's Village* gives us Christmas in June.

Get your picture taken with Santa before you lose your summer tan.

DID YOU KNOW?

• *Santa's Village in Skyforest, California is the last remaining official Santa's Village.*

• *Originally there were three: the one in Skyforest, another one in Santa Cruz, California, and another in Dundee, Illinois.*

• *Santa's Village is closed Christmas day.*

• *Santa's Village used to feature a piano playing duck.*

Santa's Village
Skyforest
(909) 337-2481

From Los Angeles:
Take the 10 Freeway East to the 215 North. Go about four miles to the 30 Freeway East to the "Mountain Resorts" turnoff. Stay on Mountain Resorts Freeway and exit on Waterman Ave. Turn left on Waterman (Highway 18) and proceed to *Santa's Village. Santa's Village* is about two miles past the Lake Arrowhead turnoff on Highway 18. The drive should take about two hours.

Reliving the golden age of burlesque at *Exotic World*

Nineteen miles off the 15 freeway by way of a series of dusty desert roads lies the jewel in the navel of Helendale, California: **Exotic World**. *Exotic World* sits on the ranch property that was once the home of burlesque star Jennie Lee. Jennie, who was familiar to her fans as "The Bazoom Girl" or "Miss 44 and Plenty More," was a dancer famous for her twirling tasseled pasties, as well as a pin-up model who starred in several films (*Hollywood Bustout, Ding Dong, Night at the Moulin Rouge*). Established in an effort to honor the bodacious gals of burlesque and to preserve its history, Jennie opened *Exotic World*—"A Burlesque Hall of Fame and Historical Museum"—in 1980. After Jennie's unfortunate death to cancer in 1989, her old pal and fellow burlesque queen Dixie Evans moved onto the ranch, sharing the property with Jennie's widower ("We're not intimate," claims Dixie) and assumed the position of *Exotic World*'s president, a labor of love to which she has loyally committed herself ever since.

Hot Pants Are Optional

Exotic World must be seen to be believed. As you drive past the sign "Chivos Goats For Sale" and reach the end of the paved portion of Wild Road, "*Exotic World*" is spelled out in wrought iron, arching majestically over the front gates. "Lili St. Cyr," "Tempest Storm," "Gypsy Rose Lee" and a bevy of burlesque's more well-known names are hand-painted on plywood signs lining the dirt road that leads to the museum and private residence of Miss Evans. A myriad of chickens, goats and horses make their home here too, the latter all named after old strippers.

Pulling into the parking area, you'll see a sign instructing you to "honk three times." Faster than you can kill your ignition and say "breakaway beaded gown," out struts the one and only Miss Evans. Wearing hot pants and white cowboy boots with a full face of freshly applied makeup, lips a glossy ruby-red and her golden blond cotton candy hair perfectly coiffed, Dixie introduces herself and begins the tour posthaste.

Billed as "The Marilyn Monroe of Burlesque" Dixie Evans began her career in the late 40s and has never really retired. No stranger to the talk show circuit, Dixie's made her rounds on *Joan Rivers, Donahue, Jenny Jones, Montel Williams, Jerry Springer, Sally Jesse Raphael, A Current Affair* and even *MTV*. Dixie's the sweetest burlesque queen you'll ever meet. It's a rare privilege to make her acquaintance and an honor to be her guest on the tour.

The main museum at *Exotic World* is a skillfully converted goat shed which now more resembles a tract house, finished with cottage cheese ceilings and powder blue-sculpted wall-to-wall carpet. The tour starts simply enough in the driveway to the main house with Jennie Lee's 1961 Rolls Royce. Moving into the anteroom you're hit with a visual barrage of burlesque overload. Every square inch is cram packed with sequined pasties, feather boas, shrines to deceased strippers, marabou mules under glass—even the ashes of Jennie Lee are on display. The walls are covered with hundreds of original 8 x 10s from the 1940s to the present that once graced the lobbies of burlesque houses and the box office windows of classier strip joints across the country. Blaze Star, Liz Renay, Patti Waggin, Sheri Champagne, Kitten Natividad, Candy Barr and Lili Christine the "New Orleans Cat Girl" are just a few of the bra-busters who create a virtual kaleidoscope against the white plasterboard walls. As you begin to lose any sense of depth perception, Dixie immediately pops in a cassette of classic stripper instrumentals and begins her non-stop spiel providing a crash course in the history of burlesque. Regaling you with stories, stripper minutiae and personal histories, Dixie leads you through a series of ten overstocked rooms as she yammers away and brandishes her point-

ing stick like Norman Schwarzkopf, pausing only to answer truly pertinent questions. Her interminable, lightning speed, stream of consciousness delivery leaves a listener very little time to process the information. Just as you begin to assimilate *Exotic World*'s unique milieu, Dixie pops in a videotape of vintage Kodacolor 8mm peepshow striptease loops and begins rambling on about Shirley Jean, the "Little Rascal" child actor-turned-stripper, or the hard-luck life story of Candy Barr. There are a few puzzling items in the museum that seem incongruous with burlesque, like a color poster of Miss Piggy, a nude portrait of Farrah Fawcett Majors on black "velvet" and an assortment of dolls and stuffed animals; spurious perhaps, but all in keeping with *Exotic World*'s inimitable decor.

Her job as president keeps Dixie quite busy, so she doesn't always have time to tend to her curatorial duties. The collection is sort of haphazardly displayed, and it's been a while since anyone's been through there with a feather duster. Piles of unopened mail sit on Dixie's desk. "People don't think we have anything to do out here in the desert, but running this museum is a full-time job," she says as her eye wanders to the corner of the ceiling directly above a pink velvet heart-shaped bassinet custom-made for Jayne Mansfield's son, Mickey Hargitay, Jr. "Oh my, look at those spiders!" Occasionally, Dixie will use her shirttail to wipe away a thick layer of dust so we can get a better look at a photo, or an item under glass. This kind of service you just don't get at M.O.C.A.

The tour concludes in a gift-shopish area, the only part of the museum in which photos of current, surgically enhanced strippers are on display like Staci Staxx and Crystal Storm (who both sport inhuman 100+" busts.) "We really don't like to put up too many of *those* kind of pictures," Dixie says with a hint of disapproval. Reprints of many of the photos displayed in the museum are for sale as well as original Jennie Lee fanzines, burlesque autobiographies and an assortment of *Exotic World* souvenirs.

Annually *Exotic World* plays host to an event where hundreds gather in the blistering desert heat to watch strippers from across the country compete for the much-coveted *"Miss Exotic World"* title.

Hours are flexible. We strongly suggest you call ahead and make sure Dixie knows you're coming. If you should cancel your plans be sure and let her know not to expect you. *Exotic World* is a non-profit organization; there is no admission fee. Donations are appreciated—please be generous, it's tax deductible.

FROM LOS ANGELES:
The drive to *Exotic World* should take you about two hours. Take the 10 freeway east to the 15 freeway north. Just after Victorville, take the D Street #18 (National Trails Highway/Route 66) exit and turn left. You'll travel on National Trails Highway for about 17 miles to Vista Road and turn left. Vista Road is easy to pass—watch carefully. You'll cross some railroad tracks and a small bridge. You'll see a corner supermarket at Helendale Road, turn right. Keep going to Wild Road, turn right. Wild Road takes a square turn to the left, but remains Wild Road. Don't let that confuse you; you're headed in the right direction, and yes, it's worth it. Towards the end of the paved portion of Wild Road you can't miss the *"Exotic World"* gates on your right. Take the dirt driveway to the clearly marked parking area and honk three times. Say hi to Dixie for us.

HIGHLY RECOMMENDED:
Stop for lunch at *Emma Jean's Holland Burger*, 171431-2 National Trails Highway, just a few miles after you get off the freeway on the way to *Exotic World*. Emma Jean's is a near-dilapidated yet charming lunch counter-style diner with next to nothing hours. If you get there before 3:00 on weekdays they're sure to be open.

If the sight of a good junk heap whips you into a state of delirium, you won't be able to resist stopping at *Stubb's Auction/Antique Mall*, 19176 National Trails Highway—you'll pass it on the way to *Exotic World*.

ALTERNATE ROUTE BACK TO THE 15 FREEWAY NORTH:

Exotic World leave you with a craving for red meat? Try *The Cocky Bull*, a rib joint, bar and opry hall with an unbelievable western decor. A carnivore's delight. It's worth stopping just to see the covered wagon salad bar.

To *The Cocky Bull*: As you leave the *Exotic World* gates, turn left (Wild Road). Take Wild Road to Helendale Road and turn left. Stay on Helendale until you hit Shadow Mountain Road and turn right. Travel about nine miles to highway 395, and turn left. Stay on highway 395, and just when you think you're going entirely in the wrong direction, you'll see *The Cocky Bull* on your left. Keep traveling on the 395 to get to the 15 freeway south.

Exotic World
29053 Wild Road
Helendale
(619) 243-5261

OUT-AND-ABOUT

Let's Do Coke!

If you'd like to pay homage to Coca Cola, one of the few mega-companies to ever bother correcting one of its most cataclysmic blunders— namely, New Coke, which some will argue was a brilliant pre-planned PR move all along— you can go downtown and kowtow outside their incredibly cool L.A. headquarters, with its exterior fashioned in the style of an art-deco oceanliner, portholes, deckrails and all. Designed and built between 1936 and 1937 by architect Robert V. Derrah, this block-long edifice also boasts rounded corners and a faux bridge up atop.

Good thing the Coca Cola Co. ditched the New Coke idea, otherwise this place might have gone the way of another classic oceanliner, namely the S.S. Titanic.

The Coca-Cola Building
1334 South Central Avenue
Los Angeles

Reliving Reagan's Salad Days at the **Ronald Reagan Presidential Library**

Amazingly, there are still Americans who actually believe Ronald Reagan was some kind of hero, much less a great president. Granted, most of these twits are rich, selfish, cold-hearted bastards who obviously didn't lose their life savings in the Savings and Loan scandal or relied on the gutted HUD to help them put roofs over their heads. In Southern California, you'll find a concentration of such types in Orange County, but that still doesn't stop them from making the arduous freeway journey north to the Simi Valley to visit the **Ronald Reagan Presidential Library**. Hell, you can't miss it, since it's just off the Ronald Reagan Freeway (118), formerly known as the Simi Valley Freeway.

It's Ronny Doody Time!

Unfortunately, you won't find the most noteworthy moments of the Reagan administration at the museum. There's no audio clip of Ron saying, "We begin bombing in five minutes." There's no diorama of the invasion of Grenada or the kidnapping of Panamanian lackey Noriega. Nor is there a memorial plaque to all the millions upon millions of lost dollars looted by Ron's cronies from the coffers of HUD and a myriad of S&Ls—presumably while Ron was taking his afternoon nap. Instead, you'll find the pre-dictable chest-thumping propaganda, including the ludicrous intimation that Reagan singlehandedly brought down the damn commies and the Berlin Wall, too (there's a big chunk of it out in the garden just to prove the point). The truth is that Ron was simply lucky enough to be in office when the failed high school project called Soviet communism finally bit the big one. His claiming responsibility for the fall of the Soviet Union and its satellites is akin to Clinton taking credit for the Northridge earthquake. Wait—maybe Ron is responsible for that, too.

Frothing-at-the-mouth Limbaugh-lovers will undoubtedly revel in the act of rummaging through Reagan's glorious history, from chimp co-star to Commander-in-Chief, but for the rest of us, it's a pretty boring place to which one would only bring the kids as an act of punishment. Then again, if you've ever wondered what the Oval Office really looks like, you'll thrill to the full-scale replica from Ronnie's heyday. Nancy Reagan fans will delight in The First Lady's Gallery, packed with all sorts of fascinating facts and paraphernalia, while shopping hounds will take undue pleasure in perusing the plethora of gifts received by Ron and Nancy from Heads of State around the world. And to think that these are but a few of the exciting exhibits that await you at the *Ronald Reagan Presidential Library*!

The Ronald Reagan Presidential Library
40 Presidential Drive
Simi Valley
(805) 522-8444

But wait—there's more! The bronze bust of Ronny which sits just outside the front doors is almost as amusing as his entire eight-year tenure in the White House. Despite the untold cost of erecting this facility to one of our country's most dubious leaders, they certainly botched it when it came to making the damn bust look like Reagan. In fact, most of the visitors who stop and look at the statue share the same perplexed look of "Who the hell is that?" until it dawns on them that it is, in fact, the one and only Ronald Reagan. And who said Republicans weren't a clever lot?

A recent polling of museum patrons came up with the following answers to the question, "Who does this bust really look like?" *Howdy Doody*
The responses were nothing less than astounding: *Van Johnson*

Alfred E. Newman, the mascot of Mad Magazine

Most people, however, thought the bust looked like
Answer #1, Howdy Doody, who, coinicidentally,
was also a puppet.

Bonzo, the chimp
"That guy who sells used cars on TV."
"Marlo Thomas' father from That Girl."

Enjoying a bird's-eye view of the birds above *California City Skydiving School*

"Who needs wings to fly..."

-Theme from "The Flying Nun"

There's nothing quite as exhilarating as falling thousands of feet through empty space with nothing but a billowing nylon bag strapped to your back. If the antics of Peter Pan or The Flying Nun ever had you pining for a life of flight, then get out your datebook, flip to your next available opening, and write (in pen) *"Jump out of airplane at California City, 8:00 A.M."* It doesn't require someone of great courage or superior athletic ability to take a successful skydive. You must, however, be over 18 and under 225 pounds—but that's nothing a fake ID and a handful of Dulcolax can't take care of in a pinch.

Adrenaline 'R Us

As any seasoned skydiver will tell you, the experience is more life-altering than life-threatening, and like the worst-case scenario of just about any other form of reckless behavior, the odds of getting mangled in a grizzly car wreck on the 405 freeway are far greater. Any seasoned skydiver will also tell you that **California City Skydiving School** is one of the best in the state—and since it's only a couple hours out of Los Angeles, what's your excuse?

As you'll learn, the skydiving community is an odd lot, exhibiting all the eccentricities one might expect of a group who makes a hobby out of jumping from airplanes (not to be confused with the MTV mentality of a bungee jumper, the skydiver I.Q. is considerably higher). Male or female, they're a take-life-by-the-balls bunch and at times may come off as a bit abrasive. They also seem to have no trouble whatsoever rising at ungodly, one-digit hours of the morning; your day at **California City Skydiving School** begins early. During your training period you'll learn the dynamics of parachute flight and operation, the important difference between a "malfunction" and a "problem," practice your jumps and rolls, work with a simulator to master turning and landing, and run through emergency back-up procedure. Ultimately, even after you've completed your ground work and drilling, it's the jumpmaster who determines whether or not you're up-to-snuff. In that respect, it's kind of fun to pretend you're a Navy S.E.A.L. in training—just for a day.

For many, the ride up in the plane is the scariest part. Imagine leaving the runway in a Cessna 206 (a tin can), crouched on the floor just inches from a big gaping hole where the door used to be! After the jumpmaster gives you your count (*"1-2-3-SKYDIVE!!"*) and helps shove you out into the open air, you'll be astonished how—like a knee-jerk reaction—any long-abandoned religious investments snap right back into practice as you gaze up to your all-important parachute and mutter prayers that held no meaning for you ten minutes prior. Any fear is soon eclipsed by the flight down, an experience that tends to turn people one of two ways: forever hooked on the rush of skydiving, or forever worshipping the ground they walk on. Either way, there's absolutely nothing like it, and you won't feel short-changed. Touchdown—if you do as you were trained—can be executed as gracefully as a sparrow landing on the thin branch of a bottle brush tree. If you're an idiot and do it wrong, you can break an ankle—or worse.

California City Skydiving School offers three kinds of jumps, varying in degrees of terror. The Static Line jump ($169.00) is a popular one among first-timers and it's also the cheapest. After about five hours of training, you jump from a height of 3,500 feet (sometimes a little higher if the pilot's in a good mood), and your ripcord is automatically pulled for you by the static line hooked inside the plane. Though technically not a "freefall" jump, you do get the "freefall" sensation for a second or two before your chute completely opens.

The advantage of the Tandem jump ($199.00) is that you get to freefall for almost a full sixty seconds, and you're only required thirty minutes of ground instruction. The disadvantage is that you're strapped doggy-style to your jumpmaster (which may not be so bad depending on who your jumpmaster might be), so the experience isn't as personal. If you're a big chicken, this is the jump for you.

With the Freefall jump ($299.00) you're on your own, with very little help from the jumpmasters. They'll get you out of the plane, but that's about it. And after enduring seven tedious hours of training and drilling, you'll want them off your back anyway.

You can take as many repeat jumps as the day and your wallet will allow; the price drops with your second jump (Tandem exempt) and *California City* offers mid-week discounts. The skydiving experience isn't without a myriad of perks: you'll receive a photograph of yourself taken upon mid-air exit of the aircraft, with your face hideously contorted into a look of abject horror. You'll also get a personal logbook completed by your instructor charting the details of each jump, and you'll be presented with a much-deserved certificate of achievement. A video service is available too, but best of all, *you'll have a sensational reserve of cocktail chatter for months to come!*

Fear of heights? Get over it, sissy! A day at *California City Skydiving School* will change your life forever—one way or the other. The very worst that can happen is that you'll plummet a few thousand feet to your death—*but what a way to go!*

California City Skydiving School
5999 Curtiss Place
California City
(800) 2-JUMP-HI
(619) 373-4826

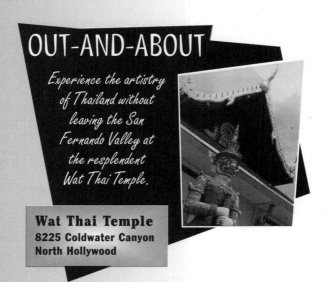

OUT-AND-ABOUT

Experience the artistry of Thailand without leaving the San Fernando Valley at the resplendent Wat Thai Temple.

Wat Thai Temple
8225 Coldwater Canyon
North Hollywood

Pondering the lost art of taxidermy at *The Roy Rogers and Dale Evans Museum*

he wood-paneled, western-style lobby decorated with several portraits of Roy and Dale (one in tooled leather) suggests that the museum consists of not much more than some glittery cowboy outfits, some fancy saddles and a few family photos. "This is Our Life" is routered into a shellacked wooden plaque hanging on the wall next to the entrance.

He Stuffed His Horse! Cute. Sweet.

So who'd have guessed that past the pecky-cedar entrance lies a taxidermied hyena, shrines to dead children and a three-dimensional portrait of Billy Graham?

Judging from the amount of crap they've acquired during their combined lifetimes, I'd venture to say that Roy Rogers and Dale Evans have never, *ever*, thrown anything away. Items that should have been trashed or donated to the Salvation Army decades ago have been fashioned into "collections" and placed on display under glass as though they were priceless treasures from the tomb of Tutankhamen. Apparently, the criteria for selecting the items on exhibit was considerably low. Anything that Dale didn't want cluttering up the closets at home seems to have been boxed up and sent here. A bunch of Roy's fishing lures were important enough to include, as was a lifetime's worth of Roy's watches scattered in a glass case along with a sign that simply reads, "A few of my wristwatches that have kept me on time for fifty years." Actually, the watch display sign was one of the more lengthy and informative explanations to be had in the museum.

In fact, there is virtually no visible explanation for *any* of the items in the museum, which makes for nothing much more than a meaningless parade of objects and images that somehow have something to do with the first couple of B-westerns. This notable absence of explication prompts many rudimentary questions from the observer. Who hung the 8 x 10 glossy of Christa McAuliffe in here? Why are those chunks of the Berlin wall mixed in with Roy's cuff links? To add further confusion to the already puzzling collection, instead of country western Muzak or some of Roy and Dale's signature tunes to accompany us during our leisurely tour, we were subjected to an interminable Barbra Streisand marathon. Every period of Miss Streisand's vexatious career was represented in this relentless, aural assault as we ogled collections of rifles and cowboy boots. We wondered if Barbra knew that Roy and Dale were using her dulcet voice to coax along the visitors to their museum. And if not, how much could she possibly sue them for?

The occasional surprises, like the creepy and tasteless shrines to three of Roy and Dale's children who died unfortunate, young deaths, are alone worth the price of admission. The shrines are arranged in separate glass cases—each one devoted to a different ill-fated Rogers' child. Case #1 contains the shrine to their adopted Korean daughter, In Ai Lee, whose name was changed to the cowgirlish "Deborah Lee," possibly to tie in with Roy and Dale's life long western theme. Poor Debbie Lee died at the age of twelve from Lord knows what because, again, there is no explanation provided. Many of Deborah's personal effects—troll doll, report card (never absent, never tardy) and slippers—are on view.

Box #2 belongs to Robin Elizabeth Rogers. Robin, a biological child, had an obvious physical problem judging from her photo, but zero explanation is given regarding her death at the age of two. Do we see a pattern developing here?

Just a few steps away you can experience the anguish and torment of John "Sandy" Rogers in shrine #3! Sandy, also adopted, who Dale describes as having "impossible chal-

lenges," died (no explanation given) at eighteen. The most haunting and disconcerting item of the museum is contained in Sandy's shrine: a childhood letter to his parents written from military school circa 1950s. Riddled with telltale misspellings, the letter is one boy's sad and desperate plea to enroll in a different school because he's constantly being beaten by his classmates. In labored cursive handwriting, he describes how he's continually kicked and hit, and how one boy even gave him a sprained wrist. He goes on to make his Christmas requests (a training rifle—the apple doesn't fall far from the tree) and again begs his parents to let him move elsewhere, closing with "Your Unhappy Son." The letter is truly pathetic and painful to read, especially with Barbra singing "People Who Need People" in the background.

Like every good mother, Dale took it upon herself to write books about each of these children and their untimely deaths. Deborah Lee's book, *Dearest Debbie*, Sandy's, *Salute to Sandy* and Robin Elizabeth's: *Angel Unaware* are all for sale in the museum gift shop. In addition to immortalizing her deceased children in hardcover, she has knocked out a veritable dime-store library of work. Are you a teen in trouble? *Cool It or Lose It: Dale Evans Rogers Raps with Youth* might be your life-saving answer. Dale speaks to the important issues facing women in her bra-burning tome *WOMAN (Be All You Can Be)* and gets a lot of mileage out of Jesus with several books about Christmas, finding "The Way" and prayer. Over twenty titles in all and every one is under glass in first edition. Who knew that Dale was a women of letters? Unfortunately most are out of print. Sorry. You'll have to comb the used bookshops to find yourself a copy of *Dale Evans Rogers: Trials, Tears and Triumph.*

Just as Barbra began wailing "On A Clear Day," we came across a completely appalling, very politically incorrect "trophy" display of over nearly ONE HUNDRED varieties of mammals, fish and reptiles that Roy himself personally killed. Among the more note-worthy works of taxidermy are the three wall-mounted baboons contorted into "hear no evil, see no evil, speak no evil" poses. Also on view are "safari photos" of Roy beaming proudly next to freshly killed, now-endangered, African wildlife.

And yes, it's true, there's Trigger. Dead Trigger. Stuffed Trigger. The horse that Roy worked into the ground with nearly 200 films is flawlessly preserved behind a plate-glass window, standing in a frozen rear as if to say, "Get me the hell out of here and give me a proper burial!" On either side of Trigger, grouped in a western diorama, are the nicely maintained carcasses of Dale's horse Buttermilk and Roy's german shepherd co-star, Bullet. Trigger Jr., too, is on display. The lesser-known of the Triggers stands separately, alone, in front of a six-foot crucifix made of rusted, welded-together horseshoes. With Roy's obvious affinity for preser-vation, I was a bit surprised that the Rogers' late children weren't also stuffed, adorned in rhinestone cowboy outfits, and attractively perched sidesaddle atop each of the celebrity equines.

There are large collections of Jesus and Republican memorabilia, including photos of both Roy and Dale shaking hands with the Reagans. There's also an entire glass case devoted to Roy's Masonic Temple junk, verifying our distrust with years and years worth of membership cards. Hundreds of photos documenting nearly every moment of their careers line the wood-shingled halls, in addition to a myriad of embarrassing family photos with cute 'n corny captions.

BULLET

The noxious Barbrathon followed us outside into the deadening Victorville heat to the museum's courtyard which features yet another taxidermy diorama—this time an Arctic theme with a snarling polar bear and a man-eating penguin. There's also an installation in honor of the famous Mr. Art Rush—their manager since 1964. Photos of Mr. Rush's other illustrious clients hang on the wall, like Lionel Cartwright, Ann Kaestner and the Liberace protege "Little Scotty Plummer."

As expected, the museum does house an extraordinary collection of western artifacts and Roy Rogers and Dale Evans memorabilia dating from the 1940s and 50s. Take a few moments to savor the beauty of American culture with the Rogers' customized Bonneville convertible. Unduly detailed with bullets, miniature horseheads, rifles and six-shooters, the car also features tooled leather upholstery, a dashboard set with silver coins, a silver saddle console and the perfunctory steer's horn hood ornamentation. Just don't ask about the gas mileage.

The gift shop, the best part of any museum, is filled with an overwhelming stock of every Roy and Dale item imaginable, most of which are surprisingly classic. Bring a wad of cash; this Gracelandish collection of souvenirs will solve your birthday, Christmas and wedding gift dilemmas for years to come.

You'll lose and gain respect for Roy and Dale several times throughout your viewing of this peculiar collection, finally losing it again as you leave with bags full of souvenirs. And as you drive off into the dusty desert sunset, you can almost hear these two right-wing taxidermy fetishists singing an eerie "Happy Trails"—with Barbra providing backing vocals.

—MM

The Roy Rogers and Dale Evans Museum
15650 Seneca Road
Victorville
(619) 243-4547

FROM LOS ANGELES:
Take the 10 freeway east to the 15 freeway north. Exit on Roy Rogers Drive and turn left. You'll see the museum from the freeway before you exit. Can't miss it. The drive should take about an hour and a half. Remember: Speed kills.

Losing our tan lines and scouting for genitals at the

Nude Beach

The most wonderful thing about nude beaches—aside from lots of naked people—is that they incite repugnance from the very same beachgoers who make a place like Santa Monica or Malibu so completely unbearable. The result is a fortuitous screening process that effectively elimi- nates the conflux of sun-seeking cretins overpopulating so many of Southern California's sandy shores, so that in addition to a lack of swimsuits, you'll find your nude beach expe- rience also pleasingly absent of the following:

There's nothing quite as exhilarating as splashing through a cool surf with wet sand beneath your feet, an ocean breeze gently moving over your body, and nothing but a little SPF 50 between you and the warmth of the sun on your skin. Contrary to popular misconception, it's this simple pleasure, this let-it-all-hang-out-groovin'-to-the-waves-at-one-with-Mother-Earth- peace-loving-live-and-let-live-nature-buzz that most are seeking at a nude beach. Can you dig? Whereas the scene at Manhattan Beach, Playa Del Rey or Malibu is all about showcasing your washboard abs, new breast implants or designer swimwear, at a nude beach—and one might not guess this to be true—when the swimsuits come off, virtually no one looks good. People basi- cally just look like people. There's something pleasantly equalizing about being naked in the bright daylight.

But make no mistake, nude beaches are not without their sexual under- current. Even so, nude beach protocol should be observed. The vibe is one of common respect—everyone's there to enjoy the beach without a swimsuit, and no one wants to be bothered because of it. But in all honesty, it's fun to look at naked people, though it's very uncool to stare. As we're sure many of the folks who frequent nude beaches are shameless exhibitionists who may even encourage gawkers, most are not—so if you must stare, at least do it surrep- titiously or wear sunglasses with reflective lenses so no one will be able to tell. If you're going to engage in sex, which is not altogether inappropriate at a nude beach depending on the circumstances, be discreet—unless of course it's all about being watched, in which case be conscientious. You wouldn't want a little seaside blowjob to land you in the slammer just because a small child was hunting for sand dollars in the wrong place at the wrong time. And if you're going to drop acid or pass a big fat joint—certainly not an uncom- mon pastime among Southern California nude beaches—use some tact.

–**Children, except for the children of nudist hippie parents, who are not really like children at all**

–**Beer-guzzling yahoos/ frat boys/bikers**

–**Virtually all tourists, except naked Europeans, which are OK**

–**Gang members**

–**Anyone with a portable CD player**

–**Rollerbladers**

–**Street performers, especially breakdancers**

–**Skateboarders**

–**Cyclists**

–**Unicyclists**

Is That A Tube Of Suntan Lotion In Your Pocket Or Are You Just Plain Naked?

ATTENTION

BEYOND THIS SIGN YOU MAY ENCOUNTER NUDE SUNBATHERS

Don't bring a boom box! The sound of the ocean is just fine thank you. A camera can freak people out—and is better left at home with your swimsuit. And men: just because a girl happens to be naked it doesn't necessarily mean she's more likely to have sex with you. Don't be a letch.

And don't *ever*, under any circumstances, for any reason—*even if you have permission from God himself*—never, *never* leave any piece—no matter how small or biodegradable—of TRASH ON THE BEACH. There are few sights more vile than seeing a healthy tide pool sustaining a myriad of starfish and sea anemones thoughtlessly strewn with an empty bag of Cheetos—or a shoreline dotted with plastic forks and empty Styrofoam containers that once held mayonnaise-heavy potato salad. If the packaging containing a twelve-pack of Budweiser or a prefab picnic lunch wasn't too heavy to carry *in* full, it's certainly isn't too heavy to carry *out* empty! There's always a garbage can within walking distance, and even if there isn't you should have a bag with you. Clean up after yourself. Furthermore, pick up any nearby garbage you see that isn't yours too. If you don't clean up your trash, no one will. In spite of Beverly Hills folklore, Bette Midler doesn't come out in the middle of the night and clean up all the garbage that you were too fucking lazy to pick up yourself. The tide simply comes in and washes most of that trash out to sea, which is not a workable alternative.

Keep in mind that while all these beaches have played host to public nudity for decades, remarkably enough not a single one of them is legally zoned as "clothing optional." The chances that you'd actually be arrested are next to nil, but take heed nonetheless.

Gaviota Beach, Gaviota

This is a scenic and very secluded beach with clear, swim-friendly waters. The shore stretches on forever, and you can experience that surreal feeling of walking hundreds of yards along the shoreline stark naked without ever passing another human. There are only a couple dozen people here at any one time—a varied and unassuming bunch—and because the location is somewhat remote, those that make the trip are looking for a peaceful and quiet escape. It's not unusual to spot a school of dolphin jumping along near the shoreline, or giant starfish holding tightly to the rocky points of the beach. The perfect place to groove away a sunny day—and evening sunset.

TO GAVIOTA FROM LOS ANGELES:

This beach is a godsend; not only is it gorgeous—and dotted with naked people—it's easy to locate. Take the 101 freeway north past Santa Barbara. About 30 miles north of Santa Barbara you'll take the Mariposa Riena exit. Make a U-turn back onto the freeway going south and drive a half-mile to a dirt parking area just to the side of the road on your right—look for railroad crossing lights as a landmark. There are a cluster of blue garbage cans left of the wide and well-worn trail down to the beach. The trail provides an easy and beautiful walk to the water, but portions of it are lined with poison oak, so wait till you reach the sand before you get naked!

More Mesa Beach, Goleta

This beach is one of the most active, and in many ways, the most fun. It attracts a wide cross section of people, mostly from the Santa Barbara area. Septuagenarian health-food nudists, "alternative" looking college kids, hetero and gay couples, hippie families, and those oiled up and questing for a George-Hamilton-on-a-rotisserie terminal tan. A naked boheme under an umbrella does a little songwriting on an acoustic guitar, an older couple walks their dogs along the shore, a group of kids work on a sandcastle, a gay contingent has a picnic lunch: if you like people-watching in a shopping mall, you'll have an absolute ball scanning the crowd here. At More Mesa the beach activities that would normally be really annoying—like frisbee tossing and volleyball—somehow seem perfectly acceptable when performed naked. The vibe is friendly and the people are cute. It's one of the very few nude beaches where light-handed, innocent flirtation doesn't come off as sleazy. You'll spot an occasional swimsuit here, but those wearing them are embarrassingly conspicuous, and stay outnumbered by about 20 to 1.

There's another portion of the beach beyond the rocky point at the end of the shore farthest from the entry mark, for those in search of a more private stretch of shoreline.

TO MORE MESA FROM LOS ANGELES:

It's a bit of a schlepp, but well worth it. Take the 101 freeway north just beyond Santa Barbara. Exit on Turnpike Road and turn left. Take Turnpike to Hollister Ave. and turn left. Take Hollister to Puente Drive and turn right. Take Puente to Vieja Drive and turn right. Start looking for Mockingbird Lane: you're going to park on Veija, as close to the intersection of Mockingbird as you can get (parking is prohibited on Mockingbird Lane.) After you park, walk all the way down Mockingbird; it will end at a dirt trail. Take that trail (it's an easy walk, but not a short one) to a steep, seemingly endless log stairway down to the beach.

Summerland Beach, Summerland

Things generally stay pretty quiet here even on weekends. Though popularly known as "the gay beach," it attracts all types. There's a lengthy stretch of shoreline and the water is swim-friendly, but you see oil rigs on the horizon line which is kind of a bummer. All the naked action takes place on the other side of the rocky point that has been reinforced with steel (to prevent landslides), and which is easily passed through. It's a perfectly decent nude beach conveniently close to Los Angeles, but not especially noteworthy for any particular reason.

TO SUMMERLAND FROM LOS ANGELES:

Take the 101 freeway north about five miles beyond Carpinteria. Take the Summerland exit and turn left. When you reach Evans Ave., turn left again and pass under the freeway. Once you're on the other side of the freeway, make the first and only left you can onto Wallace Ave. Take Wallace Ave. to Finney Street and turn right—watch closely for Finney, it's almost nonexistent. There's ample parking on Wallace, as well as a lot just off Finney, and it's all very obvious where to go. There's a paved pathway off the parking lot that leads down to the water. Once your down to the sand, go left towards the rocky point, past which lies unadulterated nakedness.

Rincon Beach, Carpinteria

This beach is smack dab in the center of a county park, complete with picnic areas and public restrooms. The beach rambles on for about a mile, and as with most nude beaches, the farther out you walk to the most remote end of the beach, the more naked people you'll find frolicking in the surf. The farthest end of this beach also happens to be the most beautiful—an excellent spot to get lost in a mental tide pool—and though long portions of the shoreline can get a little rocky, there are sections private enough so that just about anything goes. This is also a great beach to take a long, naked walk along the shoreline while dripping with seawater. The section of the beach closest to the picnic area can be iffy when it comes to nudity, so do as the natives do—or walk further down the shore. This beach is a favorite spot for surfers too, except they wear wetsuits.

TO RINCON FROM LOS ANGELES:

Take the 101 freeway north in Carpinteria. Take the Bates Road exit and turn left. Bates will lead you straight down to the parking area. Bear right into the lot marked Rincon Park. You'll find a pathway down to the water just to the edge of the picnic area.

Point Dume, Malibu

Though miniscule, the nude beach at Point Dume does have an advantage being that it's so nearby. Sometimes this beach is a total skin-show, sometimes 50/50, sometimes not at all. Generally, during the week is a pretty safe time to get naked, but weekends can be hit and miss—always have a swimsuit nearby just in case the coast guard gives you any trouble. This beach is also a favorite for amateur porn photographers and often serves as a location for many adult video box-cover shoots as well. Get there early and you might get an eyeful!

TO POINT DUME FROM LOS ANGELES:

Take Pacific Coast Highway North into Malibu. Turn left onto Westward Beach Road and follow it all the way down to the end of the parking lot (they gouge you with the parking rates). Walk to the southernmost end of the beach to the rocky edge. Follow the path through the rocks to the other side of the beach (it can be difficult to carry anything larger than a backpack over these rocks).

Abalone Cove, Palos Verdes

Though the shores can get a little rocky, there are several hundred yards of smooth, sandy beaches, and the water is clear. The crowd here is fairly mixed, with the distant, more secluded areas of the beaches frequented mostly by gay men. Though this is a popular beach, it's never too crowded and stays very low-key. The big plus of Abalone Cove are the tide pools located towards the tips of the rocky points. These tide pools are teeming with sea life: Starfish, sea urchins, anemones, small fish and crabs can all be closely observed and even carefully touched—*all while completely nude!* It sure as hell beats a trip to Sea World. There are actually two beaches at Abalone Cove, and although there really is no single trail that leads to either of them, they're pretty hard to miss. Hiking the trails can be a pretty wild experience too.

TO ABALONE COVE FROM LOS ANGELES:

Take Pacific Coast Highway (1) South to Palos Verdes Blvd. and turn right. Take Palos Verdes Blvd. to Palos Verdes Drive West and bear to the right. Palos Verdes Drive West will turn into Palos Verdes Drive South. Watch for *The Wayfarer's Chapel* on your left. Parking is a pain in the ass. You can pay to park in the Abalone Cove lot just north of *Wafarer's*, but you can't enter this lot after 4:00 P.M. Many people park in the lot of *The Wayfarer's Chapel* even though it's clearly marked "NO BEACH PARKING," but do this at your own risk; you can be cited. These beaches can be a bit tricky to locate if you've never been before. Using *The Wayfarer's Chapel* as a landmark, walk south on the opposite edge of Palos Verdes Drive South until you reach a gated road with signs reading "ABALONE COVE TIDE POOLS" and "NO NUDE SUNBATHING" (a dead giveaway). Take that black gravel road and watch for a worn path darting off to the left side just as you begin to approach the fencing on the edge of the cliff. Take that rather steep (but bearable) trail down to the sand.

Farther beyond the Abalone Cove gate, there's another trail that leads to the other beach. This trail is well worn into the roadside brush just on the oceanside edge of Palos Verdes Drive South. A good marker is the intersection of Peppertree Drive across the street. About 100 feet south of that cross street you'll find the trail.

How a seemingly harmless tourist lure unfolds into a living
nightmare at a *Live Television Taping*

Live television tapings are like the cole slaw on the greasy plate of Los Angeles tourism. Though virtually devoid of nutritional value, it's still a portion of the tourist meal that should at least be poked at just to see what it tastes like.

I Was Held Prisoner In A Soundstage!

The poor unsuspecting out-of-towner is baited with free tickets handed out by the thousands at the most populated tourist traps (*Mann's Chinese Theater, Universal Studios*, et al.), and snared with the promise of seeing their TV favorites live and up-close. But as life's lessons often show us, nothing is without a price in this world, and an audience member pays *dearly* for the opportunity to witness stellar talent like Leeza, David Schwimmer, Jackeé, or Dustin "Screech" Diamond at work. Baking in direct sunlight while lined up for hours outside a studio, like cattle being sent to slaughter, audience enthusiasm begins to wane and the real experience officially commences. Unbeknownst to them, they're about to become just another poorly treated, disposable commodity of Hollywood.

After being chilled to the bone by the sub-arctic temperatures of an overly air-conditioned television studio, the audience's joy-ride takes the first in a series of particularly ugly turns with the obligatory appearance of the so-called warm-up comic. Not to be confused with a *stand-up* comic, the warm-up comic serves not necessarily to *entertain* but only to keep the crowd from falling asleep or walking out during the several hours worth of down time. The warm-up comic's full-volume, endless onslaught of well-worn jokes and mediocre celebrity impressions (apparently it's a law that if you're a warm-up comic you *must* do celebrity impressions no matter how lacking your ability) are curtailed only by *lots* of audience interaction. Apparently feeling limited by the small stage of a real comedy club, a warm-up comic finds it necessary to roam freely throughout the audience, to touch you, pull at you, or make fun of the way you dress—all in good humor of course. How might this wear on one's nerves after, say, three-and-a-half hours? Imagine being placed inside a 40-gallon aluminum garbage can with the lid placed securely on top. Then imagine the exterior of the can being slammed with baseball bats while you count from 1 to 5000. There you have it.

Understandably, an audience would make the assumption that they are there to be entertained—to *watch* a show. After all, that's what an audience does, right? Well...wrong. An assistant director will be quick to repeatedly shout "MORE ENERGY!!" towards the bleachers, reminding the audience that they too have a job to do—though they won't receive the inordinate sums of money that the on-screen "talent" gets. Make no mistake, you too are acting: you're *playing* an audience member. So hours after you've lost interest, you and hundreds of other restless and disgruntled audience members are still held hostage in a dark, algid studio and are yet required to laugh *uproariously*, take after take, at punch lines that weren't funny when they were written, delivered by actors who are being paid several thousand dollars per episode and still can't get it right. Heck, if only monkeys could talk, imagine the money Hollywood could save!

During the fraction of time spent actually taping the show, much of what the audience is there to see in the first place is blocked from view by cameras and boom mics. Instead of seeing a live taping, the audience is reduced to watching the proceedings as transmitted from color monitors mounted above the stage. In essence, the poor fools are forced to *watch television in a live television studio!* After the longest afternoon of their lives, tourists once wide-eyed and hopeful are released from the soundstage back out into the daylight as jaded, bitter, and hard-boiled as Joey Heatherton.

Now, *that's entertainment!*

For show information, tickets, and reservations, call:

Paramount Studios
(213) 956-1777
Audiences Unlimited
(818) 506-0043

chapter seven

Kulture Schlock

When Is a Culture Not a Culture?

*Is "L.A. Culture" an oxymoron? Probably.
Yet while most Americans may consider the words "L.A." and
"culture" to be mutually exclusive, we Angelenos take a
certain perverse pride in those enlightening facets of our
city that make it so...unique.*

*Think about it:
We have bubbling tar pits and Tori Spelling. Cal Worthington and
Wolfgang Puck. Sci-fi religions and self-aggrandizing museums.
Pastoral slaughterhouse murals and hyperactive graffiti artists.
Phallic religious statues and see-thru cathedrals. Orange County
neo-Nazis and West Hollywood ultra-liberals. Gay Pride Parades
and a homophobic beanery in the heart of the gay community
whose motto once read, "No Fags Allowed."*

*New Yorkers love to turn up their noses at "uncultured" L.A.,
probably because they've had a lot of practice turning up their
noses at the stench of garbage strikes and urine-scented subway
stations. But when it comes to nonsensical, non-sequitor
contradictions in culture, L.A. has the Big Apple beat by a mile.
So what if we don't have a bustling theatre district like New York's
Broadway? We have "Cats," which is all you really need, isn't it?
Plus, L.A. boasts more multi-theater movie complexes with
postage-stamp-sized screens than all the bad off-Broadway plays
from the past ten years combined. And what's so great about
New York's Metropolitan Museum? Sure, it may have a bunch of
dusty old mummies, but can you find Madonna's corset there?
No—because it's at the Fredrick's of Hollywood
Lingerie Museum in Hollywood.*

*Central Park?
Hey, you can get mugged or drugged just as easily at MacArthur
Park—which has a bitchin' Richard Harris/Donna Summer song
named after it, to boot. Gridlock? We got it. Pollution? Please,
we invented it! The Statue of Liberty? The French gave it to us,
so there must be something wrong with it. On the other hand,
the Rocky and Bullwinkle statue just across from the Chateau
Marmont wasn't given to us by a country that hates our guts,
and it's a lot more fun to look at, anyway. Okay, so maybe we
don't have an underground transportation system so stressful
that it causes its passengers to go on shooting sprees every
once in a while, but give us time—we're building one.*

*In the interim, we have enough traffic jams and shitty
drivers to account for a preponderance of freeway shootings and
windshield smashings. And while the L.A. Times isn't half as
snooty as its New York counterpart, nor a fraction as sleazy
as the Post (which is almost like getting the Weekly World News
on a daily basis), we hope that this particular chapter
will make up up for that latter noteworthy discrepancy....*

Taking in the Mural Art at *The Farmer John Slaughterhouse*

The World's Happiest Abattoir!

Dodger baseball fans are well familiar with the folks at **Farmer John's Meats**, who have been supplying the world-famous proprietary "Dodger Dogs" to the stadium since 1964. That was the year when *Farmer John's* biggest advertising vehicle, the local TV show "Polka Parade," went national and was forced to lose all local advertisers. By chance, the Dodgers were looking for sponsors for their new TV and radio telecasts, and as fate would have it, a legendary union was born. Since then, anyone tuning into a game has heard the announcers sings the praises of the "superior Eastern-bred, corn-fed pork that is *Farmer John's Meats*."

Located in the decidedly dismal industrial area of Vernon, *Farmer John's* is but one of two remaining slaughterhouses in a region that once thrived with businesses that turned mammals into meat. During the 70s, most of the competition closed down or moved to the rural Midwest in order to mitigate shipping costs for both the animals and the grain on which they fed. But not *Farmer John's:* They narrowed their lucrative beef, lamb, and pork processing empire to accommodate hogs alone, and in doing so, eventually built a $325 million-a-year pork industry that proudly stands as the biggest west of Oklahoma—and L.A.'s best-selling brand.

Not that there actually is a *Farmer John*, of course. The fictitious agrarian was created when the owners, the Clougherty (Klow-er-tee) family, correctly realized that no one would get their name right, and decided to create the congenial namesake—in his trademark overalls and straw cowboy hat—to represent the company. That was back in 1953. Four years later, in 1957, work began on what I consider to be the company's crowning achievement (next to the ubiquitous Dodger Dog, of course): I'm talking about the gloriously underrated and virtually unknown *Famer John's* murals.

I first came upon these immense, idyllic paintings on the exterior walls of the factory when I took a wrong freeway exit one foggy Sunday morning in 1980. My head was pounding from a rather nasty hangover and I was cursing my bad luck when suddenly they appeared out of the mist like a hallucinogenic vision. Here was a continuous, wraparound work of art that depicted a bustling, bucolic scenario that covered every inch of *Farmer John's* outside wall, sometimes as high and wide as a Cinerama screen. Originally painted by Hollywood movie scene artist Les Grimes, and later augmented by Arno Jordan, the murals were meant to appear three-dimensional when viewed from a passing car, and indeed, they were striking even in the early morning fog.

These grand vistas depict the peaceful pastoral existence of pigs who seem nowhere near slaughter, and if they are, they certainly don't seem stressed about it. Add to this the images of children playing on the grass of the green, rolling hills, and it seems almost like something you'd see painted on the walls of a kindergarten or petting zoo. Indeed, the happy walls give no indication of the less-than-pretty business going on just within their confines, much as if our penal institutions were to decorate their outer walls with scenes of men gleefully going about the process of rehabilitation: reading books, lifting weights, and otherwise walking a path of righteousness—instead of dealing drugs, carving shivs from soap bars, and being gang-raped by hulking brutes with racist tattoos on their bellies.

The murals at *Famer John* are the company's way of putting a positive spin on the 10-acre death factory and its plentiful yet delicious output. And you know something? It works. No matter how pristine and computerized a slaughterhouse may be, the process of turning live pigs into crates of wieners, breakfast sausages, and holiday hams is not exactly what one would call pleasant...unless one happens to be Jeffrey Dahmer, of course. But it's amazing how a huge, jolly mural of life on the farm can make all that blood and guts seem somehow palatable. Rarely do art and industry collide in such an ironically effective fashion, so take the time to make some ham sandwiches, grab the kids and head down to Vernon to take in *Farmer John's* gigantic paintings. You may never look at slaughterhouses the same way again.

—ARL

DID YOU KNOW?

The Federal Humane Slaughter Act of 1958 requires that animals be electrically stunned prior to slaughter so that they will feel no pain?

Farmer John's
3049 East Vernon
Vernon
(213) 583-4621

Slumming at *Wigwam Village Motel*

n 1955, the marquee in front of **Wigwam Village**—one of the campier motor hotels designed for those traveling down route 66—read "Sleep in a Wigwam, Get More for Your Wampum." These days 66 is a road far less traveled, and as we approach the next millennium, the slightly more desperate "Do it in A Tee Pee" is the catchy phrase employed to attract potential guests. A sign of the times.

The clientele to which *Wigwam Village* originally catered are now long gone. You won't see any apple-cheeked American families on summer vacations frolicking among the rambling green lawns that encompass the motel's eighteen gigantic stucco teepee units. Nor will you hear them echoing Marco Polo or splashing with a gaily colored beachball in the kidney shaped swimming pool. Whoever used to care for the landscape must have been scalped around the same time that the 10 freeway offered an alternative, high-speed route through Rialto; the grounds—once grassy green—are now as dried out and crunchy as Loni Anderson's coiffure. Baking at 100+ degrees in the summer months, the arid overgrown groundcover seems to be at great risk of spontaneous combustion. The tee-pees look inhabitable at a distance, but upon closer examination bear squarish patches of mismatched paint slapped over mysterious graffiti. Bars secure the tiny windows, and *squalid* is about the most delineative term one could use with respect to the accommodations themselves. The pool now sits absent of its cooling, over-chlorinated water, which was either drained or simply evaporated over years of neglect and the hole now serves mostly as a dead leaf catch-all for San Bernardino County. But what do you want for $35 bucks a night, the *Ahwahnee Hotel*?

Indian Squaw-Lor: No Reservation Required

We'd never advise anyone in their right mind to actually stay a night at *Wigwam Village*, but if you do find yourself whiling away the day in Rialto be sure not to miss this nonpareil slice of route 66, mid-century Americana. They don't make 'em like this any-more—
thank god.

Wigwam Village Motel

2728 Foothill Blvd.

(route 66)

Rialto

OUT-AND-ABOUT

The snow never melts in Anaheim.

Alpine Motel
715 West Katella
Anaheim

Time-traveling with the *Los Angeles Conservancy Walking Tours*

Most Angelenos recoil in horror at the prospect of a visit to downtown Los Angeles—and who can blame them? In spite of all the revitalization projects and earnest attempts to bring new commerce downtown, what was once the bustling nerve center of our city is now—and will forever be—a crumbling, putrefied, God-forsaken wasteland, and everyone knows it.

Because of downtown L.A.'s somewhat besmirched reputation, a surprising few ever take the time to explore eastward beyond the iron curtain of Vermont Ave. It's a damn shame too, because downtown holds some of Los Angeles' richest history, especially when it comes to our single most noteworthy export: movies.

The stretch of Broadway Street between 9th and 3rd is the largest historic theater district in the world, and since 1979 has been listed on the National Register of Historic Places. Beginning with the nickelodeons and vaudeville houses of the early 1900s, Sid Grauman helped to establish Broadway as the city's theater center when he built the first of his hyper-sumptuous movie palaces here, *The Million Dollar Theater*, in 1918. By the early 30s there were a dozen major theaters operating on Broadway, but the burgeoning theater district began to lose speed after Grauman opened the *Chinese Theater* on Hollywood Blvd. in 1927, moving the focus considerably west, thus putting the first nail in the coffin of downtown Los Angeles and its theater district.

Amazingly, many of the original downtown movie palaces—the same theaters originally built as vaudeville houses and later converted for films—are still open to this day showing first-run movies, albeit with Spanish subtitles. Some are closed, and their futures murky.

The *Los Angeles Conservancy* is an organization dedicated to the preservation of what little architectural history Los Angeles has left. Though not commonly known, the Conservancy offers an unequalled opportunity to experience the wealth of historic structures in downtown Los Angeles with their series of Saturday morning walking tours.

A Gaping Glory Hole, The Stench Of Urine, And Miss Mary Pickford!

Without question, the Conservancy tours are the only good reason to wake up early on the weekend. All the L.A. Conservancy docents ensure an informative and enlightening look at the all-but-forgotten armpit of our City of Angels, covering the very best of downtown design with a program of eleven different tours including *The Biltmore Hotel, City Hall, Little Tokyo, Marble Masterpieces, Art Deco* and *Union Station*. By far their most popular tour—often booked months in advance—is the tour of the remaining Broadway theaters.

Trekking through the dense and chaotic street scene of downtown Los Angeles on a Saturday is an experience unto itself. The noise level alone is enough to make a reasonably sane person tear off all their clothes and run screaming down the middle of Broadway; the oppressive din from the abundance of audio-video stores and mega-arcades is matched only by the barkers in front of jewelry shops and the pushy street vendors peddling everything from Selina T-shirts and electroplated gold chains, to live turtles and home-grown produce. On virtually every street corner is stationed a toothless wheelchair-bound religious zealot screaming passages from the Bible, as well as non-religious zealots who stand on the street corners screaming simply because they just have a lot to say to the world. A multitude of languages are spoken here, and fortunately English isn't one of them; that the cacophony of Broadway is indistinguishable is its only saving grace.

The experience of the Conservancy tour is much like that of an urban archaeological dig. Among the crumbling and neglected ruins of downtown Broadway is scattered some of the most awe-inspiring theater architecture Los Angeles has to offer. Like the Pyramids of Giza, the austere facades of the Broadway theaters belie the grandeur and opulence of their mammoth interiors. To pass through the portals of these breath-taking movie palaces is to step into another time—a time that predates shopping mall cineplexes by almost 100 years.

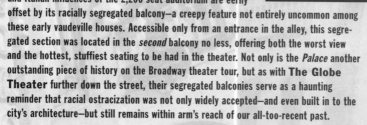

Harry Houdini and Sarah Bernhardt were among those who took the stage at **The Palace Theater**, built in 1911 as a showcase for the Orpheum vaudeville circuit. The *Palace* is the oldest of the remaining Broadway theaters, and is one of several that originally featured live entertainment, later being converted to screen silent films, then eventually talkies. Remarkably, *The Palace* is still in operation. The stately French and Italian influences of the 2,200 seat auditorium are eerily offset by its racially segregated balcony—a creepy feature not entirely uncommon among these early vaudeville houses. Accessible only from an entrance in the alley, this segregated section was located in the *second* balcony no less, offering both the worst view and the hottest, stuffiest seating to be had in the theater. Not only is the *Palace* another outstanding piece of history on the Broadway theater tour, but as with **The Globe Theater** further down the street, their segregated balconies serve as a haunting reminder that racial ostracization was not only widely accepted—and even built in to the city's architecture—but still remains within arm's reach of our all-too-recent past.

Only three of the twelve theaters on Broadway remain open to the public. Some theaters have closed down altogether, while some have taken on bizarre—often pathetic—metamorphosis. *The Globe Theater* is possibly the most dramatic example of the juxtaposition between the charming downtown Los Angeles of yesteryear and the depraved shantytown it has become. The Morosco, as it was formerly known, opened in 1913 with the play *The Fortune Hunter* and remained a successful theatrical venue until the depression, when it was converted to a movie theater and renamed *The Globe*. Although it continued to run movies through the 1980s, it soon after transmutated into a swap meet. It's been augmented almost beyond recognition although the exterior still bears the old *Globe* marquee (behind which is the original Morosco sign). The raked theater floor has been leveled out with concrete and the interior of what was formerly the lobby now houses a cramped network of makeshift booths hawking the same wares found in Tijuana. At eye level, piles of cheap underwear, baseball caps and Mexican leather goods fill your field of vision and all elements of the theater architecture are conspic-uously absent. Until you look up. Above the mess of cut-rate vendibles, the gaping remains of the theater stretch four stories overhead, unacknowledged. Gold gilded box seats are positioned on each side of the proscenium arch, behind which hangs the original hand-painted asbestos curtain. The empty balcony reaches to the high corners of the ceiling, with the segregated portion still visible. In the far rear of the building, you can see what once was backstage, stacked with three stories of small dressing rooms now like a mini-vaudevillian ghost town: one of the many mind-boggling moments on your jaunt down Broadway.

Regardless of their specific architectural influences, a design theme of undue, fantasy-scale opulence prevailed. These palaces served only one purpose: to provide a place for people to completely lose touch with reality. **The State Theater** combines Medieval, Spanish, Moorish and Greek elements, with a large gold Buddha sitting atop the proscenium arch. Both live acts and film were offered here when it opened in 1921. This was one of the early venues for Judy Garland—while she was still Frances Gumm—long before she would become immortalized by hundreds of thousands of female imperson-ators. If the crinkling of candy wrappers or the smacking of popcorn during a movie drives you into a homicidal rage, you have the *State* to blame: it was the first theater to feature a snack concession, originally offered only for the kiddie matinees. It's still open as a movie theater today, showing first-run films subtitled in Spanish. The auditorium smells like urine, despite the fact that restrooms are available.

The **Orpheum Theater** is one of Broadway's most spectaclular, and features the only operating pipe organ left among the downtown theaters. *The Los Angeles Theater Organ Society* still plays the earth-shaking, orchestral monster between films on weekends. This theater was designed after a Parisian opera house; heavy brocade drapery, tri-level box seats, and gargantuan chandeliers complete the auditorium. Downstairs beneath the lobby, a spacious dark-wood paneled lounge was available for adults to socialize. In its glory years, the *Orpheum* was home to The Marx Bros., Gypsy Rose Lee, Sally Rand, Eddie Cantor, and Sophie Tucker, among other vaudeville notables. Now *The Orpheum* is home to whatever transient sets up camp inside the tiled portico. It's a popular film location, having appeared in everything from *Hart to Hart* to *Ed Wood*. What your tour guide may gloss over—but has historical significance nontheless—are the glory holes bored through the solid marble walls of the men's bathroom stalls. Some have since been covered with steel plates or filled with concrete, but one can't help but imagine a horny Groucho running down for a quick blow before the 8:00 show.

The imposing, almost Gaudi-like Gothic/Spanish cathedral-style design of the **United Artists Theater** is markedly unlike the others on Broadway—and its cathedral design was not entirely without purpose. Mary Pickford and Douglas Fairbanks built the theater in 1927 with the intention of creating a veritable shrine to the motion picture

as well as a showcase for their new venture, *United Artists*. Rudolph Valentino, John Barrymore, Norma Talmadge, Errol Flynn and other movie actors from the period are featured in the elaborate murals on the walls inside the theater near the balcony. Crowning the auditorium high above, a dome lined with hanging crystals originally became animated when the theater was air-cooled, and the interior of the dome itself changes color depending on your vantage point—so who needs a movie? Like *The State*, *The United Artists Theater* transmogrified into something other than what was originally intended. Certainly Mr. and Mrs. Fairbanks would have become apoplectic upon learning that just a few decades after its glamorous star-studded opening, their house of film-worship would be running porno flicks, and soon after would serve as a panaderia that made use of the theater's large auditorium and lobby as the exhaust duct for its large ovens, eventually covering the ornate mirrored and frescoed walls with a thick layer of soot.

Stranger still, the *U.A.'s* cathedral prophecy was eventually fulfilled, and it's now an honest-to-goodness church! The infamous Dr. Eugene Scott and his congregation have not only saved the theater from potential demolition, they have painstakingly worked to restore its architectural integrity. "Integrity" is the operative word here, as Dr. Scott has augmented the original frescoes with a little handiwork of his own, like his twist on Michelangelo's "The Creation of Adam." Above one of the balcony exits, we see the hand of "God" passing Adam a cigar, Dr. Scott's trademark. An antique Bible display now replaces the popcorn counter, and among the Bibles encased behind glass is a 1631 edition containing the badly bungled commandment "Thall shalt commit adultery." Also featured is the wife-beaters Bible of 1545 which offers some sage advice to all good Christian men bearing the burden of a disobedient spouse: "...beate the fear of God into her heade." *The United Artists Theater* men's room is also punctuated with spackled-over glory holes as an option for those who didn't want to blow Groucho at the *Orpheum*.

The Conservancy tour also provides a fascinating and informative look at some of the other noteworthy buildings along Broadway, as well as histories on the other theaters still standing but no longer open to the public. **The Tower Theater**—said to be one of the most outstanding—was the first of the downtown theaters to feature sound movies. Today it sits in a state of disrepair, and is only used as a film location. The original stained-glass window above the lobby features a design of celluloid filmstrips, still intact and visible. If you look closely you'll spot some of the original marquees running along the top of the structure's heavily ornamented facade, bearing the ghostly remains of the words "NEWS REELS."

The **Los Angeles Theater** is the stuff Liberace's wet dreams were made of—but even Liberace didn't dream this big. With a French Baroque design influence of inordinate magnitude for an establishment functioning only as a place for people to watch movies, the lobby alone features dramatic sweeping marble stairways, bronze bannisters, a multi-tiered fountain dripping with crystals and several herculean chandeliers suspended from vaulted ceilings rivaling those of the Sistine Chapel. The level beneath the lobby originally featured a restaurant, a smoking room with built-in cigarette lighters, a children's playroom decorated in a circus theme, cavernous marble restrooms (featuring sixteen individual marble vanities in the ladies room), and a periscope setup that projected the movie onto a smaller screen in an adult lounge so that you could socialize without missing too much of the film. The *Los Angeles Theater* is as lavish as architecture gets in our city, and sadly, its doors are closed.

Though the *Los Angeles Theater* is no longer open to the public, and you most likely aren't interested in watching the latest Steven Seagal vehicle dubbed in Spanish (or in English for that matter) just for the purpose of checking out the interior of these munificent movie palaces, *The Los Angeles Conservancy* hosts an event called *Last Remaining Seats* that annually resuscitates new life into aged theaters like the *Los Angeles* and *The Orpheum*. On Wednesdays through the month of June, each theater runs a different classic film. The turnout is phenomenal. The theaters, most with a seating capacity over 2,000, are packed to the rafters. Enthusiastic film history aficionados line up for blocks in anticipation of gaining entry into one of Broadway's forgotten wonders. The *Last Remaining Seats* series is undoubtedly the only opportunity you'll ever have to see one of these downtown theaters running an uncut classic film, seated with an audience civilized enough not to urinate in their seats or make use of the many glory holes down in the men's room. One of their most popular offerings is their silent film night, with a pipe organ and full orchestra providing a live score. George Lucas take note: THX sound can't hold a candle to this.

The *Conservancy* events are the best thing going for anyone interested in exploring the rich history and lost elegance of downtown Los Angeles. Their tours offer a fascinating look—and an entirely different vantage point—at what most dismiss as the long-collapsed heart of our city.

Get up early one Saturday, it won't kill you.

For reservations, call the
Los Angeles Conservancy
at (213) 623-CITY, weekdays

Tours:

Art Deco
Every Saturday, 10:00 A.M.

Biltmore Hotel
Second Saturday, 11:00 A.M.

Broadway Theaters
Every Saturday, 10:00 A.M.

City Hall
Fourth Saturday, 10:00 A.M.

Little Tokyo
First Saturday, 10:00 A.M.

Marble Masterpieces
Second Saturday, 10:00 A.M.

Mecca for Merchants
Fourth Saturday, 10:00 A.M.

Palaces of Finance
Third Saturday, 10:00 A.M.

Pershing Square
Every Saturday, 10:00 A.M.

Terra Cotta
First Saturday, 10:00 A.M.

Union Station
Third Saturday, 10:00 A.M.

Tours are free to Los Angeles Conservancy Members, $5.00 to the general public. Tours run between 1-2 hours.

On a pilgrimage to
Jayne Mansfield's Former Home

She was as famous for opening supermarkets and splitting her dresses as she was for her movies (among them the stupendous *Will Success Spoil Rock Hunter?* and the shitty classics *Promises! Promises!* and *Las Vegas Hillbillies*), but her greatest talent was inventing herself; Jayne Mansfield's former home is a shining monument to that brilliant talent.

Within these walls Jayne had some of her worst acid trips (including one where she climbed the bookcases screaming about "THE FUCKING LIZARDS!!") and developed her habit of polishing off a quart of bourbon (often disguised in coke bottles) a day. It was also in this house that her nine-year-old son Miklos—apparently a rebellious little tyke—dragged a mattress down to the basement and set it ablaze in an effort to burn the pink palace to the ground. An unabashed publicity whore, Jayne made herself readily available to the paparazzi and her adoring fans by sunbathing in the front yard or standing out on the balcony in her nightgown, waving to idling tour buses.

The Girl Can't Help It

Mansfield purchased this three-story, eight-bedroom Spanish-style mansion with her celebrated body-builder husband Mickey Hargitay in 1957. Remodeling the place with an impeccable sense of personal style and extremely low-brow taste (you can take the girl out of Dallas...), she splashed the house a shade of Pepto-Bismol pink. Pink marble heart-shaped sinks were installed among the house's thirteen bathrooms, and a pink marble heart-shaped fireplace graces Jayne's former bedroom. Fuzzy pink super-shag carpet was put down on the floors (and applied to many of the ceilings), and was permanently stained soon after by a myriad of Chihuahuas. The heart-shaped swimming pool flanked with cherubs and bubbling fountains remains as the most celebrated feature, and details like purple sofas, religious statuary, and walls paneled in gold-veined mirror completed the gloriously garish picture.

Today, the exterior of the house appears exactly as it did when Jayne lived there thanks to current owner Engelbert Humperdinck who repainted it in its original pink in homage to Jayne (much to the dismay of his neighbors), with whom he was once involved. It now stands as a shrine for Mansfield enthusiasts, who relish the opportunity to genuflect at the front gates festooned with an ornate "JM" in wrought iron.

With thanks to Engelbert, we can now pass the house and pretend that Jayne's still with us—and that nasty car accident was just a bad dream. And on a hot day—when the convective waves are just right—you can almost see her, sheathed in a nightgown, guzzling bourbon on the front balcony, tripping her brains out, blowing kisses, and waving adoringly at passersby.

Jayne Mansfield's Former Home
10100 Carolwood Drive
Beverly Hills
NO TRESPASSING! Don't bother the residents!

Paying homage to *Angelyne*

She's the muse of the Southland, the undisputed enigma of Hollywood, she's our only-in-Los Angeles phenomenon, **Angelyne**.

Her age, and the source of her seemingly endless supply of money (literally millions have been spent to keep her on billboards and bus stop shelters), may remain Hollywood's two best kept secrets. A long-ago altered driver's license (bearing the improbable surname "L'lyne"), and an extremely vague and ever-changing recollection of her past (as well as a carefully composed present) keep her veiled in mystery.

The Girl Who Put The "Bust" In Bus Stop Shelters

I immediately became transfixed by this human cartoon when I first arrived to Los Angeles in 1984, during *Angelyne*'s first major billboard blitz. My fixation quickly turned to obsession, and then a career; I was determined to become *Angelyne*'s sidekick. A fortuitous meeting led to a lunch date, then an inseparable but short-lived friendship. Life was never the same after I rode shotgun in the white bucket seat of her '82 pearly, toenail-polish-fuchsia-pink Corvette.

**The Angelyne
Fan Club**
(310) 289-4469

Hanging out with her in the tiny apartment she keeps on the edge of West Hollywood—a place fashioned into a shrine for self-worship, with billboard-sized photos and posters of herself covering the walls—I gained some insight into this odd and extra-ordinary character: The more you know about *Angelyne*, the less you know. She's a hall of mirrors wrapped in pink spandex. And she never lets anyone get too close.

She is, like any great artist, hopelessly misinterpreted. People commonly assume that she aspires to *be* something, while entirely missing what she *is*. She has only ever aspired to be *Angelyne*, and no one can deny that she's done an excellent job. She's a living, breathing, multi-media work-in-progress; *Angelyne* is *Angelyne*'s medium. Like a Christo with cleavage, she aims to give the Los Angeles landscape some color, a shot of whimsy, and a little mystique—and she hasn't been sponging off the N.E.A. to do it. In a city where we endure a relentless, daily onslaught of in-our-face advertising, it's a god-

send to have a few billboards around town that aren't dictating standards in order to sell us a product we don't need. *Angelyne* is simply there to say hi and sprinkle her pixie dust—a harmless bit of cheesecake; a peroxided Betty Boopish pituitary case. The worst you could say about her is that she's a little self obsessed, but honestly, aren't we all?

I've never understood why she's judged so harshly. Why do people snicker at *Angelyne* but stand in line to give Demi Moore a rim job at a Planet Hollywood opening? *Angelyne* should be L.A.'s goodwill ambassador, she should be our spokesmodel for the "Together We're the Best" campaign, she should be grand marshall of the Rose Parade. At the very least, the mayor should present her with a key to our city, because I can't imagine Los Angeles without her.

—MM

Partner swapping with

The Double R Squares

T he coolest dance club in town isn't held in a downtown warehouse. It isn't owned by a celebrity. Patrons aren't handpicked at the door. It doesn't have a V.I.P. room and it doesn't feature bloodletting performances or play-piercing demos. Best of all, you won't find any ladies in the men's room.

Deep in the industrial section of Van Nuys—deeper than you'd go for a sex club or drug deal—and set back behind a grouping of nondescript commercial buildings, you'll find a place called *Mc Donald's Barn*. Step into the scene at *Mc Donald's Barn* and you'll swear that someone slipped something in your lemonade.

Mc Donald's Barn isn't exactly a barn, but a barn-esque dancehall that has inconspicuously kept its place off Saticoy Street for nearly forty years. Real wagon wheel lamps hang from the ceiling, and ancient turquoise metal folding chairs line the squeaky wood floor, well-pummeled by ardent square dancers from decades gone by. Felt banners bearing square dance clubs' insignia dating back to the late forties hang from the raw wood beams, and the walls and curtains are aged with a discoloration that can only occur with years of dust and smoke. The cowboy murals painted over the windows fluoresce with the natural light at sunset. *Mc Donald's Barn* is a special place. It's a rare, unspoiled step back into time. It's also home to **The Double R Squares**.

The Double R Squares is L.A.'s premiere square dance club, and on any given night you'll find *Mc Donald's Barn* packed to the rafters with septuagenarian couples; women painted and wigged-up like Dolly Parton in full square dance regalia and an equal number of bolo-tied, hearing-aided, Porter Wagneresque men, whirling, twirling and do si do-ing to the tunes of classic country fiddlin' played from scratchy 45s blaring over a tinny amp system.

The Double R Squares are led by Ray and Donna Rose, the royal couple of the Southern California square dance scene. Ray, a man not too proud to wear blinding white cowboy boots and purple gingham western shirts, is probably a little younger than his toupee might lead you to believe. Every bit a southern gentleman, he speaks in a deep, rich voice with just enough twang to let you know he's from Arkansas. Ray teaches the classes, singin' n' callin' to traditional old-time country tunes like "Apple Jack" or "Rocky Top, Tennessee," but occasionally throws in square dance versions of a Bob Dylan ditty or a pop hit like "Neutron Dance" making every song *unmistakably* his own. Ray instructs the class over a microphone from a small stage as his wife Donna, a full-figured gal up to her armpits in crinolines, helps out on the floor by jerking beginning square dancers into place with the yank of an arm or a shove in the back. Donna also teaches her own country line-dancing classes. Their young son Steve instructs the clogging classes.

After each "tip"—that's square dance lingo for "dance"—the group takes a fifteen-minute break and gathers 'round the cut glass punch bowl sipping Crystal Lite from Styrofoam cups and nibbling chocolate-covered graham crackers. At *Mc Donald's Barn*, it seems that reality has been suspended. Appearing like gaily costumed square dancing gnomes, one tends to wonder where all these people disappear to during the daylight hours. Their enthusiasm and spirit of celebration is awe-inspiring. These are enlightened masters in rhinestones and lurex. It's an acid party without acid. *The Double R Squares* could have given the Merry Pranksters a lesson or two (incidentally, "Mystery Bus Trips" are regularly scheduled throughout their usual calendar of club events.)

If you took mandatory square dancing in grammar school and secretly loved it, or if you've ever had the fantasy of being a regular cast member of "Hee Haw," give *The*

Double R Squares a look-see. Your life will surely change. Where else do you have the opportunity to dress in sparkly, fringed western wear, join hands, sing and socialize with people old enough to be your grandparents?

"Come have fun and forget your troubles" reads *The Double R Squares'* class flyer. "Relax with fun-loving, caring people." Ray and Donna Rose offer an invaluable break from the less embroidered, agreed upon reality we all live inside. A break that most people won't stop watching television long enough to allow time for. These kinds of breaks are rare.

And these folks know where it's at.

The Barn/
The Double R Squares
13201 Saticoy Street
(rear building)
Van Nuys
Class Information:
(818) 994-6327
(818) 994-0376
(818) 765-9283

OUT-AND-ABOUT

A tasty bite of high-style, mid-century donut signage on Historic Route 66.

Winchell's Donut House
**887 West Foothill Blvd.
La Verne**

Passing the bucket at
Wild Bill's Wild West
Dinner Extravaganza

You're probably some elitist snob who thinks a place like **Wild Bill's Wild West Dinner Extravaganza** is beneath you. You probably think *Wild Bill's Wild West Dinner Extravaganza* isn't cool enough for your cutting-edge, esoteric sensibility. You'd probably consider an evening spent at *Wild Bill's Wild West Dinner Extravaganza* an evening wasted. Well fuck you and the high-falutin' horse you rode in on! Sometimes life (especially life in Los Angeles) is chock-full of surprises, so don't let a half-hour drive to Buena Park and a bucket of beef-barley soup stand between you and one of Orange County's finest attractions. Come on, *live a little!*

A profusion of American flags, taxidermied animal parts and Native American head-dresses help trash up the squeaky-clean pre-fab "wild west emporium" of *Wild Bill's*, located along a stretch of Beach Boulevard in Buena Park that resembles a small-scale Las Vegas... if it's nighttime and you can't read. The folks at *Wild Bill's* encourage you to arrive good 'n early so you can mosey on up to the bar for a shot of Big Mountain Indian Firewater and take advantage of the pre-show performed on a small stage in the "saloon." Whatever you do—*don't*. Arrive as close as you can to showtime, allowing yourself a cushion of twenty minutes, tops. The later you come, the farther back you'll be seated from the main stage, but keep in mind that if you do show up early you'll be subjected to this preshow: one butchered cover after another of classic country tunes performed at high decibel from the saloon stage *and piped throughout the entire building, preventing any possible refuge from the insufferable noise.*

"Up With People" Meets "Annie Get Your Gun" On Peyote

In spite of the fact that the theater holds nearly one thousand people, seating is somewhat of an *affair intime*, as you and several hundred sunburned tourists wearing *Universal Studios* and *Disneyland* tee shirts are crammed elbow-to-elbow at long narrow banquet tables underneath wagon wheel ceiling lamps. All the dishware you need for the evening's selection of vile vittles—plates, soup bowls, glasses, etc.—is neatly stacked in front of you, including pitchers of cold beer, Coke and water. The waiters do next to nothing, so tip accordingly. As you labor to wedge yourself into your chair, one of the *Wild Bill's* paparazzi makes every guest feel like a star by screaming SMILE and blasting a flashbulb in your face. Later you will be presented with a big ugly *Wild Bill*'s key chain bearing your photo. Just in case you make the hideous mistake of thinking these key chains are on the house, you're slipped a little piece of paper on which has a message printed in eight languages informing you that no, it is not on the house, and that it will cost you $5.00 "to cover our costs." Somehow you'll justify the expense, because they're just too god-awful to pass up.

The show begins posthaste (there are no empty moments at *Wild Bill's*) with a line of chorus girls reminiscent of the Dallas Cowboys cheerleaders' glory days, accompanied by The Buckboards and Buckaroos hammering out a rapid-fire medley of old-time country songs. As the evening's star host and hostess—Wild Bill and Miss Annie—open the show, a Buena Park teenaged waiter slams down a pewter bucket of lukewarm beef barley soup and a basket piled high with dried-out biscuits on the table in front of you. YUM! But not before Miss Annie and Wild Bill give the soup undue fanfare with a introductory song. In fact, they have a song to present every course: the "S-A-L-A-D!" and "Pork and Beans" songs being real crowd-pleasers. There's no such thing as substitutions or "dressing on the side" here; the menu is preset and if you don't like what's dumped in front of you, don't eat it. Really, the only way to choke down *Wild Bill's* bill of fare is to not eat all day so that you arrive so ravenous you're at that point where *anything* tastes good. Or, smoke a *lot* of pot beforehand, so that by the time the meal hits the table, your case of the munchies will make up for what the chefs at *Wild Bill's* obviously lack. You can't aim too low underestimating the food here.

The show starts out strong and stays there with a series of featured acts, all of which are surprisingly sensational, each in their own inimitable way. You'll thrill to *Wild Bill's* veteran performer Bonnie West as she twirls fifteen-foot lariats in a skintight, spandex cowgirl outfit trimmed in rhinestones and lots of fringe. Finally whipping off her cowboy hat to reveal a long mane of silken hair, she falls to her knees in a backbend whirling "the world's biggest wedding ring" while several men in the audience start grinding in their seats. Bonnie also spins six-shooters on her fingertips and performs a she-devil whip-cracking exhibition with the poise, grace, and frozen ear-to-ear smile of a Miss America contestant.

Black lights aren't something usually associated with the Wild West, but this *is* Buena Park after all. The pageantry of Native American dance is only enhanced by *Wild Bill's* liberal use of Day-Glo paint and ultraviolet illumination. Before a backdrop of psychedelic wigwams, pseudo-squaws wearing white bodysuits and fluorescent headdresses do a torrid pony to a synthesized Indian-cum-B-52s score. Upon their exit the black lights are killed, and three men of the Native American persuasion—fully war-painted and feathered—take it from there, doing marvelously well without the aid of psychedelic visuals. The young Johnny Depp look-alike Indian does a frantic hoop dance, contorting and tangling different parts of his body into an elaborate network of wooden hoops. This time, it's the female members of the audience grinding in their chairs; he wears a loin cloth slit up to his hips, and manages to ever-so-unintentionally flash the seat or crotch of his tight briefs as he slips another hoop past his waist or over his legs. As they say at *Chippendales*, there wasn't a dry seat in the house.

Periodically, Miss Annie or Wild Bill will remind us how absolutely famished we all must be, providing themselves a segue into another food song upon which the waiters haul in and slam down more pewter buckets filled to the rim with near-inedible "grub."

Wild Bill and Miss Annie want you real "rowdy" for the sing-a-long, "She'll Be Coming Round the Mountain." You'll be ordered to whoop, howl or bah like sheep depending on what section of the house you're seated in. There's something unforgettably Buena Park about watching several hundred people—most of whom are adults—make farm animal noises while trying to stuff greasy ribs and fried chicken in their faces with their fingers.

The show closes with the dessert, apple pie—and don't think there isn't a song to go along with it. For the grand finale, Miss Annie and Wild Bill sing a rousing "You're a Grand Ole Flag" and "Yankee Doodle Dandee" as the bitter teenaged wait staff reluctantly prances out from the kitchen waving large American flags, filling the house with forced patriotism.

"An Enthralling and Entrancing Embroglio of Entertainments Effectively Executed By Our Extraordinary Ensemble to Edify and Enchant!" claims Wild Bill's. And they aren't lying—after all, they never claimed the food was good.

How many times in your life do you have the opportunity to see Day-Glo dancing Indians, spandexed whip-crackers and "the world's fastest can-can" all in the same two hours?

Don't cheat yourself, come discover "how the West was fun!"

Wild Bill's Wild
West Dinner
Extravaganza
7600 Beach Blvd.
Buena Park
(714) 522-6414

Getting into Photography at *Camera Obscura*

You young folk may be surprised as to just how many fun things there are to do at the Senior Recreation Center in Santa Monica. You can play a spirited card game with a septuagenarian, get your ass whipped on the shuffleboard court by a woman older than your grandmother, or just relax on the benches that line the bluff that overlook the Santa Monica beach and bay. Best of all, you can turn in your driver's license for the key that opens the door to *Camera Obscura*.

Smile, You're On Camera Obscura

We don't know what we like better: the sign out front or the camera obscura itself, but believe us when we say both are a feast for the eyes. Located up a flight of stairs near the restrooms—don't let the overwhelming scent of urine discourage you—*Camera Obscura* is an attraction as obscure as its name implies (although *Camera Obscura* is Latin for "darkened room"). Conceived by Aristotle, invented by an unknown optical freak, and named by Johann Kepler, *Camera Obscura* is indeed a darkened room, and the basis for the single lens reflex camera that we know and love today.

Santa Monica's *Camera Obscura* is one of the less-frequented tourist sites in the city, and one of the most relaxing (except on a hot August day when the room more resembles a sauna). It works like this: On the roof of the building is a rotating metal turret set over a hole in the ceiling. An opening on the side of the turret allows light to hit the angled mirror within, which then reflects the image downward through a convex lens onto a large white disk on the floor of the room. The disk is also angled at 45 degrees, and placed at the proper focal length to receive the scene coming through the lens. In this case, the scene is the view of Santa Monica from the roof of the building. A skipper's wheel mounted in front of the disk allows you two rotate the turret 360 degrees in order to get a full view of the park, bay, and Ocean Boulevard just inside. Of course, the effect doesn't work unless the room's lights are off, and overcast or rainy days may provide less spectacular images than those of the usual sunny California day.

The *Camera Obscura* room is small and somewhat stuffy, but that's okay because you probably won't be spending a lot of time in there. There are a few seats available for the weary, lazy, or elderly, and although we noticed an exhaust fan in the side of the wall, the switch next to it didn't seem to do a damn thing. Still, if you're looking to avoid the overwhelming crowds of *Disneyland* and *Universal Citywalk*, *Camera Obscura* will offer you brief respite. Then again, "brief" is the operative word in that sentence, since there isn't much more to do in the room once you've spun the captain's wheel a few times.

The large metal moniker that adorns the stone facade of the building is truly one of L.A.'s most beautiful works of art. Dating back to 1955, when the exhibit was moved from its original location in North Beach (where it first opened in 1899!) to the newly built rec center, the sign exudes a minimalist yet sassy style that has given way to the hyperbolic retro-plundering we see so often today. Enjoy both the magic of the darkened room and the enlightened inspiration of the sign at the Senior Recreational Center at 1450 Ocean Avenue in Santa Monica.

And on your way out, why not stop for a cup of coffee and a feisty game of canasta with a couple of the spunky seniors who frequent the center? Don't worry, they don't bite. They lost their teeth long ago.

Camera Obscura
Senior Recreational Center
1450 Ocean Avenue
Santa Monica

Mixing Sex and Religion at the

Statue of Santa Monica

My, That's A Big One

'm probably going to go to Hell for this one, but since that post-mortem destination is already preordained, I figure why not?

Michelangelo took his subtle potshot at the Roman Catholic Church on the ceiling of the Sistine Chapel (take note of God's outstretched hand and man's lazy, I-can-barely-hold-the-remote-control pose in the Creation scenario). There's no telling if the sculptor who created the **Statue of Santa Monica** had similar intentions—conscious or otherwise—or maybe was simply a streamlined kind of guy, but there is without a doubt a physical double entendre to the piece of art, and I'm not the only one to have noticed it. In the light of day, the *Statue* after which the seaside town is named doesn't seem so phallic. But at night—and especially with the enhancement of an overexposed photograph which erases all detail—the thing suddenly appears to be a combination dildo/rocket ship, ready to blast off to parts unknown. No matter what your interpretation, I personally find this to be yet another one of Santa Monica's shining artistic jewels (along with the Camera Obscura sign and the Shangri-La Hotel), but that probably isn't enough of a mitigating factor to quell those who would like to burn me at the stake as a heretic.

In which case, bring marshmallows.

—ARL

The Statue of Santa Monica
Ocean Avenue and
Sunset Boulevard
Santa Monica

Lost Strangeles

Stovall's Best Western
Yesterday's Inn of Tomorrow

White vinyl donkeys and silver-foiled elephants wearing space helmets once hung from the ceiling in the lobby; there was a topiary garden out front, and rooms were appointed with "daring new interior colors" and "a newer than tomorrow space-age decor." This was *Stovall's Inn of Tomorrow*: a Best Western Motel that offered a Monsanto-cum-Small World alternative to Anaheim's overabundance of cut-rate lodging for *Disneyland*-bound families. They boasted "Moon level luxury...Down to earth rates."

Unfortunately, "tomorrow" didn't end up looking anything like the *Stovall's* ebullient prognosis, and although the motel is still in business, today the decor is relatively earthbound.

Stovall's Best Western
Formerly Stovall's Inn of Tomorrow
1110 West Katella
Anaheim

Suckling the Bosom of Culture at *Frederick's of Hollywood Lingerie Museum*

The authors would like to take this opportunity to make an important announcement:

We're breast men.

And we like lingerie, too, though preferably when worn by women. So it would only make sense that one of our favorite museums in L.A. would be devoted to bras and stockings and garters and corsets and...whew, is it just us, or did someone turn up the heat in here? You know, we just can't help getting a little worked up whenever we think about **Frederick's of Hollywood.**

How Much Is That Brassiere In The Window?

Frederick's has gotten a bad rap lately, or at least been forced into the backseat of the underwear juggernaut now guided by the glossy supermodel Wonderbra overhype that has made *Victoria's Secret* anything but. And while *V.S.'s* mass mailings cannot be discounted as some of the best masturbatory material to arrive in the guise of underwear catalogs, they and the evil empire they represent are still nothing more than chi-chi pretenders to the throne of the otherwise unchallenged king of lingerie, Mr. Frederick himself. In our opinion, there is simply no place for gilded taste and phony snootiness in the world of seamed stockings, push-up bras, and pumps—and no one knew that better than Mr. Frederick!

Of course, the other side of the *Victoria's Secret* coin is a store like **Trashy Lingerie**, which attempts to play up the tawdry side of putting on a pair of crotchless panties by, well, being downright *trashy* about it. Although *Trashy Lingerie* does offer up some unusual fashions not found in either *Frederick's* or *Victoria's Secret*, and will custom-tailor the catsuit (or whatever) of your dreams, you'll find that the quality of both the service and the merchandise are unreliable. Not only have we encountered rude, petulant salespeople at *Trashy Lingerie*, but we've also been disappointed to discover that some of their products live up to their moniker in more ways than one. Add to this the insult of rather exorbitant prices and an annual $2 "membership fee" just to walk in the store, and the free admission to *Frederick's Lingerie Museum* seems more philanthropic than ever.

When it comes to shoddy merchandise, *Frederick's* has been unfairly slapped with a less than quality reputation, though for our part, we've found their product to be consistently sturdy, albeit ever so cheesy (How else would one describe a pair of red sheer crotchless panties, laced with black frill, and sporting a small toy gun that hangs from a string over a most strategic position?). As the saying goes, "Everything in moderation," and *Frederick's* is definitely the middle-ground between the guile of *Victoria's Secret* and the gaudiness of *Trashy Lingerie.*

Most importantly, does the competition even care enough to create a loving museum devoted entirely to the lacy and leathery underthings that make a girl a woman? Of course not—they're too busy trying to be classy or trashy! But in the back of *Frederick's* flagship store on Hollywood Boulevard, you'll be dumbfounded by the collection of the bustiers and such, once worn by some of Hollywood's most glamorous women—and men! Whether you have a serious silk fetish or simply appreciate the graceful curve of a seamed stocking running up a well-developed calf, you'll find plenty to ogle at behind the glass doors and within the glass cases of the *Frederick's Lingerie Museum.*

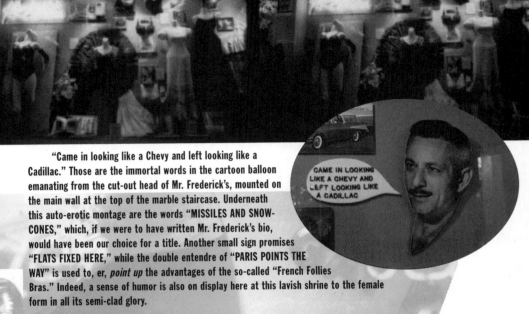

"Came in looking like a Chevy and left looking like a Cadillac." Those are the immortal words in the cartoon balloon emanating from the cut-out head of Mr. Frederick's, mounted on the main wall at the top of the marble staircase. Underneath this auto-erotic montage are the words "MISSILES AND SNOW-CONES," which, if we were to have written Mr. Frederick's bio, would have been our choice for a title. Another small sign promises "FLATS FIXED HERE," while the double entendre of "PARIS POINTS THE WAY" is used to, er, *point up* the advantages of the so-called "French Follies Bras." Indeed, a sense of humor is also on display here at this lavish shrine to the female form in all its semi-clad glory.

Then there are the bras, happily displayed on the wall along with the date of their creation and their special name. "Depth Charge," "Pointette," and "Sexpose," are but a few of the clever names devised by Mr. Frederick for his sundry inventions. And the descriptions are equally as delicious. Just check out this description for the "Sexpose" model:

"Bare your nipples but be smart and PUT YOUR BREASTS ON A SHELF!

Firm shelves under each breast leave you FREE but SUPPORTED.

You feel soft, look firm."

Want to see the strapless bra that Marilyn wore in the movie *Let's Make Love*? It's here. Did Natalie Wood drive you crazy sitting in bed with only a pink brassiere in *Bob & Carol, Ted & Alice*? It's here. Are you mad for Madonna's famous black corset? Have you

always wondered what cradled Isabel Sanford's ample bosom during the shooting of TV's "The Jeffersons"? And what about Zsa Zsa Gabor's lingerie? All of them are here for your enjoyment. Fans of celluloid transvestism will revel in the wig and bra worn by "Uncle Miltie," as well as the bra worn by Tony Curtis in *Some Like It Hot*. And these items are just the tip of the proverbial underwear iceberg, if you'll pardon the pun.

You know, if only they had museums like this when we were growing up, then perhaps all those field trips would have amounted to something other than learning how to sing "100 Barrels of Beer on the Wall."

We could have learned what all those bras we were snapping really looked like.

Frederick's of Hollywood
6608 Hollywood Blvd.
Hollywood
(213) 466-8506

Trashy Lingerie
402 N. La Cienega
West Hollywood
(310) 652-4543

The L. Ron Hubbard
Life Exhibition

We don't want to say too much about Dianetics and The Church of Scientology here because, quite frankly, they scare the living poop out of us. One gander at *The L.A. Times* six-part series on the church in 1990, *Time* magazine's cover story in May of 1991 called "Scientology: The Cult of Greed," or a perusal of books like *Bare Faced Messiah* and *L. Ron Hubbard: Messiah or Madman*, would make it appear that our fear is not unwarranted—and exactly what the church intends. And you know we *must* be scared if we're not afraid to take on a sue-happy behemoth like *Disney* but are intimidated by what purports to be a religion dedicated to healing and helping.

The fact of the matter is that Los Angeles has practically as many Scientology and Dianetics centers as it does frozen yogurt stores, and that's no coincidence since the founder, L. Ron Hubbard, spent a great deal of time here before he switched careers from science fiction writer to savior. The proliferation of Scientology Churches and Dianetics centers in L.A. is almost, well, *omnipresent*. It seems like you can't drive a mile without seeing the distinctive yellow-and-blue logos atop a building or in a storefront window. And Hollywood is a particularly popular site for these shrines to Hubbard's billion-dollar brainchild, boasting the tony *Manor Hotel and Celebrity Center* (which, as the name implies, caters to celebrities), as well as the "Big Blue Building" on Sunset, the Scientology building on Hollywood Boulevard, and the **L. Ron Hubbard Life Exhibition**, also on Hollywood Boulevard, which opened in April of 1991 with the customary bigger-than-life fanfare that marks any Scientology fête.

There's been a lot of debate about the legitimacy of the facts of Hubbard's life as presented by Scientology. Even the fact that he's "dead" is debatable since Scientologists claim that Hubbard *voluntarily* shucked his mortal coil because it had become a hindrance to his research—which one can only assume he now continues on the same astral plane as occupied by Casper the Friendly Ghost and his friends. Sure, plenty of sour Scientology defectors loathe Hubbard and his legacy, and there are a number of researchers and biographers whose own exhumations of Ron's past have come up with decidedly different details of the Official Story. On the other hand, you have millions of faithful followers who will attest to the fact that Dianetics and/or Scientology has changed their lives—if not saved them altogether. Taking a cue from the situation in Northern Ireland, we find it prudent to stay out of the line of fire of all religious debates, especially considering the extremely litigious nature of Scientology and their propensity for destroying perceived enemies. After all, we're just a couple of smartass heathens, not self-destructive martyrs.

So, if you're in the Hollywood area and just dying to delve into Hubbard's fascinating life, stop into the museum for what will surely be an eye-opening experience. First, you'll be astounded by just how much money went into this living homage to the man known to some as "The Commodore." Lavishly designed, well-organized, and almost fanatically exuberant in its exaltation of its namesake, the *L. Ron Hubbard Life Exhibition* features over 30 displays and multimedia presentations that include the typewriter on which he created the original Dianetics book, artifacts from his many global jaunts, and a truckload of awards and proclamations lauding Hubbard's "humanitarian" work.

And if your life has turned into a steaming pile of shit and you need a helping hand from the world's fastest growing cult—sorry, make that *religion*—then drop by any one of their Southland sites and let one of their helpful staff lead you to the "bridge" that will eventually allow you to become "clear." And if you don't know what that last sentence means, you definitely will once you let them into your brain....

The L. Ron Hubbard Life Exhibition

6331 Hollywood Blvd.

Los Angeles

(213) 960-3511

Rewriting History at the **_Richard Nixon Presidential Library & Birthplace_**

A more apt and complete name for this living tribute to the dead 37th President would be "The **Richard Nixon Presidential Library**, Birthplace, Garden, Gravesite, and Gift Shops." However, as the only Presidential library to be operated *without* taxpayers' funds, this place actually redeems some of Nixon's tarnished and somewhat ill-begotten image. If there is any justice in history, as far as Republican presidents go, Nixon will be remembered as a far better leader than Ronald Reagan. Fact is, poor ol' Dick merely got caught doing the wrong thing at the right time, and lacked the well-honed B-movie thespian skills to lie his way out of it—like some other presidents with political blood on their hands.

Nixon was a true foreign statesman and opened doors to Russia and China that Ronnie couldn't have even found the keys for—though Reagan still takes the credit for the fall of his much-beloved "Evil Empire." Despite all his nasty secret bombings and excursions into Laos and Cambodia, Nixon did put an end to the war in Vietnam. Still, that doesn't make our jowliest Commander-in-Chief an angel—just the lesser of two comparative evils.

While Reagan's library is located in the brushy, blighted landscape of Simi Valley, Nixon's architectural homage is in one of Orange County's less-upscale regions, surrounded by middle-class homes, mini-malls, and fast-food establishments. Other than the gravesite and birthplace featured in Yorba Linda, there isn't much difference between these two museums. Both are fraught with endless exhibits and interactive displays aimed at making the former politicians look like real human beings. Surprisingly, the *Nixon Library* does have more of a sense of humor, on the other hand. How else could one describe an exhibit of 23 never-before-seen gifts from Tricia Nixon's wedding, glibly entitled "But they didn't get a blender"? Likewise, the memorial to Nixon's funeral is called "Farewell, Mr. President," which may not be a gut-buster, but is about as smirk-inducing as Nancy Reagan's mushy, maudlin tribute to her husband at the 1996 Republican Convention.

If you happen to be a Republican and admired Nixon, then you'll be sure to enjoy this place almost as much as you will the other nearby entertainment travesty known as Disneyland. If you're a cynical American with a wanderlust, then the *Nixon Library* will delightfully disgust you and reconfirm all your worst beliefs about our nation's putrid political system. Best of all, the gift shop opens 30 minutes early so you can get in some extra shopping time. After all, it's hard to decide what to buy when faced with a vast selection of sundry gift items bearing the "RN" insignia, much less books like *Pat Nixon: The Untold Story*. Who knows, by the time you get there, they may even have an exhibit entitled "Those Wacky Presidential Expletives."

Then again, maybe not, goddamnit.

The Richard Nixon Library & Birthplace
18001 Yorba Linda Blvd.
Yorba Linda
(714) 993-3393

OUT-AND-ABOUT

Beverly Hills: the city that tries way too hard.

Beverly Hills/ Cannes, France sign
Coldwater Cyn. at Monte Cielo Drive

Oh, for those gentile times when the **Santa Monica Pier** was frequented by ladies with parasols and gentlemen with handle-bar mustaches and full-body bathing suits. It was a kinder, gentler era, one without assault weapons, crack pipes, and graffiti...without the cocky young men with bad haircuts who wear ill-fitting, baggy jeans and flash hand-signals that more resemble the nervous spasms of an unfortunate autistic child.

Santa Monica takes great pride in being "The Home of the Homeless," or so it seems. But it's not the shopping-cart crowd that made the pier such an unsavory place to take the family. It was the hordes of the aforementioned gang members, who, as they did with Westwood, adopted the *Pier* as their own personal "crib" in which to hang, chill, and generally terrorize people in LaCoste shirts. And while people in LaCoste shirts could use a little terrorizing now and then—just for good measure—when it comes down to killing them, perhaps that's where we should draw the line. That's what the cops decided, anyway, when they put a police station right on the *Pier* in August of 1995, the frosting on the cake following a few years of beefed-up pier patrols.

Is That A Corndog In Your Pocket Or Are You Just Happy To See Me?

And their presence seems to have put a damper on the activities of those who prefer drive-bys to drive-ins, forcing them to find other popular tourist sites at which to wreak havoc (May we kindly suggest Rodeo Drive, *Planet Hollywood* or *Disneyland*, perhaps?). Though the wonderful bumper cars that made the *Pier* a must for those who enjoy whiplash are now gone, their site has been replaced with a roller coaster, ferris wheel, and a number of other rides designed to induce regurgitation. The *Pier*'s greasy fish stick stands of yore have given way to more greasy fish stick stands with new fronts, as well as a conglomeration of eye-catching fast-food joints that will make you feel like you're at your local mall.

The ancient carousel at the beginning of the *Pier* was spared in the wake of renovation, and still sits in the wooden building that has housed it for years. Best of all, the horses still go up and down, the music still plays, and the thing still turns. Likewise, the arcade just down the way may be packed with new state-of-the-art video games, but it still features a bank of well-maintained skee-ball lanes. And despite the pre-existing slogan for baseball, the fact of the matter is that skee-ball is truly "America's Game." Why it's not an Olympic event is beyond us.

You can still fish from the *Pier* (no overhead casting, please), though considering the toxic content of the surrounding waters, you may be well-advised not to consume anything you catch until it has been checked out by the scientists at Lawrence-Livermore. Then again, visitors from Three Mile Island and Chernobyl will find the freshly caught seafood unusually palatable.

The *Pier* has always been a popular tourist attraction, now even more so since its recent renovation and security upgrade. Don't be surprised to hear a myriad of tower-of-Babel languages being spoken all around you, and a selection of visitors from Lithuania to Louisiana. Most of all, don't be afraid to ask the *Pier* patrol for directions to the bathroom. These are perhaps the friendliest law enforcement officers in L.A. Then again, Santa Monica is its own city with its own police force, which may explain the cops' kindness.

So if you've been hesitating to revisit the *Pier* for fear of getting caught in some child-ish gang crossfire, let us assure you that your chances of dying here are far less than that of contracting some hideous disease from taking a dip in the polluted Santa Monica Bay.

And if you do happen to run into some idiotic-looking teenagers with their humon-gous, butt-crack-revealing pants about to fall off their tattooed bodies, don't be afraid to yell out, "Hey, Bozo, pull up your damn pants! You look like a jackass!" And while you're at it, be sure to flash them some spastic gang signs with your hands.

They'll like it. They'll really like it.

The Santa Monica Pier
Colorado and Ocean Ave.
Santa Monica

Lost Strangeles

The Ambassador Hotel *Someone's in the Kitchen with Sirhan...*

The **Ambassador Hotel** and the **Coconut Grove** were once the crowning jewels in Mid-Wilshire's crown. The hotel was one of the finest in L.A., and the *Grove*, with its Lucite railings and tiered cocktail-table seating, was a venue for top talent and a hotspot for Hollywood's elite. The *Ambassador* even boasted its own branch of the U.S. Postal Service down on the first floor. In its final years, the *Grove* was reduced to such service as playing host to an awards ceremony for porno movies (which were smoke-bombed one year). The *Ambassador* closed in the late 80s, was bought by Donald Trump, and has been at the center of a debate as to whether or not to turn it into yet another overcrowded extension of the Los Angeles School District. In the interim, the vacant hotel frequently serves as a film location (Meryl Streep's hotel in *Defending Your Life*, for example).

Speaking of defending one's life, the *Ambassador* is unfortunately best known as Bobby Kennedy's unintended last stop on his seemingly unstoppable 1968 campaign juggernaut to the White House. It was here, as Bobby was attempting to leave the hotel after defeating Eugene McCarthy in the California Democratic primary, that Sirhan Sirhan caught up with the candidate as he took an ill-fated shortcut through the kitchen and gunned him down at close range. The rest is tragic history—and so, it would seem, are the glory days of this once-mighty layover of the rich and famous. Except, of course, in the movies.

The Ambassador Hotel
The Coconut Grove
3400 Wilshire Blvd.
Los Angeles

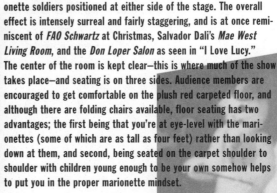

Getting lost in the surreal world of the Bob Baker Marionette Theater

f you happen to be over the age of five or six, chances are that spending a Saturday afternoon in a puppet theater doesn't top your list of weekend activities. Well, we have news for you, pal: the golf course can wait, the yard work will still be there tomorrow, and you can see that new Demi Moore spectacle when comes out on video (and the odds are that it soon will), because it's time to revamp your regular weekend agenda and make room for an excursion to the **Bob Baker Marionette Theater**. Yes, *marionette*.

Don't Look Now, But There's A One-Eyed, One-Horned, Flying Purple People Eater Sitting In Your Lap!

The *Bob Baker Marionette Theater* is the oldest operating puppet theater in the country, and though it's quite popular among the grammar school set, it's a name you don't often hear bandied about at cocktail parties—unless you happen to hang with puppeteers. But make no mistake—just because you've lost your baby teeth doesn't mean you're beyond the wild, wiggy world of puppetry—in fact, it probably means you're long overdue for a Bob Baker mental holiday.

As we've tried damn hard to illustrate throughout the pages of this opuscule of the *outré*, you never know what you'll find tucked away under a freeway overpass or scattered on the outskirts of downtown Los Angeles. Accordingly, it's dumbfounding that a place like *Bob Baker*'s even exists, let alone runs puppet shows six days a week! The theater is housed in an old warehouse that has been converted beyond recognition; the theater itself is a tall, spacious, yet cozy room, with a dramatic red velvet curtain draped at one end. Three sparkling chandeliers hang on velvet cords from the vaulted ceiling above the proscenium arch of the stage. Walls are striped like a gaily wrapped birthday gift, and liberally strung with glittering garlands, gigantic mylar bows, oversized lollipops and blinking lights. A rainbow of colored spotlights and motorized color wheels wash the otherwise dimly lit room with a dreamy, kaleidoscopic, candy-coated glow, while the orchestrated sounds of circus music come from the two large speakers topped with life-sized mari-

onette soldiers positioned at either side of the stage. The overall effect is intensely surreal and fairly staggering, and is at once reminiscent of *FAO Schwartz* at Christmas, Salvador Dali's *Mae West Living Room*, and the *Don Loper Salon* as seen in "I Love Lucy." The center of the room is kept clear—this is where much of the show takes place—and seating is on three sides. Audience members are encouraged to get comfortable on the plush red carpeted floor, and although there are folding chairs available, floor seating has two advantages; the first being that you're at eye-level with the marionettes (some of which are as tall as four feet) rather than looking down at them, and second, being seated on the carpet shoulder to shoulder with children young enough to be your own somehow helps to put you in the proper marionette mindset.

One of the puppeteers kicks the show off with a birthday announcement or two, crowning each birthday guest and naming them a member of the royal court—as well as making a polite request that the children please not grab, yank, tug, or punch at the puppets, because "if you do, the puppets will turn around and eat you" (this warning seems to be especially effective for children under the age of five). Since these puppets are *cabaret marionettes* and not limited to the confines of the boxed stage most people associate with puppet shows, they're able to roam freely on the floor (with the aid of the puppeteer of course), workin' the room and coming within close physical proximity to the audience members seated on the carpet.

For the next hour and forty-five minutes, the audience is treated to prancing French poodles, dancing ostriches, slithering sequined serpents, talking birthday cakes, flying fluorescent witches, and self-plucking fiddles—singing a program of vintage show tunes and timeless novelty songs running the gamut from "Purple People Eater" (performed by the song's namesake), to "My Heart Belongs to Daddy" (performed by a coquettish Siamese cat). Shows change seasonally and it's fairly impossible to stumble upon a flop; with 34 years behind them, the productions are time-tested and airtight, and much like Jay Ward's *Fractured Fairy Tales*, the material is suited for both the pre-pubescent and those of advanced age. The marionettes themselves are exquisitely designed and beautifully refurbished (many are as old as the theater) and will—in spite of your own disbelief—take on a life of their own.

With the exception of an occasional squalling, snot-nosed five-year-old troublemaker, the child-heavy audience is easier to take than one might expect—even for those with a W.C. Fields attitude toward kids—and the young crowd is generally more civilized and better behaved than most adults. After the curtain call, guests are invited into the party room—a *Babes in Toyland* affair—for ice cream and refreshments. Decorated like a year-round birthday celebration, the room is hung with glittery pinatas and miles of shimmering garlands. Oversized lollipops and amazonian candy-canes festoon the walls, and the place is furnished with classic ice cream parlor seating. There's also a counter where you can purchase super-cool *Bob Baker Marionette Theater* patches and buttons, as well as hand puppets, marionettes, toys and novelties. The hallways off the party room serve as a gallery of sorts, showcasing the preliminary sketches and paintings for some of the marionette designs, as well as a photo collage of the theater's history and Bob Baker's marionette work in early television—take special notice of the Liberace marionette dancing along a row of piano keys. After the ice cream, the dancing poodles, the Brobdingnagian lollipops, and the kaleidoscope of projected color—not to mention all those obscure tunes—passing through the exit and stepping back out into the glaring reality of Glendale Blvd. and First Street takes a bit of adjusting.

If you're looking for a great place to take your child—or to get in touch with your inner child—but feel some degree of trepidation when presented with the idea of a puppet show, let the folks at *Bob Baker's Marionette Theater* tune you in, turn you on, and show you where it's at.

Because when you get right down to it we're all puppets in one way or another...aren't we?

Bob Baker Marionette Theater
1345 West First Street (at Glendale Blvd.)
Los Angeles
(213) 250-9995

The Crystal Cathedral

> "...there's no business *but* show business..."
>
> — Neil Postman, *Amusing Ourselves to Death*

I don't know much about Jesus but I know what I like—and the folks at **The Crystal Cathedral** sure put on one hell of a show! One might not think that laser beams, disco fog and Siegfried and Roy-style pyrotechnic displays have their place in church, but they do in Garden Grove. Here, Christian worship means one thing: *special effects!* The days of sitting on painfully hard wood pews, listening to your priest drone on in Latin—or worse, English—are over. Slide into one of *The Crystal Cathedral*'s cushy seats worthy of an AMC movie theater and hold on tight!

It Costs More If You Want To Look Up The Angel's Dress

In addition to the architectural oddity that is *The Crystal Cathedral*, Dr. Robert Schuller and his congregation are infamous for their splashy spectaculars staged here twice yearly—each one worthy of a Las Vegas showroom. "The Glory of Easter" is their end-all passion play, with production values as slick as any *Les Mis* touring company. A cast of hundreds pile on to the Cathedral stage, including oxen, tigers, peacocks and enough barnyard animals to fill a dozen petting zoos—even Jesus makes his grand entrance down a catwalk through the center of the theater...I mean the church...on a real burro no less!

Chickenhawks will thrill to the Roman soldiers, traditionally played by the St. Paul High School football team, charging down the carpeted aisles on horseback baring their muscled thighs in short skirts and strappy sandals. Without question, however, the real showstoppers are the angels. Strung up by fine wire to an intricate block-and-tackle apparatus, they fly hundreds of feet from the far corners of the balconies, swooshing down just inches above your scalp, singing operatic songs and circling above the expensive seats down front. If you happen to be positioned in just the right spot, you can look straight up into their filmy gowns and cop a peek of some *real* heaven—perhaps that's why those tickets cost a little more.

Special effects and exotic animals are carefully paced throughout the productions to prevent any downtime—*The Crystal Cathedral* is far too savvy to blow its theatrical wad all at once—and the finales never fail to please. During the crucifixion scene, all three crosses rise from the floor through clouds of dry ice as an enormous section of the *Cathedral*'s glass wall opens like an electric garage door, bringing a gust of the cold night wind into your face while green laser beams shoot from behind the star of the show and out into the evening sky. For anyone who ever saw Kiss in concert the first time around, the resurrection sequence will take you right back to an Ace Frehley guitar solo of 1979.

While hardly shy of special effects, "The Glory of Christmas" lacks the fireworks of the Easter extravaganza—but the Easter show doesn't have camels or special guest stars! The 1995 "Glory of Christmas" featured a cheesecake-a-la-mode solo dance performance by the deaf Miss America, Heather Whitestone. Following their curtain call, cast members are stationed just outside the exits—dragging along any animal they can fit through the door—to pose for pictures and greet their public. Don't miss this excellent Christmas card photo op! There are as many as three performances a day for their month-long runs. If you can't make it to Garden Grove, call your local cable company and watch the "Glory of Christmas" or the "Glory of Easter" on Pay Per View! Buy the CD! Buy the postcard booklet! Forget to set the timer on your VCR? Buy the video! But for Christ's sake, *don't miss out!*

Even if it's not Easter or Christmas, there's still plenty to see at *The Crystal Cathedral*. In fact, free tour guides are available to show you around, and it isn't uncommon to see small groups of wide-eyed, Bermuda-shorted tourists laden with Instamatics and camcorders recording the event as though they were visiting some kind of Christian Hearst Castle. It's also fun to create your own tour, and if you do, make sure you begin at the John Crean Tower. Part Gothic, part science fiction, part Seattle World's Fair 1962, this seemingly functionless metallic and marble campanile is topped with a sharp spike that features a flashing light not too unlike the

Capitol Records building in Hollywood. With such a grand presentation, one would guess this tower must house something very special. It does. The bottom of the tower contains a small cylindrical room, with the interior circumference lined with polished marble pillars and spotlights recessed into the floor shooting beams to the ceiling. In the center of the room is a circular prie deux kneeler that encompasses a handrail surrounding a Plexiglas case containing a large piece of "crystal" positioned atop a rotating platform (reliable sources tell me it's nothing but acrylic resin, but don't let that spoil it for you). The point of all this is to kneel in front of this rotating resin chunk—which could easily be interpreted as an abstract crucifix—and stare into it, watching the play of prismatic colors and reflected light. Hours could easily be frittered away. Clearly, this is what Garden Grove Christians do instead of hallucinogens, "Stare into it long enough and it starts to move backwards," we were informed by an Orange County mother of two with a glazed look in her eye. The whole experience is very unchurchlike and the room looks more than well-equipped to contact alien spacecraft.

The *Cathedral*, too, is open for lookiloos, the architecture of which could very well set a new precedent for mega-discotheques. Equally distressing is the Schullervision screen—my term, not theirs—the football stadium-scale monitor on which Dr. Schuller is simulcast as he delivers his sermon from the stage.

Just when you thought it couldn't get any weirder, the parking lot features a "drive-in worship" section, in which followers can sit roasting in parked cars while listening to the Sunday service on giant loudspeakers positioned throughout the lot. One can only fantasize about carhops on rollerskates gliding from one driver's side window to the next carrying giant collection plates. What else would you expect from a congregation that held it's first service at the *Orange Drive-In Movie Theater* in 1955? True, all true.

If you really want to push the organized religion envelope, take a peek inside the gift shop. *Crystal Cathedral* postcards, keychains, pins, posterbooks, CDs, videos, thimbles, bells, mugs, even *Crystal Cathedral* cocktail napkins—it's all here, and it flies off the shelf. Feeling more like the housewares and stationery departments of *Macy's*, the gift shop offers bath oils, potpourri, candles, greeting cards, and totally unnecessary Keane/Hummelwareish porcelain statuary. If this is any indication of the Cathedral congregation, the selections available in the book center paints a picture even more grim: self help, self help, self help. Shelves and shelves of Christian books you'll never see anywhere else, and certainly would never open, like Cathy Lechner's *I'm Trying to Sit at His Feet, But Who's Going to Cook Dinner?* (OK, bad example, maybe you'd open that one).

If you haven't the time to attend Schuller's Sunday services or read the books he's penned, the gift shop radically simplifies the path to spiritual enlightenment; you can purchase a glittery halo here for $3.95. Also featured among the wares in the gift shop is the telling—albeit grammatically awkward—Possibility Thinkers Creed:

> **When faced with a mountain I WILL NOT QUIT!**
> **I will keep on striving until I climb over, find**
> **a pass through, tunnel underneath—**
> **or simply stay and turn the mountain into**
> **a gold mine, with God's help!**
>
> **—Robert Schuller**

Photocopied onto a thin, 5" x 7" piece of parchment paper, The Creed sells for .25 cents plus tax. How fast can you say *The Crystal Cathedral Hotel and Casino?*

—MM

The Crystal
Cathedral
12141 Lewis Street
Garden Grove
(714) 971-4000

An expensive history lesson at *Medieval Times*

If the thought of 600 screaming kids and their drunken screaming parents—all sporting paper crowns and eating with their fingers—makes you a little nervous, you might want to drop a few Xanax before visiting **Medieval Times**—or steer clear altogether.

You'd think a Medieval-themed attraction centered solely around a live jousting tournament might be somewhat of a rarity these days. Wrong! You can find *Medieval Times* as far north as Toronto, and as far south as Dallas—as far east as Lyndhurst, New Jersey, and as far west as our own backyard. Granted, *Medieval Times* probably isn't the first place you'd think of when planning a night on the town, but it's worth a look-see—even if you've never taken special interest in the period of history most noted for the Black Plague and The Spanish Inquisition.

Your medieval adventure begins as soon as you step through the doors. "Welcome to our castle!" one of the several thousand costumed employees beams as she slams a

Is That A Vaginal Pear In Your Pocket Or Are You Just Happy To See Me?

paper crown on your head (just like the ones Burger King gives away) and shoves you into a line for your medieval photo shoot with the castle's King and Queen. At *Medieval Times* no one ever asks to take your picture, they just blast a flashbulb in your face and return later to try and peddle some overpriced item bearing your startled mug.

Come showtime, crowds are ushered into the jousting arena, which faintly reeks of horse piss. The theater seating is in the round, at long tables, divided into six different color-coordinated sections (corresponding with the color of your crown—only the color blind and those short on cash will have trouble at *Medieval Times*). Shortly after you're seated—BLAST—another assault from the castle's paparazzi. Later in the evening you'll find yourself paying astronomical sums of money for these commemorative photos—just so that a picture of you wearing a *Medieval Times* paper crown doesn't fall into the wrong hands somewhere down the road.

"Hi! My name is Greg, I'll be your slave tonight," chirps a teenaged food server in medieval costume. While his greeting may raise an eyebrow or two—lest you get the wrong impression—our slave never once begged for us to shit in his mouth, flog him with a cat o' nine tails, or affix alligator clamps to his nipples (then again, we never asked). There is no boot-licking or toe-sucking or fist-fucking at *Medieval Times*; the slaves here limit their services to food, it seems. After hours, what they do is their own business. As your slave begins slinging forth steaming bowls of "Dragon Soup" from a large bucket (a soup that had the acidic taste and runny-chunky consistency akin to freshly spewed vomit), wenches peddling everything from *Medieval Times* pennants to electric roses pass your table, trying to siphon as much money as possible from your pockets before the show starts. Your wallet never gets cold at *Medieval Times*.

It's a little-known fact, but in the middle ages, jousting tournaments traditionally began with a psychedelic light show—and since the folks at *Medieval Times* have spared no detail in recreating this "evening of spectacular pageantry," the audience is treated to a second-rate LSD trip, via the rousing colored spots and freaked-out light filters swirling across the dirt floor of the jousting arena and onto the faces of bedazzled audience members. After that, the show gets iffy. Some chick brings out a live falcon and has it fly around the arena before it attacks a chunk of raw meat she's been swinging around on a leather strap. Some horses prance around and do fancy kicks in unnatural ways. There's some kind of story going on, a lot of yammering between the King and the knights—and in spite of the jousting, the sword fights and the stunts, nothing holds the audience's attention like when one of the horses takes a big dump in the arena—which eventually gets stomped over by every other horse in the arena. Well, you know what they say in show business: never work with children or animals! Try eating dinner with your fingers as you watch the rectum of an Andalusian stallion dilate and spill forth a good ten or fifteen pounds of road apples! *Slave, bring me another basted potato!*

Though the "tournament" is staged similarly to that of a WWF wrestling match, the audience is either so young, so drunk, or so ignorant that they actually scream and cheer for "their" knight (who is also color-coded with your crown and your seating assignment) throughout the competition. Full-grown adults actually leap from their chairs screaming "Go Blue Knight!!" "Kill 'em Green!" as if it's not all predetermined who's going to win! *Medieval Times* is not a good place to restore your faith in collective American I.Q.

Right about the point in the show where the victorious knight chooses his Queen of Love and Beauty—or something like that—your slave or wench will bring your dessert (a medieval Pop-Tart and perhaps the worst cup of coffee to be had in all the kingdom) as the photo wenches peddle the final portrait of the evening—plucking the last few bills from your exhausted wallet. But the evening isn't over yet! After clearing the auditorium, you're invited to the "Knight Club" for dancing and cocktails—and to meet "your" Knight in person. "Get an autograph from YOUR KNIGHT, take a picture with YOUR KNIGHT, do whatever you want to do with YOUR KNIGHT" the D.J. kept chanting like a mantra—and after spending as much money as you will undoubtedly have by that point, you'll start to feel like that damn Knight really does belong to you! As the club spins an odd assortment of tunes, from Blondie's "Call Me" to vintage polka numbers to "Funky Town," Teva-sandaled, fanny-packed tourists do the Macarena on the dance floor, and little kids start dropping like flies on the blue vinyl booths. Meanwhile, the Knights make themselves available at the bar, fluffing their long, rock 'n roll hair like a bunch of tenth-century gigolos, eager to chat up the legal-aged PYTs on summer vacation (later, you can see these same girls engrossed in intimate conversation with their Knight, now in his street clothes, outside the employee entrance of the castle at the north side of the parking lot).

You're also encouraged to spend *lots* of time in their gift shop, which is nearly as big as the arena, and features a sword concession, *Medieval Times* videos, postcards, mugs, and ashtrays, plus all the standard vendibles you'd expect to find at a Renaissance Pleasure Faire: pewter miniatures, court jester hats, crystal balls, et al. The gift shop also gives you a special peek at the *Medieval Times* equine collection, which you can see caged on the other side of a plate-glass window.

But the evening's *still* not over! Before you go, take a spin through the Museum of Torture—it's not free of course, but for $2.00 you get a crash course in medieval S&M (complete with instructions and helpful illustrations) over an array of gadgets and equipment that even *The Pleasure Chest* doesn't stock—like the fallbret, the Judas cradle, and the rectal/vaginal pear. Hang around that employees entrance and you just might find yourself a willing slave.

And you thought *Medieval Times* was just for kids.

**Medieval Times
Dinner and
Tournament**
7662 Beach Blvd.
Buena Park
(714) 521-4740
(800) 899-6600

163   KULTURE SCHLOCK

Star-fucking at *The Hollywood Wax Museum*

"The stars come to life...IN LIVING WAX."
—*Hollywood Wax Museum brochure*

O ne of the finest by-products of our celebrity-obsessed culture is appropriately located right in the heart of Hollywood Boulevard. Solely for its sheer unadulterated absurdity, **The Hollywood Wax Museum** rates as Los Angeles' #1 tourist trap.

On a tiny platform out front stands *The Hollywood Wax Museum*'s resident mime. His pores sealed shut with layers of flesh-tone pancake makeup, he keeps his post outside the ticket window doing "the robot" in a futile attempt to draw in some of the passing sidewalk traffic. Unfortunately, pancaked roboting mimes tend to scare people off these days; few buy tickets. I doubt a more known and less frequented tourist attraction exists.

The quality of the displays at the *Wax Museum* is hardly what you'd expect from a city whose chief industry is illusion—in fact I've seen better work done with chicken wire and crepe paper at a junior high school prom. Scant care has been given to upkeep. Light-

Is That A Wad Of Tin Foil In Your Pocket Or Are You Just Happy To See Me?

bulbs are burned out everywhere and most of the props are falling apart as quickly as they were slapped together. George Washington is missing his right hand, someone stuffed a wad of tissue up Franklin D. Roosevelt's nose, and many of the *Wax Museum*'s faces are as scratched up as yesterday's lottery tickets from the clawing of overzealous wax-curious patrons. The floors of the museum are sticky and the air is dank and stale, not too unlike the private viewing booths in an adult book store.

With the exception of Michael Jackson, none of the celebrity figures bear much resemblance to the celebrity, and in most cases if it weren't for the name placards you'd be clueless. It looks more like a gallery of celebrity *impersonators* with many of the women—especially Diana Ross, Dolly Parton and Cher—looking like punch-drunk drag queens. Clearly the figures are not made of wax (scratch one and you'll see for yourself,) and most are pieced together from department store mannequins. Fresh-faced tourists wander through looking puzzled, aware that something isn't quite right, unable to see the value in what appears to be a worthless and undeniably empty experience.

There are especially bad theme installations, like the USA for Africa display featuring an endless, grating audio loop of "We Are the World" along with figures of many "We Are the World" voices. But the saccharine icing on this already sickening sweet cake are the black and white photo enlargements of *real* starving African children hanging on the wall behind wax likenesses of Cindy Lauper, Lionel Richie, Elton John, David Bowie and Willie Nelson. It's an overwhelming moment that you soon won't forget. Give yourself some time to fully experience it.

Look for the hit-and-miss attention paid to male anatomical detail. Some of the men pack hefty baskets, while others were suspiciously shortchanged. George Washington and Magic Johnson feature the biggest bulges, with Henry Winkler as "Fonzie" and circus performer Gunther Gebel Williams coming in as close seconds. Patrick Swayze's crotch features almost labia-like curves, and not surprisingly, Burt Reynolds appears absent of all genitalia. Elvis' bulge—a little too high and too far to one side—looks more like a colostomy bag about ready to burst. Exactly just how far do the wax crafters take their work? Curious, I yanked down Michael J. Fox's jeans to discover that what separates the men from the boys—at least at the *Hollywood Wax Museum*—is a wad of tinfoil securely held in place with several pieces of duct tape.

The Hollywood Wax Museum
6767 Hollywood Blvd.
(at Highland)
Hollywood
(213) 462-8860

The best feature of the museum is that most of the displays are completely accessible, aside from a fence or reasonably low barrier wall. You can hop right in—as long as no one sees you—and take a few pictures. An electric eye protects some of the displays, but all they do is beep twice and there are rarely any consequences. A quick test for the photo bug: wave your hand in front of the electric eye first, most of them are broken. If you don't hear a beep, hop right in and snap away! Get on your knees and give "head" to Gary Burghoff from "M*A*S*H," or frolic doggy-style with Toto. Next year's Christmas card could prove to be quite a hoot! Just be careful not to knock anything over; you break it, you bought it.

There's a gift shop that sells some really great *Wax Museum* tee shirts, but to even enter the gift shop you have to cough up the steep $8.95 admission price. As preposterous as it may sound, it's worth every penny (if only for Michael J. Fox's tinfoil penis). And if you're prone to stalking celebrities, you can rape one here and get it out of your system before you really hurt somebody.

It's intriguing to note that of all the celebrities on display, only three of them were deemed prominent enough to be featured in the museum twice: Sylvester Stallone, Arnold Schwarzenegger, and Jesus.

–MM

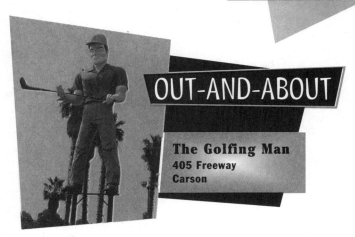

OUT-AND-ABOUT

The Golfing Man
405 Freeway
Carson

Low-rent paleontology at
The Cabazon Monsters

he Cabazon Monsters are everything a great American roadside attraction should be: they're big, they're garish, they're stupid, they're completely useless, and they're adjacent to a truck stop diner that serves honey-dipped fried chicken. Thirty years before Steven Spielberg helped make the term "Jurassic" part of our pop vernacular, a septuagenarian *Knott's Berry Farm* employee named Claude Bell was slaving away on a seemingly senseless Jurassic project of his own.

He broke ground in 1965, and when construction was completed a decade later, Claude had built himself a four-story brontosaurus—complete with little windows, a fire

Marines Piss For Free

escape, and air-conditioning, which he christened "Dinny" (pronounced *Die-nee*). Construction for a second dinosaur quickly commenced; a sixty-five-foot tyrannosaurus rex to feature a lookout tower in its mouth and a slide down its tail. Unfortunately before Claude realized that dream, he left us for the big Jurassic Park in the sky. Today the tyrannosaurus appears complete, although the steel door fitted into the side of its gut is padlocked shut and its exterior stairway is completely hacked off. In lieu of a slide, cut-rate helicopter rides are offered on the lot just behind the nameless tyrannosaurus—but the helicopter isn't shaped like a giant pterodactyl or anything, so what's the point?

Visitors are welcome to step deep, deep within Dinny's lower intestine and up a stairway leading into a "museum" and gift shop. Though the museum doesn't rival that of the *La Brea Tar Pits*, it does give a fairly comprehensive history of Dinny. The gift shop sells a lot of cheap ugly jewelry and novelties that have nothing whatsoever to do with dinosaurs, like fake spilled cans of Coke, trick brandy snifters, and mylar wind socks.

Dwarfed in the shadow of Claude Bell's inspired masterworks lies **The Wheel Inn**—a coffee shop that has kept its doors open to hungry travelers en route to Palm Springs since 1958. With a western-cum-atomic 50s decor, a phone on every table, and staff and clientele that look like they just missed the final cut of a "Hee Haw" casting call, the restaurant is as heavy on charm as it is on cholesterol. A brightly lit sign bearing the cryptic message "PUBLIC RESTROOMS .25 CENTS TO CASHIER. MARINES EXEMPT" faces you upon entering. An adjoining mini-mart just off the main dining room sells everything from Indian-head nickle belt buckles and coo-coo clocks, to single rolls of toilet paper and the Native American-inspired feather-and-leather craft catastrophes known as "dreamcatchers." The rear dining room features a "24 Hour Art Show,"—something uncommon to most truck stops—but you won't find any Brancusi sculptures or macabre Otto Dix etchings in here. What you will find are some abstract expressionist works in iridescent acrylic paint and glitter, or motel-room-style landscapes in oil. There's also a daunting selection of framed T&A posters and wall plaques crafted from real bull horns.

A trip to *The Wheel Inn* isn't complete without a spin of the postcard carousel in the lobby; for the same amount it costs to use their toilet, you can get some sensational postcards of the famed *Cabazon* dinosaurs. They also sell postcards of other celebrated dinosaur attractions too, like Bob Hope's and Frank Sinatra's Palm Springs homes.

The Wheel Inn/ The Cabazon Monsters
10 Freeway
Cabazon
(909) 849-7012

Wading through the Junk and Cliches at
Chinatown Tourist Plaza

Chinese Angelenos probably find the central tourist plaza of Chinatown just as loathsome as we do, but like all ethnic tourist traps, it seems to be accepted by its own people as a necessary evil. Just like *Santa's Village* and the *Cabazon Monsters* cater to the lowest level of Anglo sensationalism, Chinatown shamelessly fulfills the round-eye concept of Buddha-strewn wishing wells, greasy egg roll emporiums, and souvenir shops packed to the gills with cheap plastic doodads, overpriced ugly vases, and martial arts weapons. Ironically, most of these hideous items aren't even from the People's Republic of China, but from Taiwan, Hong Kong, Japan, the Philippines, and that farthest of Chinese colonies, Mexico. Worse, most of the shopkeepers treat their trashy inventory like it's Tiffany crystal, plastering their walls with quaint signs that bear sayings like, "So nice to look at, so lovely to hold, but if you break it, consider it sold"—and eyeballing your every move as if you might suddenly go berserk and start smashing all their windup, spark-spitting Godzillas. What's the big deal? Don't they know this stuff is specifically manufactured to break within an hour of purchase anyway?

Situated between Hill St. and Broadway at the Northern end of Chinatown proper, **Chinatown Plaza** was once the home of two of L.A.'s premiere punk venues, *Madame Wong's* and the *Hong Kong*. *Wong's* has long since sold out to an antique shop, and the *Hong Kong* no longer features hip new bands. What's left is a typical Chinatown tourist trap, flanked by two arched entryways on either street, and featuring a large, garish "wishing well" that more resembles one of those carnival games where you try to pitch a dime onto any one of a number of strategically poised glass dishes. Looking more like a miniature replica of the Martian landscape, this red plaster monstrosity is marked up with little signs that serve as targets for your spare change: "Health," "Love" and "Money" are but a few of the objectives at which you can toss your coinage in hopes of a rosier future. One wonders who's the first to collect the riches from this bogus money magnet: the proprietors of the plaza, or perhaps one of the many homeless citizens who populate the downtown area? If there's any justice in the world, it would be the latter.

> **Confucius Say: "He Who Buys Cheap Plastic Souvenirs Gets What He Pays for."**

If you're in the market for a full-on black Ninja outfit complete with hood, mask, gloves, and shoe covers, then you might find what you're looking for in one of the many curio shops that line the *Plaza*. Bruce Lee fans will also be pleased to know that they can purchase an assortment of nunchaks, sharpened throwing stars, knives, swords, spears, and similar killing tools at these very same boutiques. If jasmine soap and cheap plastic vibrators are more your speed, you'll find them here, too, along with imitation jade carvings, giant rubber insects, wind chimes, and the occasional odd import like the electronic multifunctional ass-cleaner that fits on the top of your toilet seat like some kind of funky lunar module.

If you're going to visit Chinatown and plan on parting with some bucks, then for God's sake, take a trip down this unique neighborhood's sidestreets before you take on the heavyweight tourist trap that sticks out like a sore—and infected—thumb. On your off-the-beaten-path trek you'll find plenty of bizarre apothecaries that sell medicinal herbs as well as rare and aged Ginseng, seafood markets stocked with creatures you never knew existed, and an assortment of other bizarre vendors you'll find nowhere else in the City of Angels. Then again, if you're after a Chinatown snow-dome that whips up a winter flurry when you shake it, you already know where to go.

Chinatown Tourist Plaza
900 Broadway
Los Angeles

See You Later...

Crying crocodile tears for

The California Alligator Farm

There once was a time when Florida had nothing on Los Angeles. The City of Angels also boasted acres of beautiful orange groves, a booming retirement community, and eventually, a bevy of coke addicts. What you may not have been aware of, however, was our once-thriving and illustrious 'gator farm!

At the time, **The California Alligator Farm** was the biggest in the world ("The Most Stupendous Aggregation of Alligators Ever Exhibited!" they proudly asserted), with a reptile population of nearly 2000, including a prodigious offering of iguanas, snakes and turtles. Here you could see reluctant alligators coerced into performing "tricks," learn how to catch a wild 'gator by way of an instructional demo, eyewitness alligator hypnosis, and even saddle up one of the giant man-eating reptiles for a ride around the park! At feeding time, crowds watched nervously as an attendee would take a full-grown live chicken by its legs and dangle it over the open jaws of a hungry adult 'gator—teasing him a bit for the sake of the spectators—before dropping the unlucky bird to its quick (and apparently tasty) demise. Afterwards, you could further demonstrate alligator appreciation in the gift shop—throwing karma to the wind—over an enticing selection of handbags, wallets, shoes and luggage.

Unfortunately our alligator farm went the way of our orange groves, and these days alligator rides are pretty tough to come by in Los Angeles—much less a decent set of luggage—and it's probably just as well. Some animal activist spoilsport like Bob Barker or Brigitte Bardot would probably picket to have the place shut down anyway.

The California Alligator Farm
Formerly adjacent to Lincoln Park
Los Angeles

Entering the twilight zone of
Santa Claus Lane

A 1950s freeway rest stop originally intended as a play on the Santa Barbara/Santa Maria/Santa Monica theme, Santa Claus, California (a.k.a. **Santa Claus Lane**) has come a long way since its modest beginning as a juice bar and gift shop. Unfortunately, over the years *Santa Claus Lane* seems to dazzle fewer and fewer passersby, with the expansions made during its prosperous heyday now as neglected as a Christmas tree lot on December 26th. Lobstertown, U.S.A.—one of two restaurants once featured in Santa Claus, California—now stands abandoned. The *Santa's Kitchen* of yesterday—an unduly charming theme restaurant featuring two Christmas trees completely decorated, skirted, and begirded with packages—is the *Nick's Steak House* of today. A cluster of shops dealing exclusively in bric-a-brac endure like a carefully composed still-life or a scene from the morning after a neutron blast—Hummelware in place, not a human in sight. It just makes you want to cry. *Santa Claus Lane* is one of those places that you feel guilty leaving without making a purchase.

We've always been worried about the fate of *Santa Claus Lane*. It's not like we're losing sleep over it or anything, but one can't help but wonder just how many more years are left for this gem among Southern California roadside attractions. To peddle a strawberry shake or a gift-pack of dried fruit in 1954, a mammoth Santa Claus was more than enough to snare a passing motorist. But as we approach the next millennium there seems to be something decidedly lacking about a Santa Claus-steepled roadside reststop—so much so that the cars keep moving right on by. A candy store and bakery, a toy emporium, a restaurant, and a string of shops that sell items so useless they can only be classified as "gifts" all sit poised, polished and eagerly awaiting business, but are almost always completely devoid of spendthrift travelers. Actually, it's pretty remarkable that *Santa Claus Lane* is able to meet its overhead peddling licorice whips, cinnamon rolls, pogo sticks and porcelain miniatures on the edge of the 101 freeway in Carpinteria.

It must have something to do with the magic of Christmas.

Santa Claus Lane
Santa Claus, California
101 Freeway
Carpinteria

OUT-AND-ABOUT

Load your camera and make a special trip out to La Puente's most famous orifice. You won't be sorry— and the donuts are great too.

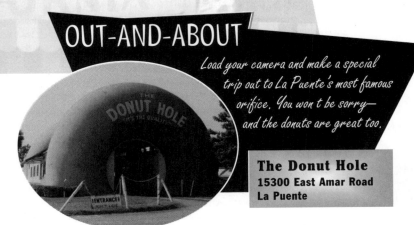

The Donut Hole
15300 East Amar Road
La Puente

The Old Town Music Hall

El Segundo's Hallucinogenic Hootenanny

ince most Angelenos have no concept of how to behave in a movie theater (much less on a freeway), the already unsavory experience of spending half a week's pay for the opportunity to sit in a small black box with a Lilliputian screen is further soured by the noisome antics of ill-bred filmgoers, proving that there's a whole hell of a lot to be said for the home video industry.

Fortunately, there is one last great bastion for public viewing of the motion picture: a place pleasingly absent of screaming babies, rowdy teens, and soda-slicked floors. **The Old Town Music Hall** is the only place left where a person can see a movie the old-fashioned way: no commercials, no labyrinth-like cineplex, no frappucino, and, on occasion, no sound! Tucked away on a tiny sidestreet in El Segundo (the less-traveled side of LAX), this micro-theater originally served as a silent movie house, and today, three quarters of a century later, still runs the odd silent flick. *Now that's progress!* In fact, their regular film calendar rarely carries a title that postdates the bombing of Pearl Harbor. Though the Shirley Temple vehicle *Dimples* may not be at the top of your list of must-sees, at least you won't have to face the crowds of the latest Schwarzenegger blood-fest. Instead, you'll find a loyal group of film enthusiasts blessed with an attention span that can bear periods longer than that of a music video.

The diminutive 188-seat auditorium is barely large enough to accommodate the two enormous chandeliers which loom from its relatively low ceiling. Semi-reclinable seats in rows no wider than four-across face a raised carpeted stage, dressed up with cherub-topped candelabra floor lamps, and a grouping of several sculptures—all of which happen to be the RCA dog ("His master's voice") in different sizes. An elaborate Chinese gong flanks the left side of the stage, and to the right, an exotic "bell piano" topped with a shiny gold Buddha encrusted with plastic gems. Also crammed onto the small stage are two concert pianos, including a 1917 Steinway once belonging to Nelson Eddy (its ivories were reportedly tickled by George Gershwin).

The Old Town Music Hall features another attraction even more unique to movie theaters than Chinese gongs, cherubic lighting schemes and RCA dog sculpture: bolted in place at center stage is their 1925 "Mighty Wurlitzer" (at *The Old Town Music Hall*, the word "Mighty" must always precede the name "Wurlitzer"). And mighty it is, because this isn't your typical theater pipe organ. A fairly unattractive "velvet" drape hangs upstage behind the organ keyboard—presumably to conceal the movie screen. But you're in El Segundo, folks, and things aren't always what they appear. As the master of the "Mighty Wurlitzer" takes his seat and starts pumping his organ, the curtain slowly peels back to reveal the vibrating, honking, rattling animation of organ innards; every pipe, air vent, drum, bell, and horn going at once like a mammoth one-man band. *So what,* you may be thinking. *Big deal, organ guts, who cares?* Well, like Ken Kesey's old school bus, these organ guts go a little "further": *because every piece is painted in different fluorescent colors and illuminated with black lights!!* The sight of shaking hot-orange tambourines and Day-Glo blue snare drums is something you just don't see every day, unless you do a lot of acid. If you've a propensity for psychoactive substances, certainly you'll agree that *The Old Town Music Hall* is a *very* special place (especially when you consider the cherubs, the pack of ceramic dogs, and the munificent chandeliers). And if you're the type who gets "high on life," hold onto your hat, because life in El Segundo doesn't get much higher than this.

The "Mighty Wurlitzer" gets fired up for a musical prologue prior to each feature presentation, and leads the audience through a quick series of sing-a-longs to time-tested old standards like "Mairzy Doats" and "My Wild Irish Rose," while the lyrics are projected on the screen from antiquated slides. If you've never sung-a-long to a psychedelic pipe organ knocking out a tune like "After the Ball" then you might as well suck the gas pipe. In addition to the sing-a-long, they run a program of short subjects—usually a rare cartoon or a live-action sound comedy—and take a brief intermission before the feature.

The Old Town Music Hall is the only movie theater in greater Los Angeles that regularly runs full-length silent films with live pipe organ accompaniment. Don't underestimate how wonderful a movie can be without hyperbolic special effects, superfluous dialogue or an obnoxious overkill of Foley art. You may be the youngest one there by seventy years, but if you'd rather face the scene at *Universal CityWalk*, go right ahead you masochistic jerk. But don't say we didn't warn you.

The Old Town Music Hall

140 Richmond Street
El Segundo
(310) 322-2592

Lost Strangeles

Remembering the heyday of Dr. Gene Scott

"JESUS SAVES.
MOSES INVESTS."

—Anonymous

God's Angry Man Is Still Pissed Off

In L.A., it's funny how so many things can converge in a strange karmic kind of way. For example, there was a time ten years ago when you could ride the voyeuristic elevators at the *Bonaventure* and at the same time get a fabulous view of the immense red neon JESUS SAVES sign that loomed prominent on a rooftop just across the street. That sign was the beckoning beacon of **Dr. Gene Scott's** ministry, a multimedia monopoly that at one time had a death-like grip on the airwaves, both TV and radio, until the spoilsports known as the FCC thought that the white-bearded, hat-wearing, horse-owning, cigar-smoking minister was a little too powerful for his own britches, and thus came down on him with much the same wrath God displayed at Sodom & Gomorrah. For me—a fan of recreational evangelism—that was the death knell for L.A.'s finest and most reliable entertainer. You wouldn't find Reverend Schuller demonstrating his contempt for a meddling federal agency by bashing a bug-eyed, wind-up monkey to bits with a baseball bat on the air, that's for damn sure!

Scott didn't dabble too much in the straight-ahead, teary-eyed, Jesus-Died-For-You-So-Send-Me-Some-Money variety of fundraising. Instead, he tended to ramble on endlessly about the power of the pyramids, or the Lost City of Atlantis, or how Jesus made a secret trip to England during the mysterious years prior to his nasty crucifixion. And when he tired of such lectures, he'd revert to a frayed video clip of some very white gospel crooners singing a ditty that must have been *Scott*'s fave: *I Want to Know*. As if picking out a victim at random, *Scott* would fix his steely gaze into the camera and bellow something like, "I need ten thousand dollars from Wilmington, North Carolina!" And until he got his ransom, he would play that musical clip over and over, introducing it with the terse, hoarse phrase, "Play *I Want to Know*." And like magic, it would play. And play. And play. Until the viewers of Wilmington broke down from either guilt or exhaustion and collectively coughed up the ten grand. Once *Scott* played *I Want to Know* eleven times in a row. Eleven times! Even though he was paying for the airtime, such a maneuver took brass balls, in our opinion, and made us love the man even more. Of course, we never sent him a dime. Two could play at his game.

Now the JESUS SAVES sign is gone and so is the vast expanse of *Scott*'s once-powerful empire. But he still spreads his word at the *United Artists Theater* in downtown L.A., where he has actually taken the time and money to spruce up the place a bit in an attempt to bring it somewhat back to its original splendor.

Still, it's not the same as it used to be. Especially when you have *I Want to Know* burned indelibly into your mind.

"Artistry they call it! Free expression!"

—Dr. Gene Scott on Modern Art

Sampling a taste of Bombay without leaving Orange County in Artesia's

Little India

Although many would argue that L.A.'s cultural and ethnic diversity spells nothing but trouble, it can't be denied that we're also one of the most enlightened and peace-loving heterogeneous societies in the country—give and take the occasional riot. Even better, this cultural comingling has produced some of Southern California's best restaurants, shopping haunts and museums!

Take **Little India** for example. This four block stretch of Pioneer Blvd. between 183rd and 187th Streets in Orange County's city of Artesia contains the highest concentration of all things Indian this side of New Dehli—and it's all just a stone's throw from *Knott's Berry Farm.*

If you're in the market for a flowing, sheeny sari as seen in any number of effulgent Indian tinctorials but have come up short at *The Beverly Center*, the only problem you'll have on Pioneer Blvd. is choosing which sari shop to visit first. You can start with the *Indian Sari Palace* (18640 Pioneer Blvd.) and work your way up the street to the biggest shops like the *Sari Niketan House of Fashion and Weddings* (18423) which also has lots of cool sundry exotica, and *Preety* (sic) *Fashions* (18327) which features one of the best display windows complete with bindied mannequins—and the fashions are indeed "preety." The sari selection of Pioneer Blvd. hardly ends there, though; there are oodles of smaller shops, and among them you should be able to find at least one sari you can't live this lifetime without.

Even if you're not in the market for a sari you're sure to find something of interest in *Little India*—if not, you can at least make a game of spotting the most misspelled English words or grammatical errors on the street's signage. A stop into *Bombay Spices* (18626)—one of the better markets on the street—is a treat for the senses where you'll not only find an excellent selection of Indian spices (the place smells heavenly) in addition to cosmetics (the darkest red lipsticks you've ever seen), bindi powder dispensers, incense, and tongue scrapers. This store also carries a dazzling collection of accessories for the altar, like little statues of Nataraja, magic lamp incense burners, and pictures of the Taj Mahal encased in acrylic resin. *Bombay Spices* also sells a comprehensive list of Indian films on video, which screen nonstop on a monitor inside the store. Indian cinema is highly prolific and often impressively stylish, and in fact they produce more films per year than Hollywood. It's worth popping in just to catch a few moments of an Indian musical. *Shree Ganesh Groceries* (18411) is one of the largest Indian markets on Pioneer, and warrants a visit just to see their selection of Indian equivalents to American products; the shape of the jars are familiar, as are the colors on the label, but it might take you a second to recognize "Rasna" = "Tang," and "Horlicks" = "Ovaltine." Can you guess what "Gello" is? You can find nearly anything in here—from sitar music on CD, to a primitive pestle and mortar setup, and you'll soon discover that Indian markets are much, much more than grocery stores. *Novelty's* (sic) (18607) has an extensive selection of gifts and cooking gadgets, as well as a large array of adhesive bindis for those unwilling to fiddle with messy powders. Take a side-trip down the cross street of 186th on the east side of Pioneer and poke into *Ziba Music and Gift Center* (11806 186th Street) for an excellent selection of Indian tunes, or the *Surati Farsan Mart* (11814 186th Street) to sample some

Unless you're looking to supplement your sari collection, you'll agree that the best thing about *Little India* is the food. If you're not in the mood for the plenitude of sweets and *chat* (snacks) peddled on Pioneer, you should sit your ass down in the *Little India Grill* (18383) in *The Pioneer Center Shopping Mall* between 183rd and 186th Streets. It's one of the best in the neighborhood, and one of the few to serve *thali* (hot food) in the middle of the day. They're dirt cheap ($5.00 for the lunch buffet and $6.00 for dinner!) and offer a sumptuous veg fare, as well as lamb and chicken, with a selection of six different breads freshly baked in their clay oven. The spicy smells wafting from the door of *The Bombay Chat House* (18511) might lure you in, but they don't serve as varied a feast as *Little India Grill*. Standard Sweets (18600) offers an exclusively vegetarian *chat* menu.

The Pioneer Center Shopping Mall* also features a must-see curiosity, and one of the few Korean businesses in *Little India*, known as *The Water Store* (18381). Guess what they sell. They probably figured the business can't fail since everyone needs water—we just wonder how they explained this to the bank when they applied for their small business loan.

If you're not Indian or Korean, shopkeepers may initially eyeball you with suspicion, but they warm up once they realize you're there to enjoy the splendors of their turf on their terms. If you're unsure about an item on a menu, a proper pronunciation, or some weird Indian widget collecting dust on a shelf, ask. They won't think you're uncool, and take great joy in sharing their culture with an ignorant occidental. One of the best things about *Little India* is that you'll inevitably leave having learned something about the Indian culture that you didn't know upon parking your car. Speaking of which, the parking on Pioneer is FREE—no meters to deal with, no valets, no public lots. Just the gutter and you.

If some nasty plague or impending famine has previously spoiled your travel plans to Calcutta, get out your *Thomas Guide*, grab your tongue scraper, and make the trek to Pioneer Blvd. in Artesia.

You won't be sari.

Little India
Pioneer Blvd.
(between 183rd
and 187th Streets)
Artesia

Preparing for the Real Illegal Alien Invasion with
The Unarius Academy of Science

I t takes a certain kind of mind to believe that soon, *very soon*, our "Space Brothers" from another planet are finally going to land here on Earth and bring with them a better life for us all. While some naysayers would label such a mentality as "fucking loony," optimists who see the glass as half-full would opt for an adjective more in the realm of "insanely hopeful." Upon reflection—and especially living in a town that seems hooked on producing movies about aliens either saving or destroying the earth—the concept certainly seems no more farfetched than our own earthbound, pixie dust-laden fantasies such as a balanced federal budget, world peace, and politicians who can keep their dicks in their pants. Heck, even when compared to the pathetically impossible notion of racial equality, alien contact seems a far more feasible event than, say, Newt Gingrich being strung up by his heels and given the Mussolini treatment—which, if there were any justice in this

Mom, There's An Alien Mothership In The Backyard!

world, would have happened a long time ago.

But enough daydreaming—we're here to talk about the coming of the aliens. And the *Unarius Society* would like nothing better than for those tiny beings with the big black eyes to quit abducting Whitley Streiber, mutilating our cattle and just *land* for Chrissakes! Unarius, an acronym for **UNiversal ARticulate Interdimensional Understanding of Science**, is one of the more way-out of the UFO fan clubs, so way-out, in fact, that it tends to be shunned by most other paranormal groups whose primary means of communication is channeling dead people and alien life forms. Channeling is an important part of the "Interdimensional Science" that is *Unarius*, and is especially helpful since MCI has yet to extend its service to the constellation of Taurus, where our space buddies the Pleiadians are planning their summer vacation on Earth in the year 2001. According to the Unarians, the Pleiadians—along with spacecraft from 31 other planets—will be landing on a rising portion of Atlantis in the Bermuda Triangle, so you'd best book your Caribbean cruise tickets now because this is one spectacle that beats the heck out of watching drunken vacationers from Indiana fall on their asses while attempting the limbo after one Mai-Tai too many!

Is the Taurus constellation too far for you to even begin to fathom? Well, according to the *Unarians*, we have space neighbors who live even closer than the Pleiadians; so close, in fact, they might even be considered to be right in our own cosmic backyard—at least as far as solar systems go. Did Paul McCartney know something we didn't when he wrote the lyrics "Venus and Mars are all right tonight" for a stupid song on his stinky album "Venus and Mars" over two decades ago? Nah, he was probably just stoned to the gills and grasping for some musical fodder, but the *Unarians* really believe that Venus and Mars *are* all right tonight—and every night, in fact—since these two planets are homes to even more of our celestial kin. And we ain't talkin' about some green moss growin' on

a rock. Did you know that Jesus Christ was from Venus? So say the *Unarians*. And they also hint that one of the races on earth is actually a bunch of migrants from Mars. So *that's* why Canadians talk funny!

Best of all, *Unarius* lets its members strut their Thespian stuff when they are given the opportunity to put on their own kind of interstellar-meets-Shirley McLaine Passion Play. In a bizarre combination of bad improv and psychic projection, the *Unarians* dress up in gaudy sci-fi costumes and pose as members of the Interplanetary Confederation (the organization who will arrive in 2001) in order to cure their psychological problems by performing off-the-cuff, past-life psychodramas. This is the kind of theater that John Waters and Kiss fans would surely enjoy, and is the perfect training ground for psychological counselors hoping to take on the most extreme cases.

Who could have devised such a nutty "science" in a world gone sane? Ernest Norman, that's who! Ernest, the author of *Cosmic Continuum and Interdimensional Physics*, and the man who founded *Unarius Science* way back in 1954, was also the reincarnation of that famous Venusian, Christ (or so he said) and the real inventor of television, which Philo T. Farnsworth stole from him when they met by chance in Logan, Utah in the 1920s (again, this is Norman's side of the story). Though Ernest died in 1971, *Unarius* carried on and even flourished under the control of his flamboyant wife and co-founder, Ruth Norman, who passed away in 1994 at the age of 94. Ruth, who was best known to *Unarians* as the Archangel Uriel (an acronym of Universal, Radiant, Infinite, Eternal Light), and to neighbors as the "Space Lady," was the one who instituted the costumed pageants, and also moved the group from its original L.A. base to the glamorous and otherworldly city of El Cajon, a San Diego suburb, shortly after Ernest's death. Ernest—also known as "The Moderator of the Universe" and "Archangel Raphiel"—allegedly approved of all of his wife's augmentations, communicating to the group from his new headquarters on Mars through Charles Spaegel, a Unarian medium who is actually the reincarnation of Charlemagne and one of the current head honchos at *Unarius*.

Trying to keep up with all the *Unarian* teachings—as well as the contradictions contained therein—is a daunting task. It's also time-consuming for anyone with a full-time job and errands to run. But if you have a hunch that 2001 will be a big year for friendly alien visitation, and have been dreaming of the day when you, too, could take part in the annual *Unarius* Conclave of Light convention—wherein the members don some of the ugliest and outrageous outfits since Sonny & Cher were on the air—then get on the *Unarius* bandwagon. They have a veritable mothership full of books and videos just waiting for you, and special seminars to prepare you for the arrival of our Space Brothers, who, hopefully, are as benevolent as the *Unarians* say they are, and won't enslave us, eat us, or worse, force us to watch *Supermarket Sweeps*.

Unarius World Headquarters
145 South Magnolia Ave.
El Cajon
(619) 444-7062

Mufon-LA

augh if you will, but UFOs are no laughing matter for the folks at **Mufon–LA** (Mutual UFO Network), the local chapter of the nationwide organization of UFO buffs. We'd been wanting to check out one of the *Mufon* meetings for quite some time—long before extraterrestrial speculation enjoyed its cheesy media renaissance—but as L.A. fate would have it, the first meeting we attended turned out to be a freakish exception to the rule. Imagine our surprise and consternation when we discovered that strange alien beings had replaced the guest speakers for the evening. These creatures, posing as a Yuppie couple, droned on more about satanic, cannibalistic torture than they did about alien encounters—which, in the end, amounted to even more torture. We wanted to see and hear about sightings, photos, videos, top secret documents, and how our government is hiding it all from us for no good reason. Well, as it turns out, we picked a *bad* night.

Sure Beats Going To An AA Meeting

Yes, the fact of the matter is that you can get all that good kind of stuff at a *Mufon* meeting, at least most of the time. The preliminary videos and speakers on our particular *hell night* were quite down-to-earth, offering up the latest evidence of something really bizarre going on *up there*. And, to be sure, there is *something* going on, or The X-Files wouldn't be wallowing in its own special brand of freakish success. Just check out any one of a number of convincing videos and books sold at the back of the room. Those of you expecting to stumble upon an audience of kooks adorned with aluminum foil receptor hats on their heads will be sorely disappointed. The *Mufon* patrons are normal folks, *good Americans like yourselves*, who just happen to harbor the same firm belief that our government is a lying, sneaking, cheating pack of toadies who'd sooner tell you how to cheat the IRS than divulge everything it knows about flying saucers and little grey men. Heck, if our elected officials lie to us about everything else, it only makes sense that they're not being forthright about the impending apocalyptic invasion from outer space.

Mufon–LA
1001 Pickwick Center
(One mile east of
Buena Vista at Main)
Burbank
(818) 450-MUFON

Mufon trades in more academic circles than, say, the Unarius and Aetherius clans, and a *Mufon* meeting makes a great first date for physicists, astronomers, and computer geeks. Just check out the scheduled speaker and/or topic before coughing up the $10 entrance fee ($5 for members). Though our first visit was a truly disturbing letdown, further sessions redeemed the experience. Heck, you may even be lucky enough to attend a session with Mr. Alien Contact himself, Whitley Strieber, who is no stranger to the *Mufon* circuit, and knows a number of spacemen on a first-name basis.

Spacing Out with *The Aetherius Society*

"God made man, but he used a monkey to do it."
—*"Jocko Homo" by Devo*

Did you know that mankind is so violent that we've completely destroyed the human race on this planet not once, but *twice?* The first time we killed each other off was when we lived on what was known as Lemuria or Mu. Never heard of them? How about Atlantis, then? Yes, the legendary sunken city was also the playing field for the second genocidal Superbowl that wiped us out many eons ago. And while we're on the subject, you probably didn't know that even before these two tragedies transpired, we lived on another planet altogether! It was called Maldek, and it was located between Mars and Jupiter until we destroyed our race and the damn planet to boot! If none of this sounds familiar to you, then perhaps you are not acquainted with the teachings of **The Aetherius Society**.

Like the *Unarius Society* and *The Church of Scientology*, *The Aetherius Society* is a melange of earthly theologies augmented by a healthy dose of sci-fi weirdness. Mixing yoga, UFOs, and a patchwork quilt of eastern and western religions, *The Aetherius Society* has developed a worldwide following since its inception in 1954 by Sir George King, and keeps its American headquarters right here in Los Angeles (other locations can be found in New Zealand, England, and Canada).

"His Eminence" Sir George King was the "Primary Terrestrial Mental Channel for the Cosmic Masters." In other words, he was the earthly conduit for messages from highly evolved beings on other planets in our solar system, who, for some reason, want to help us out of our violent rut, yet not get too close to us in the process. And with our track record for destroying planets, who can blame them? Fortunately, these "Transmissions from the Cosmic Masters" have been recorded, transcribed, and published by *The Aetherius Society* for the benefit of all those in search of the truth.

While most of the *Society*'s beliefs are sure to raise eyebrows and elicit more than an occasional chuckle of doubt and disbelief, their bottom line is surprisingly refreshing in a world of greedy cult-religions that promote self-advancement and threaten anyone who stands in their way. "Service is the most potent religion," according to *The Aetherius Society*, and following their doctrine, those who practice selfless acts to benefit their fellow man will find themselves advancing up the evolutionary ladder of enlightenment faster than those who seek to satisfy their own wants and needs alone. Indeed, much of the *Aetherius* mission is to balance mankind's crappy karma for the better, which is quite a herculean task when one considers the relative size of our collective global debt. Let's face it, as far as animals go, we may be advanced, but as creatures allegedly made in God's image, we really suck.

Is That A Spiritual Energy Radiator In Your Pocket

That's where *The Aetherius Society* hopes to lend a helping hand. Take their "Operation Prayer Power," for

Or Are You Just Happy To See Me?

example. Using "dynamic prayer, eastern mantra and mystic mudras," members of the society gather together in order to summon up "Spiritual Energy," which is then stored in a radionic battery. To fill each battery takes weeks of such sessions, with each battery storing thousands of hours of Prayer Energy. This energy is then released through something called a "Spiritual Energy Radiator," which quickly discharges the battery and dispenses the stored energy in a concentrated form. Such discharges are used when the Earth is in need of Spiritual Energy, like after a natural disaster, the onset of war, or the opening of another *Planet Hollywood*.

It's difficult to believe that prayers stored in a battery can help someone trapped under ten feet of earthquake rubble, but it's just as hard to poo-poo such claims by *The Aetherius Society*. To our knowledge, no one has ever survived a killer hurricane only to pin their fortunate outcome on a blast of prayer energy from *The Aetherius Society*'s radionic battery. But then again, how the heck would someone even know he was the lucky recipient of such an ethereal force? It boggles the mind.

The charging sessions for Operation Prayer Power are open to anyone willing to take the time and energy to be taught how to turn mere mantras into a powerful, global healing force. Be an Energizer Bunny in the name of all that is Good and Right—stop by *The Aetherius Society* to help fill their radionic battery today. And while you're there, ask about their other interesting missions to help save the world.

You'll be glad you did!

The Aetherius Society
6202 Afton Place
Los Angeles
(213) 467-HEAL

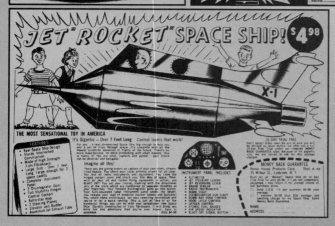

Anyone who's had first-hand experience with the teeming
throngs of L.A.'s mega-malls already knows there's a hell of a lot
to be said for agoraphobia. No wonder the Home Shopping
Network has spawned an entirely new mutation of American
consumerism. It's just too bad that the products offered by HSN,
QVC and their ilk are usually limited to questionable exercise
equipment, ugly zirconium jewelry, synthetic-blend sweater sets,
hideous porcelain figurines, commemorative plates, and monstrous
gemstone pendants the size of a baby dinosaur's head.

Imagine—in a perfect world—being able to pick up your
remote control, channel surf to a home shopping station,
punch in a few digits on your telephone, and purchase the
soiled g-string of your favorite porn star, a full-color
photo-set of bikinied amputees, or a wealth of XXX video
selections starring midgets, hermaphrodites, or worse,
Tonya Harding. Consider, if you will, the possibility of a
network where Chicken Boy products are pitched 24 hours a day,
seven days a week...where lycra swimwear with built-in
butt-plugs are fashion de rigeur...where recipes for making LSD
and TNT have replaced Martha Stewart's recipe for eggnog.

It may take some time before we see anal beads or survivalist
tracts peddled on our television screens, but don't despair;
you can still get your hands on a myriad of weird, semi-dangerous
stuff without having to lift your fat ass from your Laz-E-Boy.
If you can whip out a credit card, write a check, lick a stamp,
pick up the phone, or waddle down to your nearest mailbox,
then there's a wiggy, wonderful world of mail-order
madness waiting just for you.

Here, then, for your perusal, we offer a mere smattering
of Southern California's most eclectic and egregious mail-
order offerings. So let your fingers do the walking into
a weird and wacky world of funky-flavored fun.
Just don't forget to wash your hands afterwards.

Flat Is Where It's At!

Did you know that the Earth is flat? It is if you listen to the folks at **The Flat Earth Society**. Calling themselves "the oldest continuous Society existing on the world today," *The Flat Earth Society* eschews so-called scientific thought as the same old dogma that's been served up over the centuries by "sorcerers, witch doctors, Priests-Entertainers, and tellers of tales," the latter of which we take to be a reference to politicians and radio talk show hosts alike.

As the Society puts it, "Science consists of a weird, way-out occult concoction of gibberish theory-theology...unrelated to the world of real facts." And describing themselves, they say, "We are the sane and/or have Common Sense as contrasted to the herd who is unthinking and uncaring." Most importantly, they emphasize that "Earth Flat is a fact, not a theory." Also, that the " Sun and Moon are about 3,000 miles away and are both 32 miles across. The planets are 'tiny.' Australians do NOT hang by their feet under the world..." And so on. Whether you agree or disagree with their assertions, you have to admit that these cats are emphatic about their cause, to say the least, and are either totally nuts or have a lot of balls to espouse their radical—and some would say heretical—theories.

Perhaps the scientific community is less than noble, having freed the genie of nuclear power without first figuring a way to get it back into the bottle. Perhaps the concept of a spinning globe is merely another fantasy spun from religious doctrine. Perhaps the Earth *is* flat after all.

We started to get excited: If the Earth *is* flat then perhaps this book will shoot to #1 on the sales charts and stay there for a year or two. Perhaps Daisy Fuentes, wearing only a pair of cha-cha heels and coated in lard, will be waiting for us when we get home. Perhaps we'll win the lottery. Perhaps they'll bring the breakfast cereal *Quisp* back. Perhaps...just perhaps.

Then again, maybe not. Not to rain on *The Flat Earth Society*'s parade, but science does have its upside (Prozac and the silicon microchip immediately come to mind), and despite the *Society*'s statement that all "airplanes fly level on this plane earth," that's hardly convincing proof that we're living on a gargantuan organic pizza box. Not to say that they're wrong, but, well, either NASA has been perpetrating a major conspiracy for thirty years, or all those astronauts were hallucinating when they orbited *something* that was round, big, and blue.

Still, *The Flat Earth Society* deserves to be listened to, if only for the fact that *someone* out there is offering a semi-intelligent alternative to the scientific party line that's being sold to us hook, line and sinker. Frankly, we don't know whether the earth is flat, round, or triangular. But what we do know is that *The Flat Earth Society* prints one heck of an interesting newsletter and is a lone voice in the wilderness of otherwise blind acceptance. And if the world does turn out to be flat after all, then maybe there is a chance that our Daisy Fuentes fantasy can come true, too.

Or, at the very least, they'll bring *Quisp* back.

The Flat Earth Society
P.O. Box 2533
Lancaster, CA 93539
(805) 727-1635

Letting your fingers do the walking
through the *Ampix* catalogue

While passing time in a waiting room, are you the kind of guy that flips through an issue of *Cosmo* or *Elle* to look at the pictures of pretty girls? Are you continually disappointed to find their photo layouts conspicuously absent of amputee models? Good news! **Ampix** has served the "Amputee Devotee" since 1974, and offers the world's largest collection of female amputee photos and videos available!

For Those Without A Leg To Stand On

Please don't misunderstand the intentions of *Ampix*. This is not a mail-order freak-show out to exploit poor, innocent, nubile amputees. Quite the contrary. *Ampix* is an organization managed by and catering to "amps" and "amp" aficionados alike, in the fervid adoration of lovely ladies who are missing limbs. Surprisingly, the material that *Ampix* sells is not pornographic in nature and the business is run with an extremely high level of integrity as set forth by the three, tedious pages of "Policies and Procedures" that each client receives with the catalogue and is expected to follow.

No detail is insignificant in the fulfillment of the sophisticated fetishist. A laymen might presume that one amputee beauty is as good as another—an arm, a leg, what's the difference? Only to the discriminating amputation zealot do distinctions like "single above knee" or "double below elbow" have any importance. With true fetishistic precision, each one of their 600+ color stills listed in the catalogue are exactingly and obsessively categorized not only by the type of amputation, but also by a long code number detailing the pose (standing/sitting/walking/lying), view (full front/left front/right front/back/side) and clothing (dress/skirt & blouse/shorts/slacks/swimsuit.)

The *Ampix* catalogue includes "The Living Library," a selection of "amp" stories on audiotape like "Peg Leg Annie and the One-Armed Bandit," or "Out on a Limb." Each title is listed with a brief synopsis, like:

Volume VII - The Van
The 60s were not only the days of free love, they were the days of free spirits and a "go anywhere and see it all" attitude. Of course, it was tougher for a pretty young girl with no legs and only one arm, but with a loving companion, a VW van, and an uninhibited spirit, anything was possible. Follow these flower children in their search for happiness.

Ampix also stocks a wide variety of high-quality videos that you're not likely to find at the corner *Blockbuster*. The *Ampix* talent roster includes "Marilyn," whose video features "cheerleading routines on one leg," and "Marsha Dee"—famous for being the first amputee model to do a spread in *Nugget* magazine—who sports "a wooden peg with a clear plastic socket so you can see her stump flex and contract as she moves and dances." Whatever floats your boat.

For $5.00 (money orders only) *Ampix* sends you one sample color photo, their newest catalogue, and periodic updates on new merchandise.

Ampix
Post Office Box 864
Lawndale, CA 90260

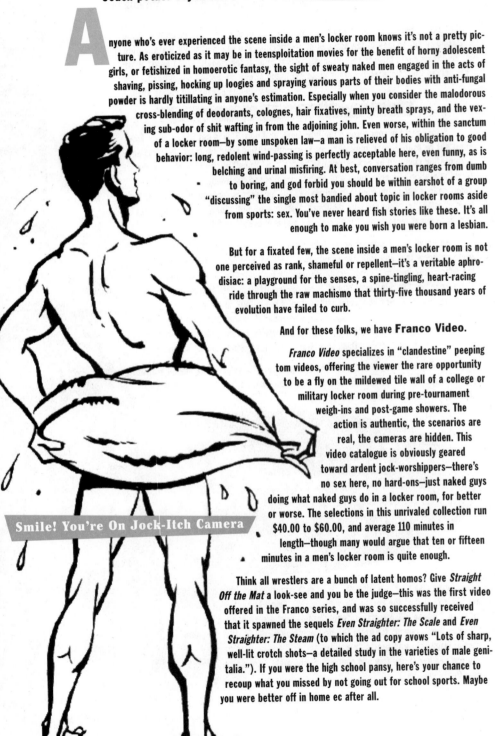

Couch potato voyeurism with *Franco Video*

Anyone who's ever experienced the scene inside a men's locker room knows it's not a pretty picture. As eroticized as it may be in teensploitation movies for the benefit of horny adolescent girls, or fetishized in homoerotic fantasy, the sight of sweaty naked men engaged in the acts of shaving, pissing, hocking up loogies and spraying various parts of their bodies with anti-fungal powder is hardly titillating in anyone's estimation. Especially when you consider the malodorous cross-blending of deodorants, colognes, hair fixatives, minty breath sprays, and the vexing sub-odor of shit wafting in from the adjoining john. Even worse, within the sanctum of a locker room—by some unspoken law—a man is relieved of his obligation to good behavior: long, redolent wind-passing is perfectly acceptable here, even funny, as is belching and urinal misfiring. At best, conversation ranges from dumb to boring, and god forbid you should be within earshot of a group "discussing" the single most bandied about topic in locker rooms aside from sports: sex. You've never heard fish stories like these. It's all enough to make you wish you were born a lesbian.

But for a fixated few, the scene inside a men's locker room is not one perceived as rank, shameful or repellent—it's a veritable aphrodisiac: a playground for the senses, a spine-tingling, heart-racing ride through the raw machismo that thirty-five thousand years of evolution have failed to curb.

And for these folks, we have **Franco Video**.

Franco Video specializes in "clandestine" peeping tom videos, offering the viewer the rare opportunity to be a fly on the mildewed tile wall of a college or military locker room during pre-tournament weigh-ins and post-game showers. The action is authentic, the scenarios are real, the cameras are hidden. This video catalogue is obviously geared toward ardent jock-worshippers—there's no sex here, no hard-ons—just naked guys doing what naked guys do in a locker room, for better or worse. The selections in this unrivaled collection run $40.00 to $60.00, and average 110 minutes in length—though many would argue that ten or fifteen minutes in a men's locker room is quite enough.

Think all wrestlers are a bunch of latent homos? Give *Straight Off the Mat* a look-see and you be the judge—this was the first video offered in the Franco series, and was so successfully received that it spawned the sequels *Even Straighter: The Scale* and *Even Straighter: The Steam* (to which the ad copy avows "Lots of sharp, well-lit crotch shots—a detailed study in the varieties of male genitalia."). If you were the high school pansy, here's your chance to recoup what you missed by not going out for school sports. Maybe you were better off in home ec after all.

Smile! You're On Jock-Itch Camera

Showers Are Regulated for Proper Temperature (a.k.a. *S.A.R.: The Football Team*) chronicles the antics of a varsity football team as they "...strip and hit the showers...display bravado and spit on the floor." But the action doesn't stop there; you'll also see the team "...let their penises flop around." If you've never treated yourself to the spectacle of a varsity football player allowing his penis to flop around, or watching him piss into a floor drain, you'll surely need to add this title to your video library!

No Cleats Beyond This Point is hyped as an "Outstanding study in hypermasculine behavior," and guarantees "a bunch of hard, straight-boy butts." Any woman who feels that gender has limited her to a lower rung on the socio-economic ladder may want to reconsider her position after witnessing these guys "...piss into the floor drains, talk about getting hard-ons, flip each other off, complain about jock itch and tug at their nuts..."

Whether you're a jock fetishist, a frustrated janitor, or a curious female (or any combination of the three), a locker room romp is always safer when experienced vicariously through the *Franco Video* series. At least there's no threat of contracting athlete's foot—and best of all, you won't need to hold your nose.

OUT-AND-ABOUT

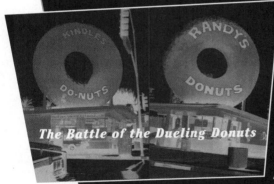

The Battle of the Dueling Donuts

Who says a donut by any other name tastes as sweet? Though they're just miles apart from one another and feature the exact same 1954 design, it's no contest: Randy's K.O.s Kindle's with their customer service, the ardent pride they take in the historic value of their building, and the cool Randy's Donuts T-shirts they offer for a mere $10.00. The folks at Kindle's don't even seem to be aware of the fact that a gigantic donut graces their rooftop.

Kindle's Do-nuts
10003 South Normandie Ave.
Los Angeles

Randy's Donuts
805 West Manchester Blvd.
Inglewood

Placing an order for the virtual
panty-raid that is *Kitten Natividad's Fantasy Polaroids*

I f you thought the only way to score a piece of lingerie formerly worn by burlesque icon and Russ Meyer legend Kitten Natividad was by landing her in the sack, you obviously don't know about **Kitten Natividad's Fantasy Polaroids**.

With her inimitable charm and impossible bust measurement, Kitten won super-celebutante status for her starring roles in the Russ Meyer classics *Up!* and *Beneath the Valley of the Ultravixens*. Her dynamic double-D form has graced the screen in scores of other films and videos (among them *Bodacious Ta Ta's*, *Titillation* and *Takin' It Off*) in addition to heating up many a go-go pad and strip joint runway throughout her illustrious career.

Kitten Natividad's Fantasy Polaroid Service is a branch of her fan club, The Kitten Klub, and works like this:

The Polaroids in question feature Kitten posed alone, dressed, half dressed, or undressed according to your fantasy. You can write Kitten a letter saying, "I'd like you wearing purple lace panties, a black waist cincher, and open-toe high-heeled marabou mules, doing splits and eating a ham-and-cheese on rye, toasted, no mayo, light mustard." Kitten doesn't discourage the detail-oriented, and does her damndest to meet every request.

Snap 'N' Sniff!

There are two different kinds of *Fantasy Polaroid* sets available, starting at $40. The "Lingerie Fantasy Polaroids" are Kitten's biggest sellers. You specify the frilly little underthings you'd like Kitten squeezed into and the position you'd like her to assume. You'll not only receive the Polaroids of Kitten posed and scanty-pantied as per your request, but you'll also get the soiled lingerie! These can get quite pricey since you don't usually find 46 DD brassieres or black satin merry widows in the bargain bin at *Woolworth's*. "Random Fantasy Polaroids" are for Kitten's frugal fans; they consist of five different shots selected by Kitten—the client has no creative input with these, and gets no lingerie.

An occasional high-roller will nab one of her rhinestoned stage costumes of the 70s—but Kitten says most of her requests are for "crotchless panties, dildos, and all that crap..."

Send requests and inquiries to:
The Kitten Klub
5917 Oak Ave., #148
Temple City, CA 91780

Reliving Karen's salad days with *Carpenters For Sale*

Question: What do Thighmaster spokeswoman Suzanne Somers, rubber-faced comedic never-was Charlie Callas, and infommercial boy-toy John Davidson have in common? Answer: They all appeared together in "Space Encounters," the 1978 television special starring Karen and Richard Carpenter! If you forgot to set your Betamax the night that show originally aired, it's still not too late to catch this stellar spectacular, thanks to Ron Garcia's **Carpenters For Sale**.

Ron offers an ever-changing list of enticing Carpenters memorabilia, with items as rare as a 1975 mint condition tour program, and as obscure as a collection of late-70s radio interviews on cassette. He's also got an impressive list of original 45s too (Remember "Calling Occupants of Interplanetary Craft"?); however, if you think you can pass on the videotape selections like "A Christmas Portrait" (with guest stars Kristy and Jimmy McNichol) or the aforementioned "Space Encounters," you'd better check your pulse.

She Ain't Skinny, She's My Sister

Next time a rainy day or a Monday has got you down, just sink into your favorite easy chair, put a bottle of Epicac on ice, and thrill to the sights and sounds of America's #1 singing sibling sensation as offered by Ron Garcia's *Carpenters For Sale*.

It really is yesterday once more.

Keeping it brief with *Koala Swimwear*

Is That A Gun In Your Man Mold Or Are You Just Happy To See Me?

Men: do you feel left out when your ladyfriends get their *Frederick's of Hollywood* or *Victoria's Secret* catalogues in the mail? Wish that you too had an entire catalogue of spandex slingshots and lamé twist-ties to choose from, just for men? Looking to wear a little less than a Speedo but a little more than a cock ring next time you hit the beach? Look no further than the **Koala Swimwear** catalogue: the sunlover's bible of butt floss.

Never in your life have you seen "swimwear" like this—it's enough to make a pornstar blush. Showcase your organs with *Koala's* mindboggling designs like "Holster," "High Rise," "The Shaft Suit," "Tied Up," or the impossible "Man Mold," and give fellow beachgoers a real eyeful. Get the most shock value for your cock value; with *Koala* on your side, you can't help but turn heads.

A sense of humor and a hyper-imaginative design team make the *Koala* catalogue a man's single best resource for infinitesimal beach wear. Video catalogues and a wide range of depilatory products are also available.

Unfortunately—even with rigorous hair removal treatments—few men can pull off the *Koala* look on a public beach. But it might be a whole lotta fun trying if you don't get arrested first.

W hen I lived near downtown L.A., one of my favorite icons—next to the neon *Jesus Saves* sign—was an odd statue that stood atop a building near the corner of Broadway and 4th. With the body of a man, the head of a chicken, and a bucket in his outstretched arms, Chicken Boy was the 22-foot-tall mutant mascot who overlooked the fried chicken joint below that bore his name. To be certain, he was an effective advertising tool, for one day I actually bothered to stop by the restaurant and sample some of their tasty fried fare. And though I soon thereafter suffered severe gastrointestinal distress, I didn't hold a grudge against that wacky icon who lured me into one of the worst, diarrhea-inducing meals of my life. If anything, I loved him even more. After all, he was merely a statue, and had nothing to do with the preparation of my gut-wrenching lunch. Then, one day in the mid-Eighties, I drove by *Chicken Boy* only to be dismayed by the fact that not only was the store gone, but so was my fine-feathered hero. While the space that once sold less-than-palatable poultry would simply be redecorated and reborn as yet another place of business, *Chicken Boy* himself was slated to be given a one-way ticket to the desert where he would become a target for gun-toting, hen-hating NRA members.

"Too Tall To Live, Too Weird To Die."

Fortunately I wasn't the only weirdo who bothered to look up (literally) to *Chicken Boy*. Not that Amy Inouye—the founder of Future Studio—is a weirdo, but she, too, also had a thing for the giant chicken-human hybrid, and saved *Chicken Boy* from being dragged to his doomed desert locale. Though dubbed as the "Statue of Liberty of Los Angeles," Chicken Boy lingered in pieces for years, first in an outdoor storage facility, then inside a parking structure—all the while enduring rejection from each and every institution to which he was offered (like the Smithsonian and the Museum of Contemporary Art). This denial turned out to be a good thing, though, for from its loins sprung the incredibly cool *Chicken Boy Catalogue for a Perfect World*™.

Using *Chicken Boy* as her beacon of inspirational light, Amy and her Future Studio began the mail-order madness of selling the world's tackiest treasures, along with custom-made *Chicken Boy* shirts, hats, keychains, underwear, watches, mugs, placemats, stationery, and heck, you name it! You can even purchase front-and-back license plate frames bearing *Chicken Boy*'s motto: "Too Tall to Live, Too Weird to Die." What started with simple Chicken Boy souvenirs for clients and family has now grown into a burgeoning business that also offers "Elvisobilia," rugs that depict dogs playing pool, pet sombreros, shopping cart purses, and "best of" accordion CDs. And whether you want to dress your cat up as a Catholic nun or a Hasidic Rabbi, you'll find both outfits in the *Chicken Boy Catalogue*.

There was a time when you could drop by Future Studio on Saturdays and stock up on *Chicken Boy* merchandise, but no longer. Worry not, however, since Amy still holds an open house every once in a while, and throws open the doors to the studio every Saturday in December for those of you looking to stock up on *Chicken Boy* Christmas gifts. Only a real Scrooge wouldn't delight in a *Chicken Boy* switchplate cover, pocket protector, or toothpick holder!

Despite the fact that Saturday visitation rights are now defunct—and that the development toadies responsible for the brightly blighted *Universal Citywalk* first proposed the idea of a *Chicken Boy* retail store to Amy and then shot it down in typical Hollywood fashion—you can still get the full flavor of what *Chicken Boy* is all about from the brilliantly written catalogue and its contents. By itself, this quirky little compendium makes for great bathroom reading, and also functions as the perfect source for your friends and relatives who share your perfectly wonderful bad taste!

As for *Chicken Boy* himself, he is once again in pieces, his parts stored here and there until the day when he can once again become whole. He did manage to come together a few years ago at ARCO Plaza in downtown L.A. for a limited engagement, but as the saying goes, "All good things must come to an end, even *Chicken Boy*."

Amy has been pitching a *Chicken Boy* show to the networks, and even hopes to create a Metrolink stop that will be centered around *Chicken Boy* and roadside culture. Perhaps the odds of these projects coming to pass are better than those Amy faced with putting up the ill-fated *Chicken Boy* emporium at *Universal Citywalk*, but probably not. Which just goes to show that *Chicken Boy* is more than just misunderstood. He's way ahead of his time.

Call or write for your own catalogue, and join the ever-growing ranks of other *Chicken Boy* fans who are working together to make this crummy planet a perfect world.

—ARL

The Chicken Boy Catalogue for a Perfect World™
P.O. Box 292000
Los Angeles, CA 90029
Order toll-free
(800) 422-0505

OUT-AND-ABOUT

Drive Me Crazy!

You never know what you'll find parked behind the plate-glass window of Barris Industries, the creative force behind Hollywood's most legendary customized cars. From Beach Blanket Bingo to Batman, Corvette Summer to Cannonball Run—if there was a weird car in the movie, chances are that Barris had something to do with it. Though their showroom is closed to the public, it's completely visible from the sidewalk; the super-bitchin' Monkeemobile, the famous golf cart shaped like Bob Hope's face, and all the Batman vehicles have made occasional pit stops here. The showroom walls sport an impressive collection of movie posters— all films that have featured a Barris auto. Remember the early Ron Howard classic "Eat My Dust"? Neither do we.

Barris Kustom Industries
10811 Riverside Drive
North Hollywood

Personal Freedom Meets Paranoia at *Eden Press*

With the Feds trying to chip away at what's left of our personal freedoms on almost a daily basis, you need a friend like **Eden Press** in your corner. Although this Fountain Valley mail order book company bills its latest catalogue as "Books for the Nineties," the euphemistic title fails to do true justice to the contents. Although you may also be able to find some of the offerings in the *Eden Press* catalogue at *Amok* and *Survival Books* (which are also featured in this book), *Eden* specializes in subversive reading materials for you Americans with more than just a modicum of distrust for your government (and rightly so), and who would like to retain what little privacy you have left...or at least the facade thereof.

Is That A Phony Passport In Your Pocket Or Are You Just Happy To See Me?

Along these lines, *Eden* offers such fascinating titles as *HOW TO USE THE FREEDOM OF INFORMATION ACT AGAINST THE I.R.S.*, *HOW BIG BROTHER INVESTIGATES YOU*, and *ARE YOU NOW OR HAVE YOU EVER BEEN IN THE F.B.I. FILES?*. Do you hate the I.R.S.? Who doesn't? Perhaps you may want to peruse *THE U.S. TAX HAVEN LOOPHOLE, DISINHERIT THE I.R.S.*, and *THE COMPLETE TAX AUDIT GUIDE*. You'll also find a wealth (if you'll pardon the pun) of info about offshore banking opportunities, get-rich-quick books, and even tomes about borrowing money (especially if you have bad credit), lawsuit and asset protection, and how to open a foreign bank account.

Paranoid about your valuables? Then texts like *THE BIG BOOK OF SECRET HIDING PLACES* and *HOW TO BURY YOUR GOODS* ought to put your mind at ease. Trying to track down a slippery slimeball or trying to get the goods on your competition at work? Read *YOU, TOO, CAN FIND ANYBODY* and *HOW TO GET ANYTHING ON ANYBODY*. Those in the throes of wreaking vengeance will be delighted at the vast selection of instructional manuals, from George Hayduke's classic *GET EVEN: THE COMPLETE BOOK OF DIRTY TRICKS*, to lesser-known, specific instruments of terror like *TENANT'S REVENGE* and *DIVORCE DIRTY TRICKS*.

If you've been thinking about acquiring a bogus passport or applying for another passport from a foreign country, *Eden Press* has the books for you. Or if you've been thinking about vanishing from the face of the earth or assuming a new identity, *THE PAPER TRIP* series and *100 WAYS TO DISAPPEAR AND LIVE FREE* are but two of the *Eden* titles that can help you achieve these ends.

If some of this sounds illegal to you, well, you're partially right. But just like you can buy books on how to grow killer marijuana, how to make L.S.D., or put together a lethal pipe-bomb, there's a big difference between reading about it and doing it. So while many of these titles have to do with screwing our oppressive government, its all-powerful ancillary agencies, and/or society at large, the underlying fact of the matter is that none of them would be available to us if we didn't have a little document in our favor called The Bill of Rights, and the Freedom of the Press that it guarantees.

For now, at least.

Eden Press
11623 Slater "E"
P.O. Box 8410
Fountain Valley,
CA 92728
Order toll-free:
(800) 338-8484

Globe Sales

Too bashful to check out of your local video store a title like "Girls Who Eat Cunt"? Or, maybe you've had your heart set on a penile pump or a long strand of anal beads but just don't have the time to comparison shop sex toy boutiques. Your problems have been solved: send for the Globe Sales catalogue and let your fingers do the walking! This glossy, full color, photo packed mail-order catalogue of XXX-rated videos, magazines, CD ROMs and adult novelties is sure to add spice to your daily load of credit card bills, junk mail, and those missing children things.

Globe Sales covers all their bases, doing their damndest to please perverts of every variety. The catalogue is heavy on videos, and offers a remarkably comprehensive list of titles. If you're a fella who digs chicks with child, check out the "Ready to Drop" series. Got a thing for pretty Asian girls? "Geisha Gash," "Stir Fry Snatch" and "Fortune Cookie Nookie" are just three of the titles Globe offers to sate your case of yellow fever. Is there a self-respecting homosexual alive who could resist a title like "10 Inches of Meat"?! Even videos featuring she-males ("Dames with Dongs"), group sex ("Too Much Twat"), anal endeavors ("Up Yours"), interracial action ("Huge Black Tits"/"Big Black Cocks") and switch-hitters ("Any Hole") all have their place at Globe Sales. Dig a little deeper and you'll find dwarves, obese women who wrestle, and a feature starring a gal with three clits! As well as offering a selection of foot, bondage and spanking fetish selections, Globe also carries an impressive line of amateur porn titles like the "America's Raunchiest Home Videos" series.

No video library should be without the stomach churning Annabel Chong vehicle "The World's Biggest Gangbang." You'll not only find Annabel, but all your fave XXX stars sprinkled between Globe's lurid pages. Kitty Fox, "The World's Sexiest Senior," bra-busters Wendy Whoppers and Pandora Peaks—even dead porn stars like John Holmes and Savannah live forever through mail-order. For those who have never seen Traci Lords on all fours wearing only cheap black pumps getting fucked like a dog and panting like the slut that we all know she is, you can find her only legal adult video, "Traci, I Love You," in this very catalogue. Watching her Melrose Place reruns will never be the same.

But lest you get the wrong impression, it's not just fulsome skin flicks that Globe Sales deals in. They also peddle rubber vibrating pussies, strap-on tools and prosthetic extensions, cock rings, the obligatory lubes and love potions, life-sized sex dolls—even an inflatable, fuckable, potbellied pig ("sex with a silent partner has never been so satisfying...she'll bring out the animal in you!!"). This is stuff you just won't find in The Sharper Image.

Cult film buffs take note: look no further for that obscure Chesty Morgan title or the classic 8 mm shorts of Betty Page and Tempest Storm et al. You'll go broke making your choices among the irresistible collections of vintage stag films, 1970s porn trailers, and the 60s and 70s Harry Novak sexploitation features like "Mantis in Lace," and "Wham-Bam-Thank You Spaceman."

Prices are competitive and you can even fax your order. If the shipping time is too long for you to wait, flip to the phone sex section of the catalogue and get your rocks off now at $2.00 per minute. Talk about convenience!

Address your catalogue request to:

Globe Sales
Box 7020
Tarzana, CA 91357

Getting on the right tract with the *Free Tract Society*

> "...every person in the world is a sinner and should be punished."
>
> —*Make This a Real Hollowe'en;* Bible Tract, author unknown

> "I'll take your mother and make her a whore."
>
> —*My Name is Cocaine;* Bible Tract, author unknown

Religion By The Pound

> "The world as we know it now is coming to an end."
>
> —*The End of the World;* Bible Tract, Eugene Turner

THE MARK OF THE
BEAST
Is It Near?

There's nothing like a Bible tract to lift your spirits—and it seems that at one time or another, we've all been the reluctant recipient of one. These crudely produced and poorly written pamphlets are usually dispersed by God-fearing maniacs eager to make you feel so completely rotten about yourself that you'll do absolutely anything to save your wretched soul, including—especially including—begging for god's forgiveness. According to the philosophy of the Bible tract, the laws of the afterlife are pretty cut and dry: if you don't accept Jesus Christ as your personal lord and savior, you will simply burn in the eternal fires of hell. Maybe worse. Not surprisingly, Bible tracts generally incite repugnance rather than Christian reverence.

The Free Tract Society doles these things out by the pound. Although they "request a donation" of a mere $7.00 per, they aren't called *The Free Tract Society* for nothing; if you're a skeptic, they'll send you a half-pound *gratis*, no questions asked! Why on God's earth would I want a half-pound of Bible tracts—free or otherwise? you may be asking. Well, no one likes to be proselytized, certainly, but Bible tracts have other uses. Consider these suggestions:

-Bible tracts have been grossly underestimated as a decorative art form. When adhered to a bathroom wall in a checkerboard pattern and coated with a thick layer of clear, oil-base sealant they make an excellent—however frightening—wall covering. Very *Carrie*!

WILL YOU TAKE THE
MARK?

—Slip a few in your pocket for when you use public restrooms. Place them faceup inside the lip of a urinal as close to the drain as possible: *urinal targets!* Really piss off some Christians!

—Take correction fluid and white out the name "Jesus" or "God" from every tract, and replace them with names from the objectionable *Friends* cast. Hand them out in front of Paramount's studio audience entrance.

—Women: toss those dangerous bottles of mace and pepper sprays from your purse, and instead carry a big stack of Bible tracts. When presented with a title like "Jesus Loves You So Much It Hurts," your would-be assailant is sure to flee the scene!

—If you just can't deal with those students peddling magazine subscriptions door-to-door, post the Bible tract titled "Hell Is No Myth" to your front porch, and they'll keep right on walking!

—Next time a pushy vagabond rattles a paper cup filled with change up against your car window at an intersection, slip him a Bible tract instead of a fin, and maybe together we can end the homeless problem.

—Next time a waiter gives you really rotten service, instead of a tip, give him a bible tract and a warm smile.

Your options don't end there, of course; be creative! After all, they're free!

Free Tract Society
P.O. Box 42544
Los Angeles, CA
90050

Beautiful tan. Beautiful skin
COPPERTONE

The Coppertone Billboard

Whenever my family took a car trip to visit relatives in Newport Beach—*Disneyland* being our ultimate destination—I knew our vacation had officially begun when we drove past the gigantic **Coppertone Billboard** on the 5 freeway. In those days of the early 70s it was still animated, with the dog bouncing up and down tugging at the little girl's bikini bottoms. *"Beautiful tan..Beautiful skin—Coppertone"*—it was the most sensational billboard I had ever seen, mostly because it moved, but also because—for me—it was the definitive symbol of summer fun: suntan lotion, bright blue skies, and sandy Southern California beaches. It was a visual I refused to miss on our long drive, like that first glimpse of the tip of the Matterhorn. It meant that we were almost there, and that I'd soon be able to unfasten my seatbelt and put on a swimsuit.

Good things—*especially* good things—don't last forever. Especially in Los Angeles. When I made the move down to Southern California in the mid-80s, it pained me to discover that my beloved *Coppertone Billboard* was in a state of disrepair. The little dog was no longer animated, and looked more rabid than playful. The little girl was beginning to get sunburned. Still, I was emphatically grateful that it was even standing and relished the thirty or forty seconds I had to soak it in from my car window whenever I drove that stretch of the Santa Ana Freeway. The ensuing years however, were not kind. Towards the early 90s, some cretinous gang members defiled it with their idiotic graffiti (where's Bernard Goetz when you need him?), and although attempts had been made to maintain the sign by retouching the vandalism, soon after it was graffitied again, then retouched, and graffitied, and eventually the battle was lost and the maintenance abandoned. The original paint began to peel considerably, and the pig-tailed little girl (urban legend says it was child-model Jodi Foster) was unable to withstand summer after summer of relentless Orange County heat—by 1993 she looked like she had been dragged from a burning building. To see this glorious billboard go to pot was like a knife through my heart.

I knew then that the days of my cherished billboard were numbered, and that the number was probably getting down to two digits. I made a special pilgrimage to Buens Park and for the first time ever, I pulled off the freeway and onto the frontage road leading to the vacant building on which the *Coppertone* sign stood, and quietly worshiped. For years my eye had been trained to scan from a car window at fifty-five mph, but standing still beneath the billboard gave me an entirely new perspective, almost like seeing it for the first time. Although it never looked worse—and the graffiti had me spewing bile—it still worked its magic. *"Beautiful Tan..Beautiful Skin"*—it took me right back to those long car trips with my dad behind the wheel, the promise of something fabulous.

Soon afterward, without any fanfare and without any fights, the billboard was taken down. Driving that portion of the 5 freeway is now like passing an old house where a childhood friend once lived. It never gets any easier seeing treasured parts of Southern California disappear.

I will always buy Coppertone.

—MM

The Coppertone Billboard
Santa Ana Freeway
at the Beach Blvd. exit
Buena Park
(former location)

Despite all appearances, writing a book like *L.A. BIZARRO* isn't an easy thing to do. For one, it doesn't pay very well. Secondly, there's never really enough room to write about all the things you really want to write about. And lastly, there's always going to be someone who's going to feel cheated and disappointed when it comes to the book—other than the authors, of course.

What we've attempted to do here—again, despite appearances—is assemble more than just an arbitrary sampling of what we feel to be especially unusual or exceptional throughout Southern California that deserved a place in our lurid spotlight. Sadly, by press time, some of our entries had proven to be too obscure for their own good. Some establishments had simply crapped out, while others had been deep-sixed by the Board of Health. Some died of old age, like the classic *Undie World of Lily St. Cyr*; or left town like *Dr. Blyth's Weird Museum*; or closed their doors, albeit temporarily, due to natural disaster. Such was the fate of Simi Valley's *Bottle Village*, which, as its name implies, is an actual locale constructed entirely of bottles—not a wise choice of building material for any dwelling located on or near the San Andreas fault. And, as in life itself, we were forced to make those happenstance decisions born from the brevity of our existence (in this example, the page length of this book), which thus forced us to excise some of our more colorful choices like *Thai Elvis*, *The Banana Museum*, *The Edy Williams Fan Club*, *The Tiki News*, *Googie Tours*, *The Ball Club*, *Bischoff's Taxidermy*, *The International Vampire Association*, *Clearman's Village*, and a company that will pick up your dead pets and dispose of them for you.

Surely, there will be more than a few Angelenos already familiar with some of our choices, some of whom may even feel a bit let down that we didn't lead you to even more new, dangerous, offbeat, and potentially lethal locations. To you, we cordially invite you to go suck an egg—and to be sure to look for the updated edition of this book for your future reference.

Speaking of which, although our files are veritably teeming with fodder for our next edition, we welcome and invite any suggestions from our readers—native or otherwise—with new, exciting, and generally weird information that would make our jobs a hell of a lot easier the next time around. If you happen to cough up some choice new tidbit, do keep in mind that you won't get your name in print for the favor. And you surely won't be paid for your info, either, but then again, you can always take solace in the fact that, when you get right down to it, neither were we. Please send any such data to:

Anthony R. Lovett & Matt Maranian
L.A. BIZARRO!
P.O. BOX 480648
Los Angeles, CA 90048

In closing, we'd just like to say that we hoped you enjoyed reading *L.A. BIZARRO* as much as we did slaving over it—whether you bothered to actually visit any of our "discoveries" or simply enjoyed them vicariously. All kidding aside, it was a fun, happy book to write, much more gratifying than, say, assembling a book about *How to Love Your Inner Child*, or worse, a ghost-writing gig for Martha Stewart.

Either of which, of course, we would undoubtedly have been paid for.

Play safely.

With warm regards,

—Anthony R. Lovett & Matt Maranian